World of Art

Dr Jiang Jiehong is Professor of Chinese Art and Director
of the Centre for Chinese Visual Arts at Birmingham City
University, and Principal Editor of the *Journal of Contemporary
Chinese Art* (Intellect). His book publications include *Burden or
Legacy: From the Chinese Cultural Revolution to Contemporary
Art* (2007), *The Revolution Continues: New Art from China*
(2008), *Red: China's Cultural Revolution* (2010) and *An Era
without Memories: Chinese Contemporary Photography
on Urban Transformation* (2015). Jiang curated the 2012
Guangzhou Triennial, 'The Unseen'; the 2014 Asia Triennial
Manchester, 'Harmonious Society'; and the 2018–19 Thailand
Biennale, 'Edge of the Wonderland'.

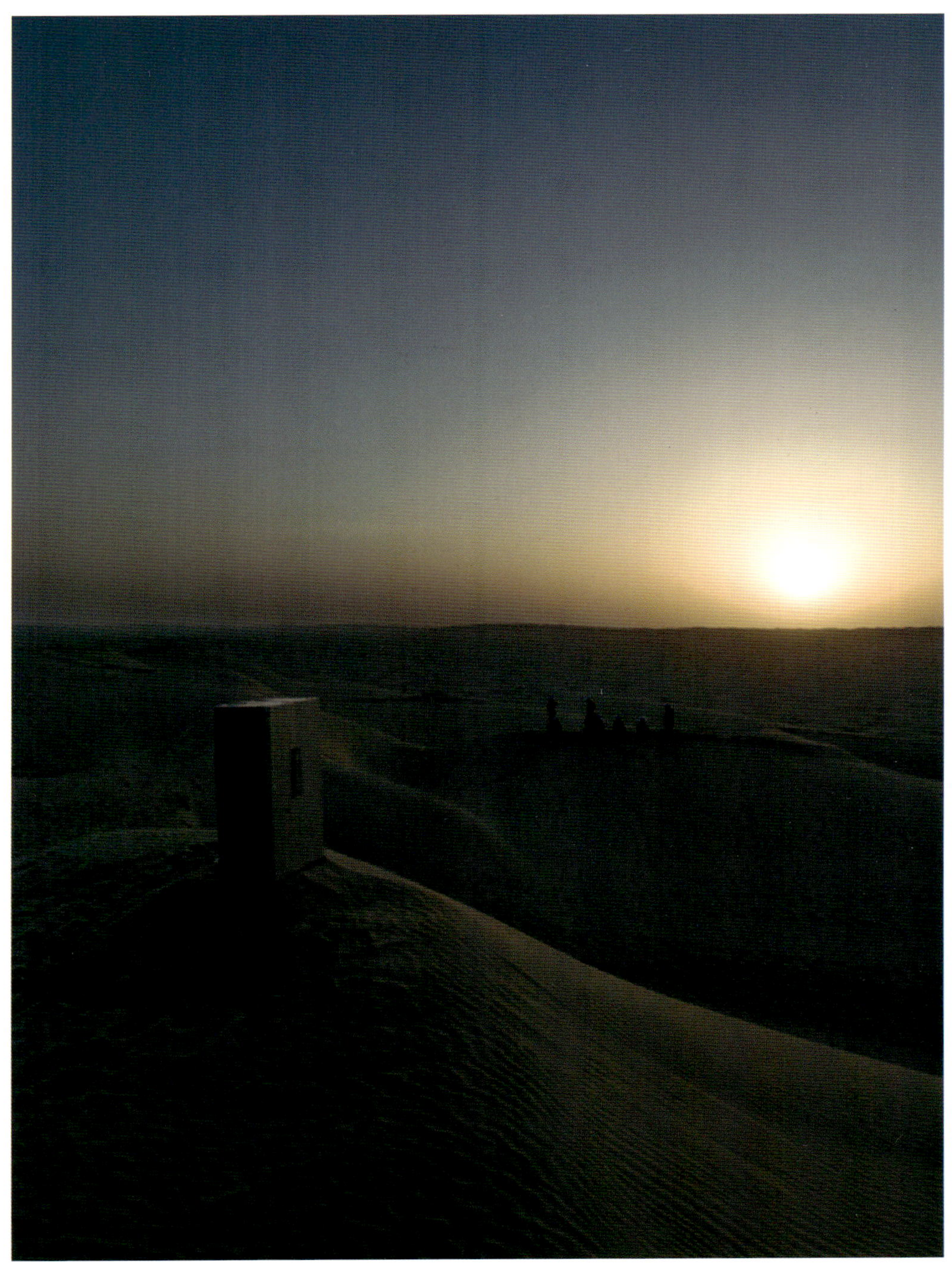

1 Zhao Zhao, *Project Taklamakan*, 2016 (detail of performance)

World of Art

The Art of Contemporary China

Jiang Jiehong

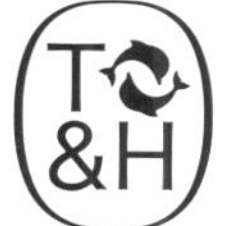

For Julia and Michelle

Acknowledgments

I owe a great debt of gratitude to all the artists whom I admire and have worked with in the past few years for their inspiration, generosity and hospitality, and for the timely help offered by their family members, studios and gallery assistants.

This project was derived from my ongoing research, curating and writing in the field. I have gratefully received support and assistance from many institutions, including AIVA Shanghai, Asia Art Archive, Beijing Commune, Boers-Li Gallery, CAFA Art Museum, Centre for Chinese Contemporary Art, Guangdong Museum of Art, Ikon Gallery, Leverhulme Trust, New Century Art Foundation, OCAT Shanghai, Open Eye Gallery, Shanghai Minsheng Art Museum, ShanghART Gallery, Tang Contemporary Art, Tate Liverpool and Today Art Museum. At Birmingham City University, I have benefited from the generous support of Research at the Faculty of Arts, Design and Media, and from exchanges with academics and doctoral students at the Centre of Chinese Visual Arts.

This book would not have come into existence without the encouragement and invitation of Constance Kaine and Roger Thorp at Thames & Hudson. I am also indebted to their team, especially Ilona de Nemethy Sanigar, Mohara Gill, Sam Ruston, Poppy David, Luke Kiley, Jenny Wilson, Adam Hay and Isabel Roldan, for their expertise in making this volume possible.

First published in 2021 in the United Kingdom
by Thames & Hudson Ltd, 181A High Holborn,
London WC1V 7QX

www.thamesandhudson.com

First published in 2021 in the United States
of America by Thames & Hudson Inc.,
500 Fifth Avenue, New York, New York 10110

www.thamesandhudsonusa.com

The Art of Contemporary China © 2021
Thames & Hudson Ltd, London

Text by Jiang Jiehong

Art direction and series design: Kummer & Herrman
Layout: Adam Hay Studio

British Library Cataloguing-in-Publication Data
A catalogue record for this book is available from
the British Library

Library of Congress Control Number 2020940728

ISBN 978-0-500-20438-2

Printed and bound in Hong Kong, China through
Asia Pacific Offset Ltd

Contents

Introduction

This book tells a special story of contemporary art in relation
to the People's Republic of China. It is about art, and it is about
China today. The discussions will not unfold in a linear way
that charts the development chronologically, as a forty-year
history of Chinese art; instead, topics will be generated through
a series of curatorial approaches that examine contemporary
art in the context of the unprecedented cultural, political and
urban transformations in post-Mao China.

The end of the Great Proletarian Cultural Revolution
(*Wuchan jieji wenhua da geming*, 1966–76) opened an entirely new
chapter for modern Chinese history, and indeed for Chinese art
too. During the last decade of the twentieth century, Chinese
art started to become more visible and to attract the world's
attention via frequent participation in important international
art events, such as Documenta and the Venice Biennale. Since
the turn of the twenty-first century, the Chinese government's
vision of urbanization, a growing national awareness of and
anxiety about developing cultural and creative industries
within urban spaces, the institution of biennials, triennials
and art fairs, the dramatic expansion of art education, and the
rise of newly founded private museums and art spaces have all
played a part in promoting the development of contemporary
art in China.

There are a variety of definitions of 'new art' in China. From
a political point of view, on the one hand, such art has been
categorized into 'official' and 'unofficial' art, or 'underground
art' in the context of a totalitarian society; it has even been
coined 'un-unofficial art', which 'encourages real freedom of
creation in an open, multi-orientational space'.[1] On the other
hand, from the point of view of artistic radicalism, the Western
idea of the avant-garde (*qianwei*) has been employed since the
1980s to signify an oppositional stance towards established
convention, or to position artists outside the domains of
institutional art. In more recent times, 'experimental art'

(*shiyan yishu*) has been adopted as a looser and broader definition. The word 'experimental' (*shiyan*) connotes the idea of radical innovation, and yet at the same time it implies something that can be exploratory, or tentative, and that appears to be somehow less determinate or less responsible in the event of anything going wrong. The term *qianwei yishu* (avant-garde art) was often used as a synonym for *xiandai yishu* (modern art) or *dangdai yishu* (contemporary art) by Chinese art critics of the 1980s, with little clear distinction.[2] The term 'contemporary art' first appeared in the West in the first half of the twentieth century,[3] and it was adopted by Chinese critics and artists in the early 1990s to proclaim a pivotal transition, from 'modern' to 'contemporary'. Today, in China, it is the most commonly used term. According to the artist and art historian Terry Smith, the term 'contemporary' has three core meanings, 'the immediate, the contemporaneous, and the cotemporal'; and its concept, 'far from being singular and simple – a neutral substitute for "modern" – signifies multiple ways of being with, in, and out of time, separately and at once, with others and without them'.[4] In the context of developing and conceptualizing new art in China, the art historian Wu Hung argues that the words 'modern' and 'contemporary' indicate two different approaches: the former, 'temporal and diachronic' to recognize artists' efforts to identify with movements of historical significance; and the latter, 'spatial and synchronic' to suggest 'a sense of rupture and demarcation – the end of an era as well as the kind of historical thinking associated with it'.[5] In this volume, the term 'contemporary art' will be used to define the latest artistic developments in China. Since the 'historical' was once 'contemporary', and the 'contemporary' will one day become 'historical', this book attempts to transcend a linear narrative of art history, and instead, through a cultural perspective, to understand Chinese artistic development beyond the Western context, for a new insight into Chinese art contributing to the globalized art world.

Arts and culture started to be developed afresh after the death of Mao Zedong, the founder of the People's Republic, and the end of the Cultural Revolution, in 1976; and, in particular, after the policy of Reform and Opening (*gaige kaifang*) was confirmed at the Third Plenum of the 11th Central Committee of the Communist Party of China in December 1978. During the first three decades of the People's Republic (founded in 1949), art, following the doctrine of Mao's 'Yan'an Talks',[6] had been through a transformation or nationalization – from the Soviet Socialist Realist style, for instance, to a more localized style – often with a sophisticated label, such as 'Revolutionary Realism' or 'Revolutionary Romanticism'. With attempts to break away from this dominant – and, indeed, only – ideology in the post-Mao era, a range of art practices came into being, including what art historians have dubbed Scar Art (*Shanghen yishu*) and Native Soil Art or Rustic Realism (*Xiangtu xieshi*). Rather than depicting or idealizing a revolutionary world, artists started to reflect upon and expose the actual situation in China. Cheng Conglin's *Snow on a Certain Day of a Certain Month, 1968* is a frequently cited example, being one of the first pieces to expose the traumatic experiences of the Mao generation and their losses during the turbulent years. Equally of significance, young artists further explored ordinary lives and the minority people whom they had encountered during their years spent working in the countryside during the Cultural Revolution. Among widely cited works, Chen Danqing's *Tibetan Series* and Luo Zhongli's 2-metre-high (over 7 ft) photorealistic painting *Father* are most representative of the turn from 'scar' to 'native soil'. These artists were not just yearning for rural and natural life; they were, more importantly, translating reality into something symbolic or monumental, as well as examining and revealing human values in everyday existence. The legacy of realism has continued.

When did art become 'contemporary' in China? From the end of the 1970s, many art groups emerged, and sixteen unofficial art exhibitions took place across the country, in Beijing, Shanghai and Xi'an. These spontaneously organized exhibitions – for instance, *Nature, Society and Man* by the April Photography Society (opened 1 April 1979), and the first show of the No Name Painting Society (opened 7 July 1979) – were deliberately 'apolitical' in order to seek out 'pure' art.[7] Arguably, the most noteworthy debut of new art in China was staged through the two *Star Art Exhibitions* (*Xingxing meizhan*) in 1979 and 1980. The Star group was initiated by the two core members Huang Rui and Ma Desheng, and the first exhibition consisted of work by twenty-three artists in total, including Wang Keping, Qu Leilei and Ai Weiwei. By rejecting the highly polished Socialist Realist style, and the approach of 'decorating' revolutionary and political events, the Star group broke the silence. Unlike in other unofficial exhibitions, the Star artists did not keep their distance from politics and the established ideology of Maoist art; in other words, they did not stay neutral or seek only to convey artistic values beyond revolutionary aesthetics. Instead, they appeared to be explicitly political and critical, and they defined an independent position further from the official Chinese art world than any other since 1949.

Why are the two *Star Art Exhibitions* generally accepted as the beginning of the development of Chinese contemporary art? There are two obvious reasons for making such a clear division between revolutionary or Maoist art and new art in China, and these are the end of an autocracy and the start of an opening to the outside world. However, this binary thinking seems to be too simplistic. First, it is superficial to attribute the advent of Chinese contemporary art to the natural termination of Mao's regime, as if contemporary art could only be produced outside totalitarianism, or as if, after Mao, China's leaders were no longer autocratic. Although intellectual freedom is generally seen as essential to developing contemporary art practice, it is not in fact a prerequisite. The development of contemporary art in China has its own path. Secondly, one might argue that it was only after the years of reform and opening up at the end of the 1970s that China began to meet the West and its world of art. However, this time frame implies a one-way system of China learning from and becoming part of the 'contemporary art' world in the Western context of development, and, at the same time, it neglects the momentum and the plurality of contemporary art that were evident in many different parts of the globe. According to the anthropologist and writer Marc Augé, 'the world's inhabitants have at last become truly contemporaneous, and yet the world's diversity is recomposed every moment: this is the paradox of our day. We must speak, therefore, of worlds in the plural, understanding that each of them communicates with the others...'[8] In fact, China's meeting with the world did not happen overnight when the Open Door reforms began; and furthermore, in the late 1970s and 1980s, there was still a lot of oppression in China, with only a limited range of knowledge or information available. As the curator Hans Ulrich Obrist has observed, a dynamic avant-garde movement took place in the very resistance of all these difficulties, and a remarkable generation formed and became to China what the 1960s generation, including Andy Warhol and Joseph Beuys, had been to America and Europe.[9]

In this new age of globalization, says the art historian and theorist Hans Belting, 'world art' appears to be 'an old idea complementary to modernism'. The term 'world art' was 'initially coined as a colonial notion' that was in use to refer to the art of 'others', although examples of their work could be found in Western museums. 'Global art', on the other hand, is 'recognized as the sudden and worldwide production of art that did not exist or did not garner attention until the late 1980s... [It] not only accelerates contemporary art's departure from the guidelines of a linear art history, it also flourishes in parts of the world where art history has never been practiced…'[10] Is contemporary art in China simply an influence from or copy of the West, or is it a consequence of the natural development of Chinese art after the Reform and Opening policy? The following chapters will analyze and re-examine contemporary art produced during China's social and cultural transformations.

Before we embark on a new exploration of Chinese contemporary art, it is worth revisiting the existing discussions and those artists, artist groups and works that have been spotlit in art history. At the First National Symposium of Oil Painting, held in April 1986, the critic and curator Gao Minglu introduced the term '85 Art Movement (*85 Meishu yudong*), or '85 Art New Wave (*85 Meishu xinchao*), thereby drawing attention to its historical and cultural context. The movement featured prominently in numerous exhibitions that sprang up after the *Sixth National Fine Arts Exhibition* (1984), spontaneously initiated by groups of young artists to promote new ideas and concepts. Nearly one hundred art groups appeared nationwide during the '85 Art Movement, and some are seen today as vital in having articulated an avant-garde agenda, tested group identity through a series of collective projects, and challenged conventional art forms, including the Northern Art Group (*Beifang yishu qunti*), the Pond Society (*Chi she*), Xiamen Dada, and the Southwest Art Research Group (*Xinan yishu yanjiu qunti*). The Northern Art Group, for example, acted as the advocator of 'rational spirit'. Among the leading members of the collective, Shu Qun noted that 'our practice has proven that the "new culture" as it was initially formed in our minds was ambiguous. Only through discussion, debate and experimentation with the creation of artistic schema did this become clearer.'[11] Likewise, Wang Guangyi's notion of 'liquidation of humanist enthusiasm' was formed to express 'a sentiment prevalent among the avant-garde artists in the second half of the 1980s, the call for the change of paradigms' (see p. 20).[12] Secondly, and running counter to this current of rationalism, according to Gao's analysis, there was a tendency to pursue 'intuitionism and a sense of mystery', which figured quite prominently in exhibitions such as the *November Painting Exhibition* in Beijing, the *New Figurative Exhibition* (*Xin juxiang zhanlan*) in Shanghai and Yunnan, the *Zero Exhibition* (*Ling zhan*) in Shenzhen, and the *Shanxi Modern Art Exhibition*. Thirdly, there was the renewal of concepts concerning the process of art making, behaviourism and Pop art, which was influenced – or, arguably, 'randomly catalyzed' – by the Robert Rauschenberg exhibition that opened at Beijing's National Art Museum in November 1985.[13]

In August 1986, the *Large-Scale Slide Exhibition of New Wave Art* (commonly referred to as the Zhuhai Symposium) showed 1,100 slides of work by regional artists and art groups. This was then followed by the *Symposium on the Making of Chinese Modern Art* at Huangshan in November 1988, also known as the Huangshan Symposium, which, similarly, attracted the participation of more than a hundred artists and critics. As a consequence of these two important events as a process of debating and planning, the *China/Avant-Garde* exhibition (the title in Chinese, *Zhongguo xiandai yishu zhan*, literally means 'Exhibition of Chinese Modern Art') was finally staged at the National Art Museum in February 1989, to conclude the movement by revealing it in all its complexity and, at the same time, to set a new point of departure for Chinese contemporary art.[14]

The notion of the so-called 'Post-89', taking the 1989 exhibition *China/Avant-Garde* as a landmark of contemporary art in China, refers to an art phenomenon whereby artists continued to develop new thinking and work derived from the '85 Art Movement. From this new phase, the two most dominant trends of painting became internationally known – both terms coined by critic and curator Li Xianting at the beginning of the 1990s – as Political Pop (*Zhengzhi bopu*) and Cynical Realism (*Wanshi xianshi zhuyi*). According to Li, the former first emerged at a time when China had become even more tightly closed at the end of the 1980s and the beginning of the 1990s. For example, it was then that Wang Guangyi started to develop his series of *Great Criticism*, in which he deconstructs the language of symbols through the juxtaposition of images of the worker-peasant-soldier of the Cultural Revolution with the logos of Coca-Cola and Marlboro, among other commercial brands imported from the West. Also making use of the significance of Mao's visual legacies, Yu Youhan re-portrayed the god-like image of the Chairman, decorating it, for instance, with floral images from Chinese folk art to flatten any political significance; and, later, Liu Dahong recorded the amplitude of the revolution – so-called 'big-character' slogans of protest, mass parades and performances, and the deified Chairman – in a festive, celebratory and almost surrealistic scenario. Political Pop included work achieved beyond direct appropriation. In *1989 Standard Pronunciation*, Zhang Peili invited Xing Zhibin, who was then a famous newscaster on CCTV (China Central Television) – metaphorically, the face, the voice and the expression of the state – to read out words from a Chinese dictionary, starting with *shui* (water), in her usual orthodox manner but using a tedious monotone. The authoritative became meaningless. With the support of curators, both domestic and international, Political Pop played the role of ambassador in the early 1990s, introducing Chinese contemporary art to the Western world.

The New Generation Art Exhibition (*Xinshengdai yishu zhan*), staged at the National Museum of Chinese History in July 1991,[15] appeared to be a major breakthrough in regard to the restriction of avant-garde art exhibitions in China after 1989, and formed a new set of aesthetics, leading to the Cynical Realism movement as a response to the socio-political environment in China at that time. For example, Liu Wei portrays what might be his own childhood, with two young children and a doll, all dressed up properly, posing and yet looking desensitized and absent-minded, in front of a gigantic

2 BELOW Wang Guangyi, *Great Criticism: Coca-Cola*, 1993
3 OPPOSITE Yu Youhan, *On the Tiananmen Tower*, 1990

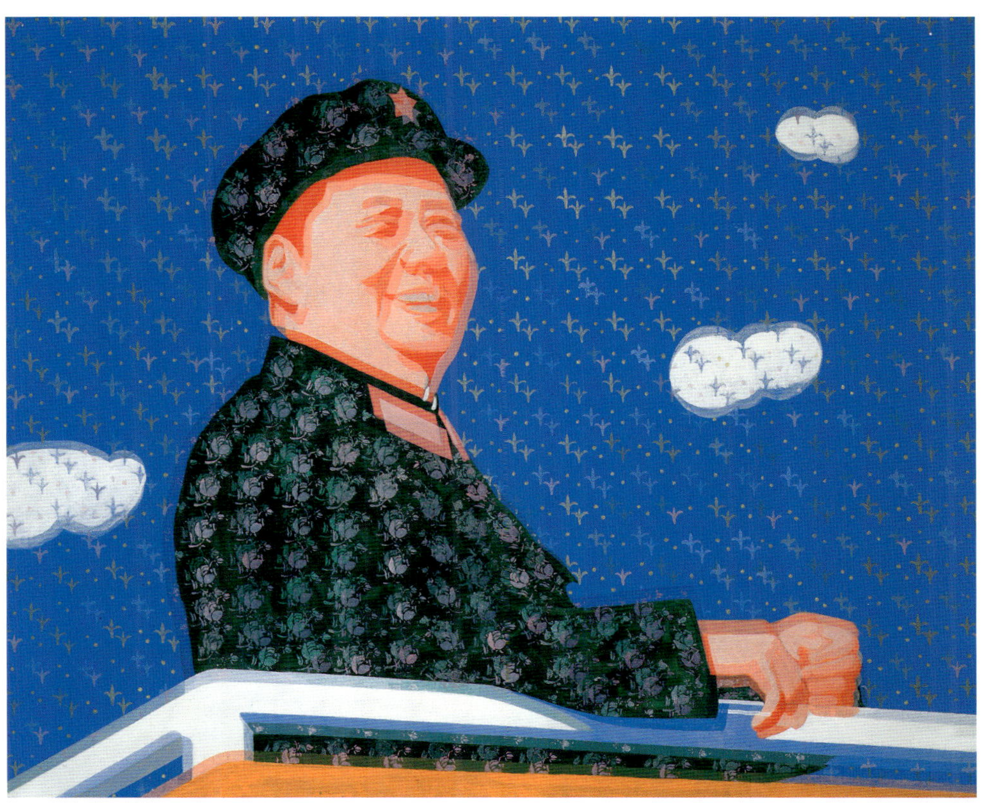

6

portrait of Mao as the defining backdrop of the generation. Liu Xiaodong, meanwhile, takes groups of urban youths as his subject matter, and represents their somehow indifferent and uncaring states. Fang Lijun's well-known image of a bald rogue has become iconic for Cynical Realism: he is, for example, depicted in the middle of a huge yawn – or what might, in fact, be a cry – to express a sense of ennui. Similarly representative are the laughing men in Yue Minjun's painting and sculpture series (see p. 52). In *Taking a Picture in Front of Tiananmen*, Wang Jinsong mocks supposedly serious and honorary moments. In this new version of such a scene, the dignified architecture of Tiananmen is depicted as a theatrical set, while the conventional image of revolutionary workers, peasants and soldiers is replaced by a group of jolly urban professionals, with blank figures at the back, either as a remembrance of the past or as an invitation to new generations to come. There is clearly a certain sense of 'apathy' in the Post-89, reflecting an anxiety

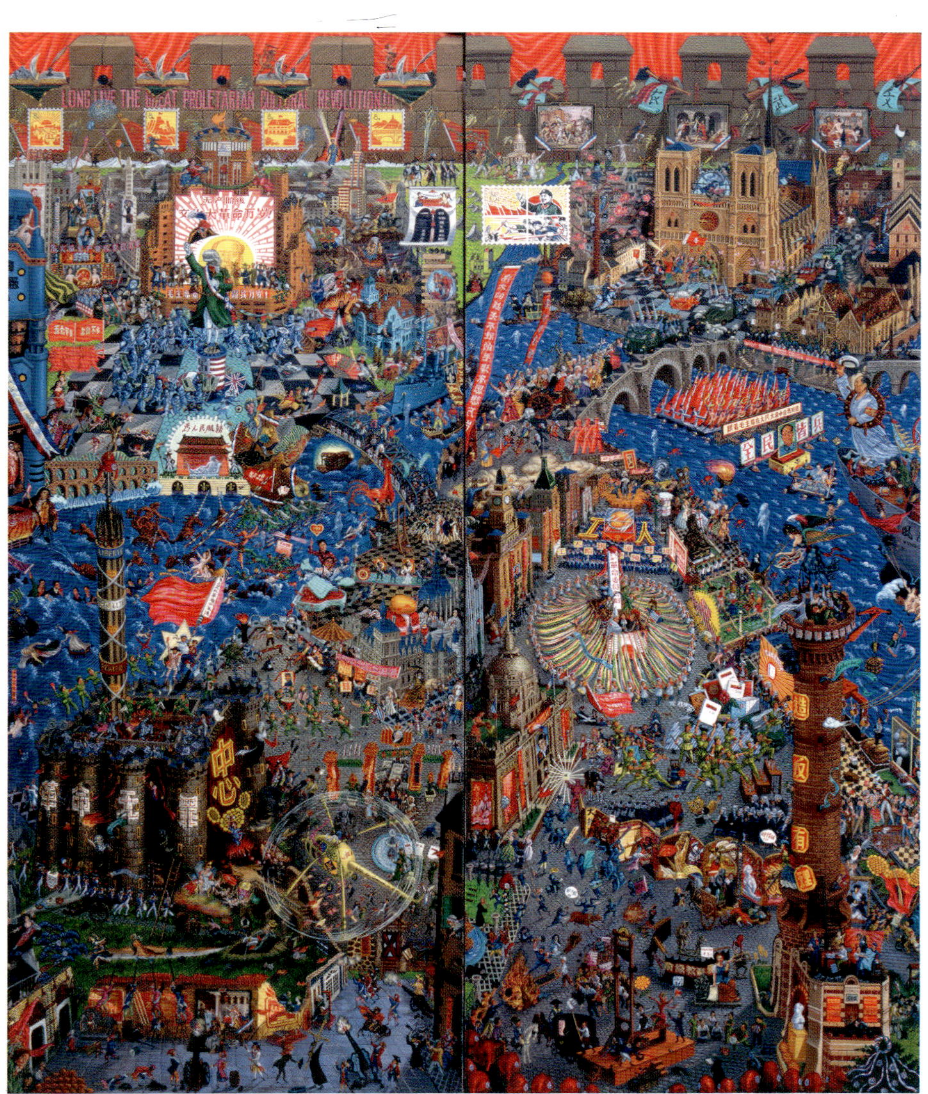

4 ABOVE Liu Dahong, *A Tale of Two Cities*, 1999
5 OPPOSITE Zhang Peili, *1989 Standard Pronunciation*, 1991 (video still)

arising from the perception of uncertainty. 'When reality fails to provide a spiritual support,' as Li Xianting discusses, 'the meaning of the meaningless becomes [an artist's] channel for assigning new meanings to art and existence. This is both their most desperate approach to entrusting new significance, as well as their most promising avenue towards self-salvation.'[16]

Artists in the post-Mao era have indeed generated a specific energy, committed as they are to breaking the boundaries of 'art' for contemporary China, and to extending their artistic and cultural understandings to the rest of the world. The key factors that have been crucial to the development of Chinese contemporary art from local to global are external as well as internal. Externally, survey shows of Chinese art were introduced to the West in the early 1990s; for instance, *Art Chinois 1990: Chine Demain pour Hier* (1990) in Aix-en-Provence in France, and *China/Avant-Garde* (1993–94), which first opened in Berlin, and subsequently travelled to Rotterdam, Oxford, Odense and Hildesheim. Notably, as a section of the 1993 Venice Biennale, *Passaggio a Oriente* marked the appearance of Chinese contemporary art on the international stage, with a presentation of fourteen Chinese artists. Since then, Chinese contemporary art has frequently contributed to long-standing biennials, triennials and art fairs, in cities like

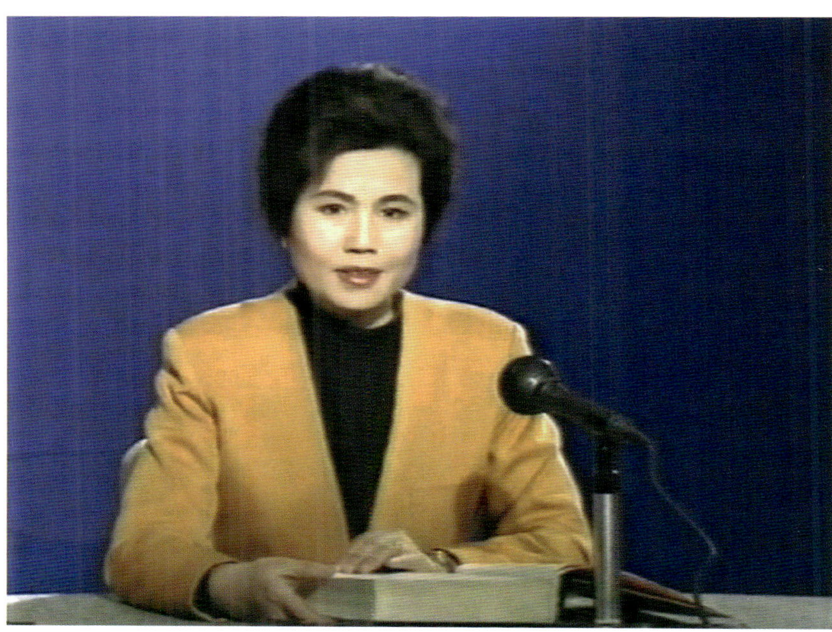

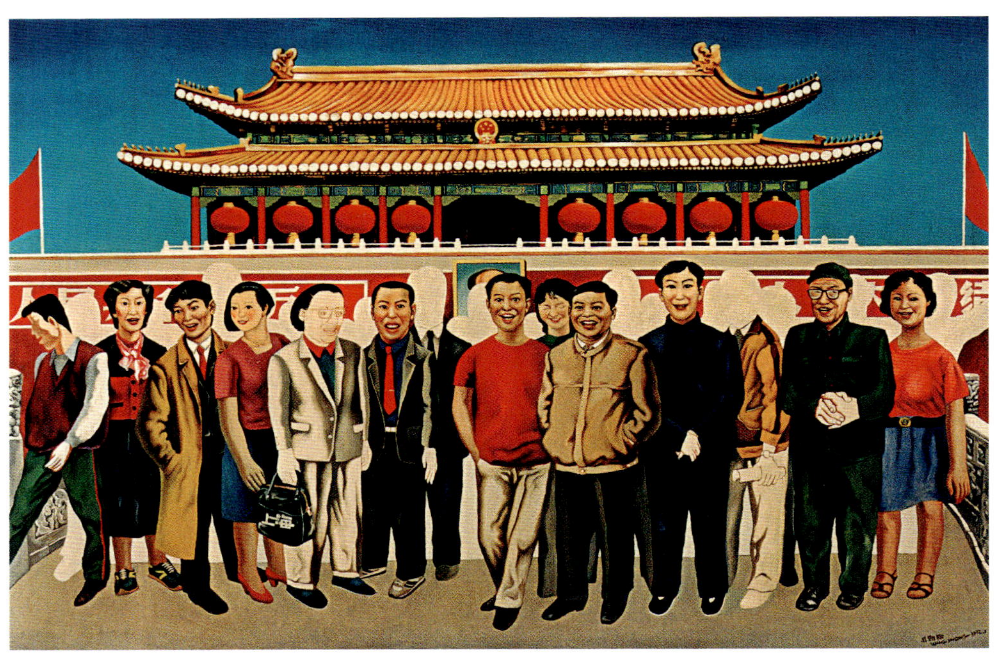

6 Wang Jinsong, *Taking a Picture in Front of Tiananmen*, 1992

Venice, Kassel, São Paulo, Basel, Istanbul, Sydney, and many more. Chinese art has rapidly become a new club member of the contemporary art world. At the same time, 'new art from China' has been a regular guest at Western art museums and galleries, including in the *Inside Out* exhibition (1999) at the San Francisco Museum of Modern Art, *The Real Thing* (2007) at Tate Liverpool, *The Revolution Continues* (2008) at the Saatchi Gallery and *Art of Change* (2012) at the Hayward Gallery, both in London, and, more recently, *Theatre of the World* (2017) at the Guggenheim in New York. Internally, by the end of the 1990s, cultural development – as well as continuing to promote the merits of economic well-being – was being picked up as one of the strategies to enhance China's entry into the World Trade Organization (achieved in 2001). Contemporary art exhibitions in China started to welcome international artists from the beginning of the twenty-first century. Following the success of the first two editions of the officially organized Shanghai Biennale (1996, 1998), major contemporary art events were considered an alternative opportunity to connect China to the world; international works were first accepted by the Shanghai Biennale in 2000. At that point, therefore, contemporary art was 'legitimized'. Using the platforms of these international art events, as well as private art museums newly established in China, more Chinese artists have exhibited their work alongside those from different cultural backgrounds and become part of the globalized art world.

Rather than following any invented genres and terminologies, however, and becoming sidetracked by many more related discussions, this book will examine the emergence and development of Chinese contemporary art in a different way. The following four chapters are constructed as a series of perspectives that are interconnected to reveal contemporary art as generated from everyday reality in the People's Republic.

The first chapter focuses on the experience of the masses and offers an account of various contemporary understandings of and artistic reflections on the notion of the 'collective', from the family unit to the *danwei* work unit, from the political parades and gatherings of Mao's period to the square dancing of the present day. It examines people's understanding of the communist leader, and the notion of the collective, and the ways in which such subjects have been widely appropriated and reflected in contemporary art. Representations of Mao's collective and the role of individuals become central to the discussion.

The twentieth century was a century of changes, in which China experienced unprecedented disruptions in the continuation of cultural traditions, and artists became entangled in the tensions of cultural anxieties. Given this unique situation in China, Chapter 2 examines the fate of artistic and cultural traditions at a time when the country was experiencing enormous political and social changes, and the ways in which contemporary artists, through their experimental practices, have played the roles of substitute inheritors of everyday legends, as well as critical commentators and pioneers for re-imaginings. The chapter reflects critically upon the interruptions, and addresses the reinterpretation of Chinese traditional art and culture in the context of contemporary art.

Social and cultural disturbance has continued with the 'revolutionary' urbanization in post-Mao China. With a population due to reach one and a half billion in a few years' time, China still continues to accelerate its economic development, and more than half the population has become urban. The third chapter uncovers the consequent impacts on individual artists who have experienced extraordinary urban transformations, and how these artists have responded to the rapid changes through their practice. The ongoing process of urbanization has provided rich material not only for alternative artistic expressions, but also for new critical perspectives 'into China's decisive transformation into an urban nation [in which artists can] conceive their art making as an approach to deconstruct the mainstream social and economic discourses promoted by Chinese policymakers'.[17]

Finally, the origin of Chinese contemporary art can be explored through a reassessment of its early development in relation to the impact of China's Cultural Revolution. Over and above the manipulation of the iconography of Mao and the colour red in early developments of Chinese contemporary art, the link between the spirit of the new generation of Chinese artists in the post-Mao era and the mood of the rebel can be established. While Mao's Cultural Revolution brought ten years of political turbulence and cultural disaster, it also gave birth to Chinese contemporary art and saw the first emergence of its visibility in the international art world. Chapter 4 of this book portrays an alternative image of art, with a status of being 'at large', in relation to the cultural and political constraints of contemporary China. These constraints have not been regarded passively, but have instead become the stimulus for creative strategies, and the driving force to generate, accumulate and deliver artistic power. The chapter reveals the rebellious position as the foremost legacy of the Cultural Revolution for art, and the work and events developed against the authorities and beyond the conventional art space. The particular notions of 'off-site' and 'incident' are employed to examine the body of selected work – the marginalized, the excluded, the unexpected and the forgotten. This chapter will reveal a series of exceptional works that were site-specifically produced, executed and performed, as well as works that have often been seen as political or social 'events', or artistic 'incidents'.

At the end of each chapter, a coda introduces perceptions of modern-day China to further extend discussions in response to the topics covered in the main texts. These codas arise out of personal experience, research, teaching and conversations over a tea set with artists, colleagues and friends on regular visits back to China over the last twenty years. Each encounter has brought fresh insights. While a journey to and from China takes place between two countries, this project takes place between two worlds, the artistic and the 'real', which combine to form the very essence of the 'world of art'.

Chapter 1
The Collective

The word 'collective', *jiti* in Chinese, can be read literally as 'grouped individuals'. For many decades, following the foundation of the People's Republic of China, the collective was developed as a means for people to learn, understand and share their lives. By being extended with a suffix, as 'collectivism', it has been valued as a particular energy generated through individuals who have a common goal, a precept of selflessness in favour of collective interests, a communist morality, or a sacred belief in Mao's world.

In the early development of the new China, mass assemblies became a prominent and familiar phenomenon, and this helped to expand the term far beyond its literal meaning. Sociological and political interpretations of the notion of 'collectiveness' in China sometimes refer to this phenomenon as a 'family' movement, whereby individuals also belong to their work unit as a focal nucleus of life, or, more precisely in the Chinese term, their *danwei*, which includes, for instance, factories in the case of workers, schools and universities for students and teachers, hospitals for doctors and nurses, and so on. According to the writer and academic David Bray, *danwei* is a generic term denoting not only the Chinese socialist workplace, but also the specific range of practices that this embodies. As he defines it:

It is the source of employment and material support for the majority of urban residents; it organizes, regulates, polices, trains, educates, and protects them; it provides them with identity and face; and, within distinct spatial units, it forms integrated communities through which urban residents derive their sense of place and social belonging.[1]

The *danwei* functions not only as the state apparatus
of political control, but also as a redistributing agency in
which rewards and opportunities are linked to individuals'
political attitudes and loyalty.[2] In the environment of the
danwei, everything is intended to be transparent within the
collective, with nothing being personal, in order to ensure
faith in communal living. The collective may be designed as a
'criterion' of daily life, and constructed as an idealistic identity
for 'the people' – allowing for no authentic independence, but
promoting an overall kind of conformity, within which one
can nonetheless, through super-conformity, be recognized
and valued with legitimate status.

The Brain

The *danwei* style of collective was effectively constructed under
Mao's regime. This is to say that, despite the country's vast
population, all the individual collectives that made up the total
collective body of China seemingly had one singular brain, that
of the Chairman. Every condition and every movement of all
the individual bodies was inspired and specifically instructed
by the brain. When, on 9 September 1976, Mao died, at the age
of 82, the entire country fell into deep mourning. An estimated
one million people filed past his flag-draped coffin laid at
the Great Hall of the People to pay their final respects. But
more than grief, there was a sense of loss and a fear for the
uncertainty of the future as China moved forward without its
leader. Life would have to carry on, but very differently. Without
the critical examination of Mao through artistic reflections,
it is impossible to truly understand the collective.

In 1988, Wang Guangyi made his monumental series of
paintings, *Mao Zedong*, representing the Chairman's 'standard
portraits' on five large canvases, two of them with red grids
and three with black grids. The series was first shown in the
1989 *China/Avant-Garde* exhibition at the National Art Museum
in Beijing, and became one of the most controversial works
of the time, marking 'a turning point in China's modern
art movement'.[3] The original intention of this series was to
conclude the artist's 'liquidation of humanist enthusiasm'.
However, after it had been exhibited, Wang suspected that
'the onlookers, with hundredfold humanist enthusiasm,
endowed Mao Zedong with even more humanist connotations'.[4]
The 'divine' images were overlaid with thick grids: practical
guides for duplicating and enlarging, and so glorifying, the
Chairman. Normally removed once pictures are completed,
here the grids remain and overlay a sombre grey Mao, serving
as a frame for measurement or analysis. In Wang's paintings,

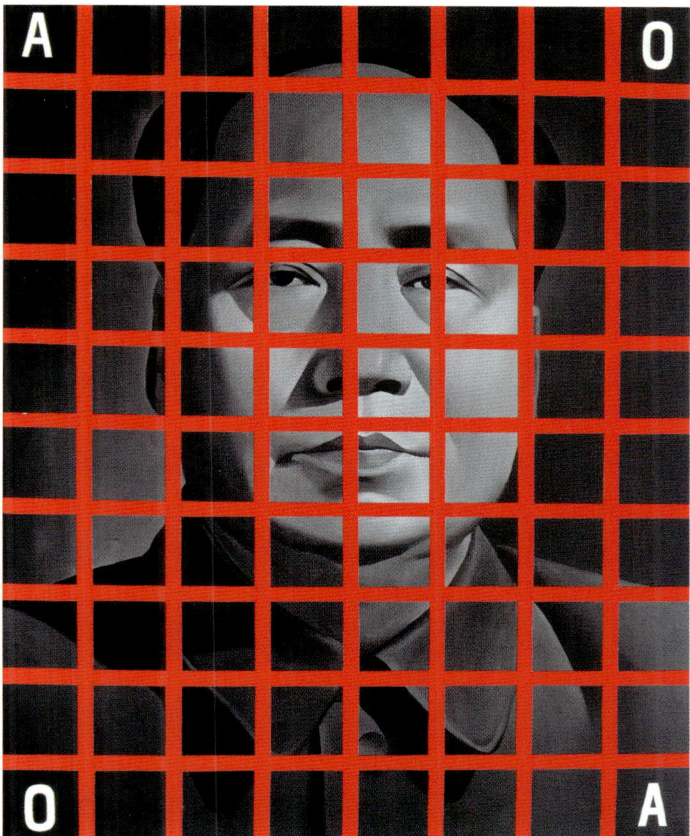

7 Wang Guangyi, *Mao Zedong: Red Grid No. 1*, 1988

as critic and curator Karen Smith discusses, the warning barrier 'required people to pause for a moment before approaching this deity', and 'forced an objective reconsideration, literally to put Mao into perspective, a sentiment reinforced by a palette of cold reds and steely blue-greys'.[5] The rationale here was simple: by bringing the grid out from beneath the surface of the picture to the forefront, the image was transformed from an object of worship into a subject of judgment.

As an artist of a slightly older generation, Yu Youhan experienced the years of the Cultural Revolution while studying in Beijing at the Central Academy of Arts and Crafts. During that time, Yu painted huge images of Mao on a wall of more than 120 square metres (over 1,290 sq. ft) opposite the Tiananmen Tower. To him, the Chairman meant everything – 'a great leader of the nation, a symbol of China or the East, a book

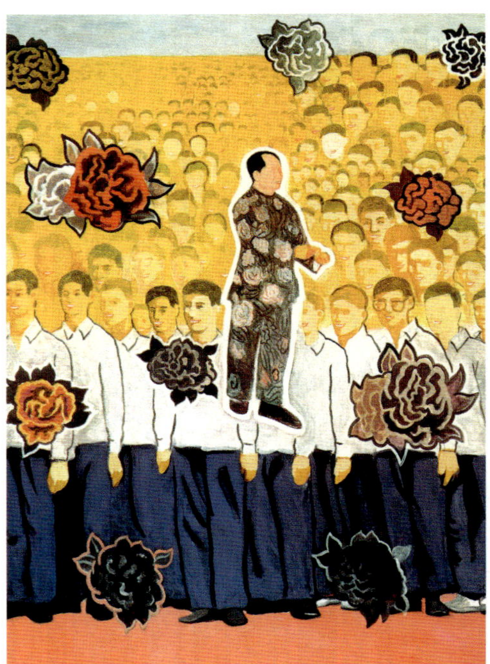 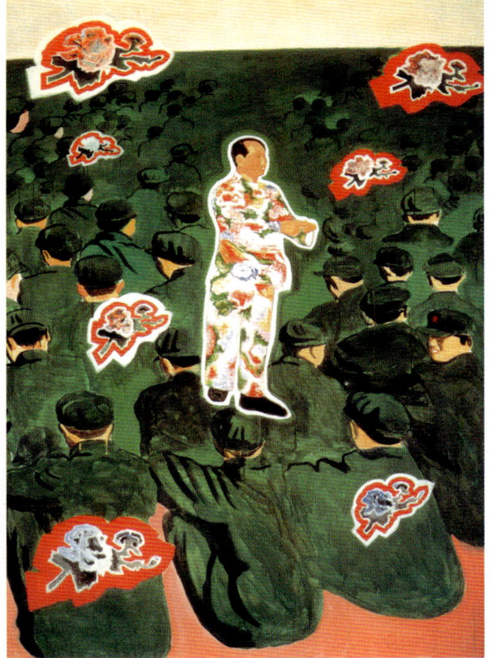

of culture or a particular period of history. Sometimes Mao is avant-garde, but sometimes rather conservative.'[6] From the end of the 1980s, however, the artist began to re-portray Mao in a completely different way. Most of his early paintings are based on journalists' photographs of Mao published in the pictorials officially sanctioned by the state. All the images that were accessible to the public were positive, as well as historically and politically significant, celebrating Mao leading the country and his people on the way to the success of the People's Republic.

[8] In Yu's series *Mao and His People*, the leader is positioned in the centre of each work, his pose appropriated from the well-known photograph of Mao at the talks in Yan'an (see p. 7). Instead of the original patched trousers, however, his suit is patterned with flowers, and these are also dotted around the painting, which is turned into a fabric-like composition. Similarly, floating flowers [9] are applied to the 1991 work *Talking with Hunan Peasants*, based on a 1950s photograph depicting Mao sitting graciously with a family of cheerfully admiring peasants – the men notably sitting, while the women stand – in his home town, Shaoshan, in Hunan Province. The floral patterns were the artist's own invention, inspired by the paper flowers used as so-called

8 OPPOSITE Yu Youhan, *Mao and His People*, 1995
9 BELOW Yu Youhan, *Talking with Hunan Peasants*, 1991

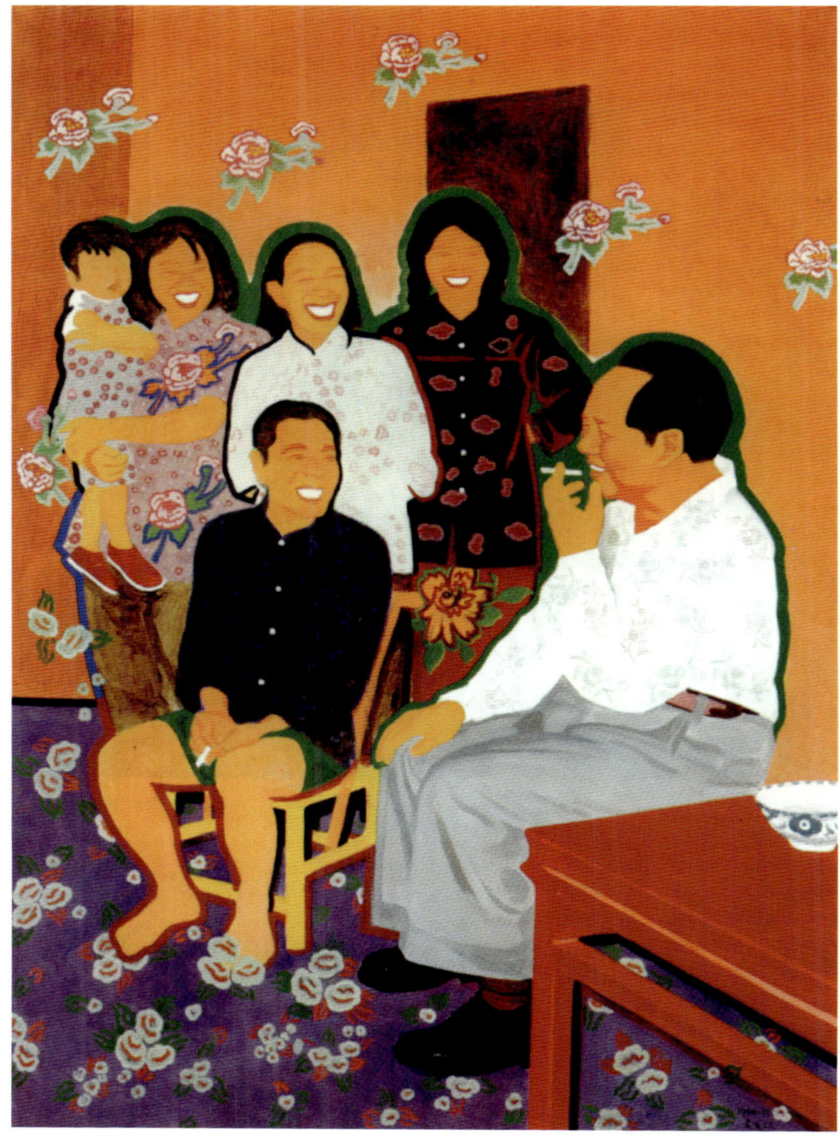

'spiritual rewards' in communist China. Imposed on Mao and the other figures, they appear everywhere in the painting, recalling the native style of folk art. As the artist has reflected, 'The floating flowers decorate the space quite nicely, and yet make it an unreal and hollow environment. Communism, which we are encouraged to dedicate our lives to, seems to be a beautiful paradise, an unreachable destination. However, people do not have the ability to expose the lie, or break away from the dream.'[7] The subjects' smile, the collective smile, joyfully in unison under the guidance of Mao, represents the over-idealized relationship between the Chairman and his people, while their ignorance of the situation is somehow divulged by their bare white teeth.

Li Shan's work seems to be even more obviously 'treasonous'. The painting series *Rouge* is based on two of the most famous photographs of Mao, one taken during the period of his guerrilla activity in the 1930s and the other comprising a benevolent-looking 'standard portrait'. The word 'rouge' (*yanzhi*) describes a hue of pink verging on fuchsia, at one time a colour particularly associated with Chinese traditional art, such as Beijing Opera and New Year painting. It is chosen here as the title for its symbolism of something superficial but, at the same time, useful for whitewashing revolutionary ideology and the real prospects of people's lives.[8] In the series, a mysterious lotus-like flower containing the colour rouge is always carried between the lips of the communist leader, who sometimes wears a red-star cap as well as lipstick. On the one hand, this 'rouge-ization' of Mao demonstrates the popularization of the Chairman's portrait and its transformation into a mass icon; on the other hand, the folksy, even vulgar taste for the colour rouge eliminates and insults the sacred meaning of the image of Mao. Art historian Francesca Dal Lago explores further:

An implicit reference is directed toward male homoerotic desire, traditionally associated in China with the theatrical world because of the convention of men playing female roles [in Beijing Opera]. This association – implied both by the use of the colour and by the androgynous, feminized features assumed by the portrait in Li's series – introduces another recurrent trope of the literary recollections of the Cultural Revolution – that of sexual freedom and liberation experienced during this period. 'Gendering' Mao becomes Li's personal way to vulgarize the figure of the leader and bring this sublime object of desire to a more accessible level. The result of this practice is the projection of the artist's sexuality onto the icon, the screen of a feminized Mao.[9]

Although these manipulated versions of Mao were explained by the artist as 'transferring' (rather than feminizing) Mao to the state of a purely unisex human being, a visual symbol, or icon of cultural identity, the images – because of Mao's political and apotheosized status in a patriarchal society – inevitably had a subversive impact.

In the numerous propagandistic visual productions of the People's Republic, Mao was always represented either standing heroically or sitting – as a saviour who never lies down. Repose was evidently excluded from the revolutionary vocabulary, except for one presentation of Mao in a horizontal position, and that was the actual body of Mao (so we are told), protected in a glass case in his mausoleum in Tiananmen Square. Sui Jianguo holds mixed feelings for the Chairman – instinctively full of respect and admiration for his political achievement and personality on the one hand, and critical of his autocracy on the other. As he notes:

In Mao's era, we were not independent individuals – we co-existed with the ideology; after his death, we started to pursue our own personal values, to denounce Mao and to attempt to make a clear distinction and separate ourselves from him. And yet, I realize that I will not be able to transcend him and his time, and unconsciously, in fact, I have been using Mao's instruments and his ways of thinking to deal with things. Undeniably, we are still part of the past, and to be criticized.[10]

Sui Jianguo's 2003 work *Sleeping Chairman Mao* expresses the artist's emotional connection with the leader and reveals the ambivalence between respect and criticism. It is a painted fibreglass sculpture, presenting Mao lying on his side asleep, with head and hand peacefully on the pillow. He is curled up comfortably in a *beiwo* (literally, a 'quilt nest' or 'quilt home'), his whole body wrapped from chin to foot in this tubular blue quilt, which is decorated with an ornate batik pattern of white quasi-floral abstractions. The original clay piece from which the fibreglass was later cast and painted was not, however, sculpted by Sui Jianguo himself, but by an artisan, Wang Wenhai, from Yan'an, the rural city in Shaanxi Province that is celebrated as a shrine of the Chinese communist revolution.

Working at Yan'an Revolution Memorial Hall since the 1970s, Wang Wenhai, together with his wife, has made thousands of Mao statues for over forty years, and enjoys a reputation as the so-called 'Yan'an Clay King'. In various sizes ranging from large to small, these always represent Mao vertically, either as full-length statues or as busts. The invitation to make a

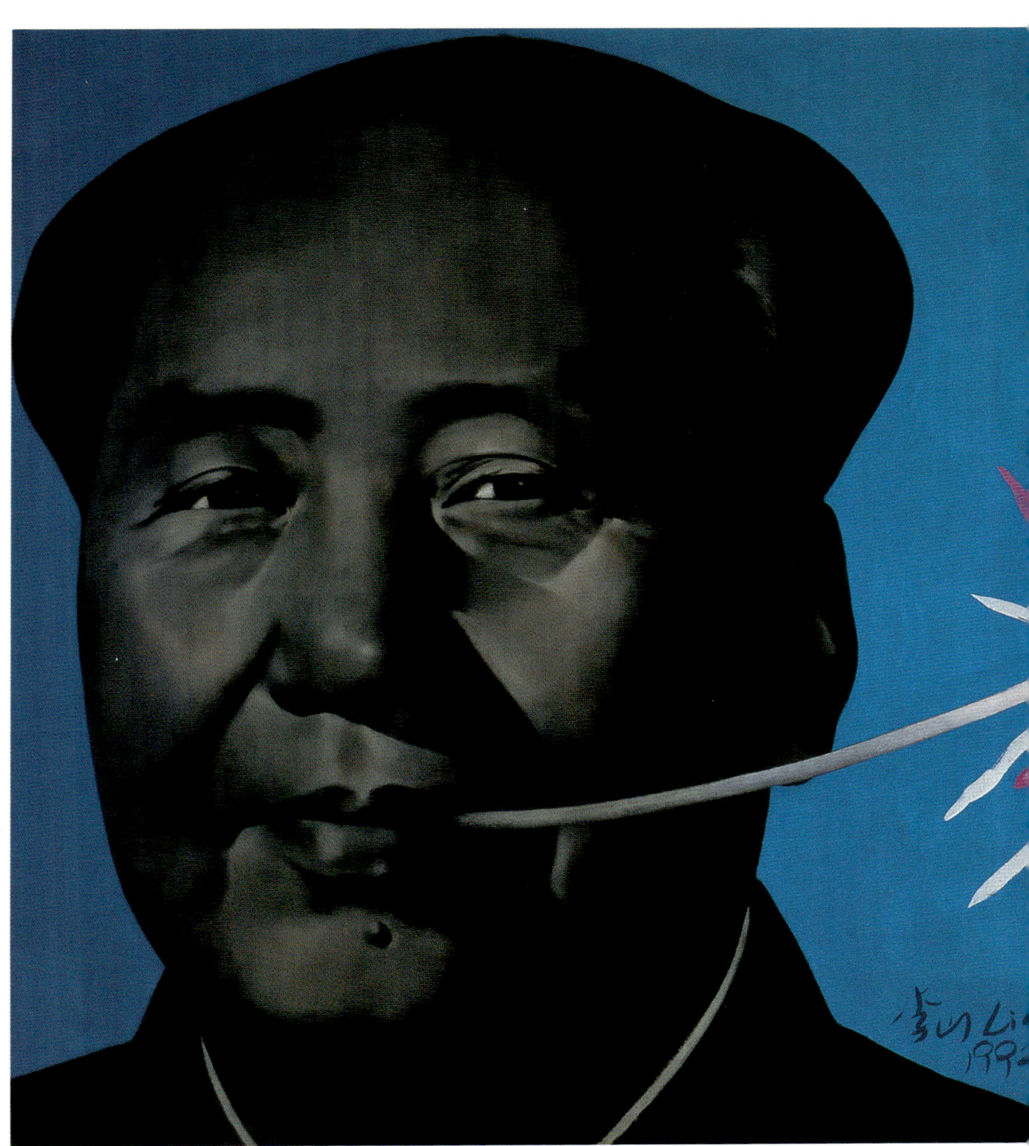

10 Li Shan, *Rouge No. 22*, 1992

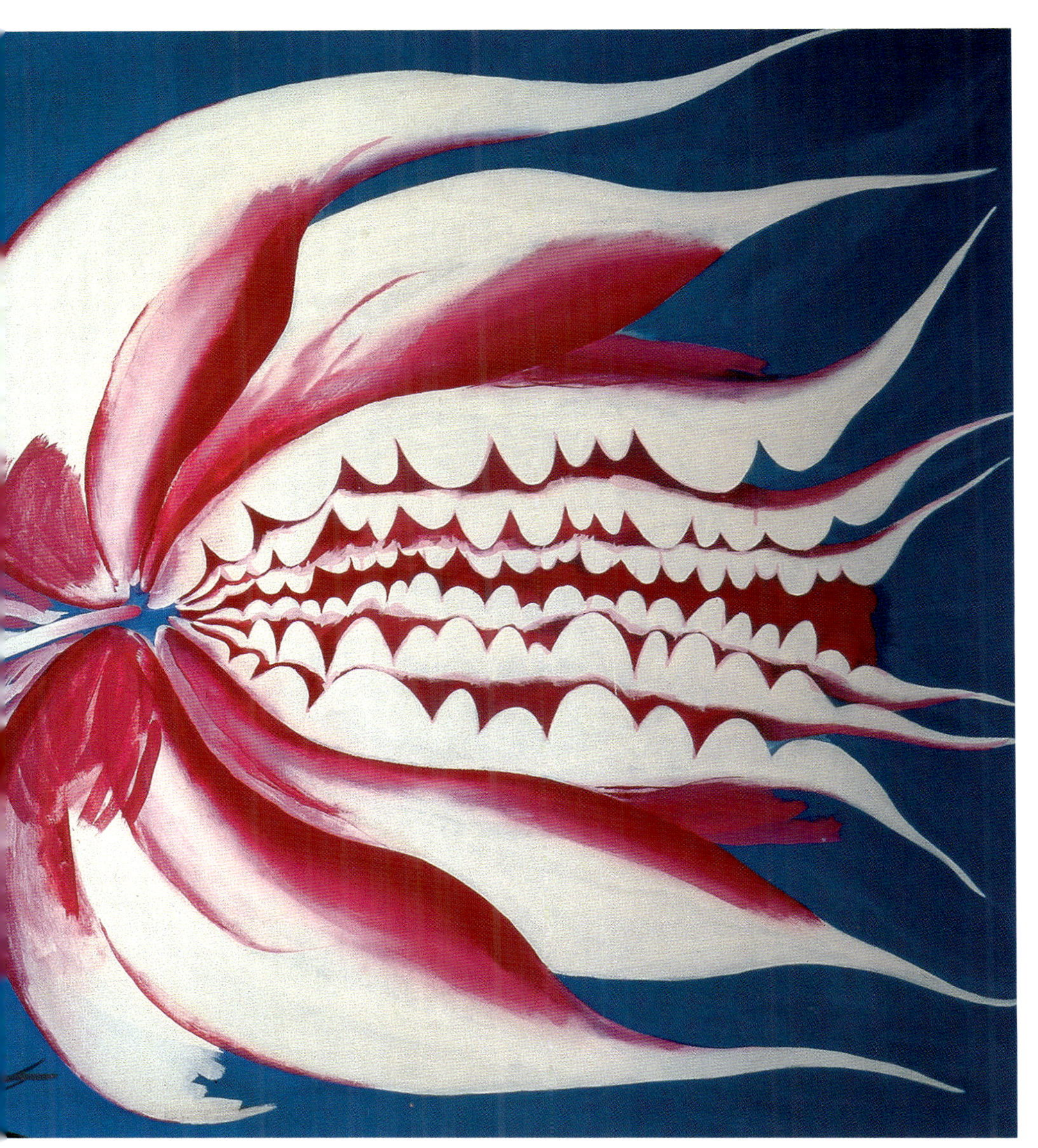

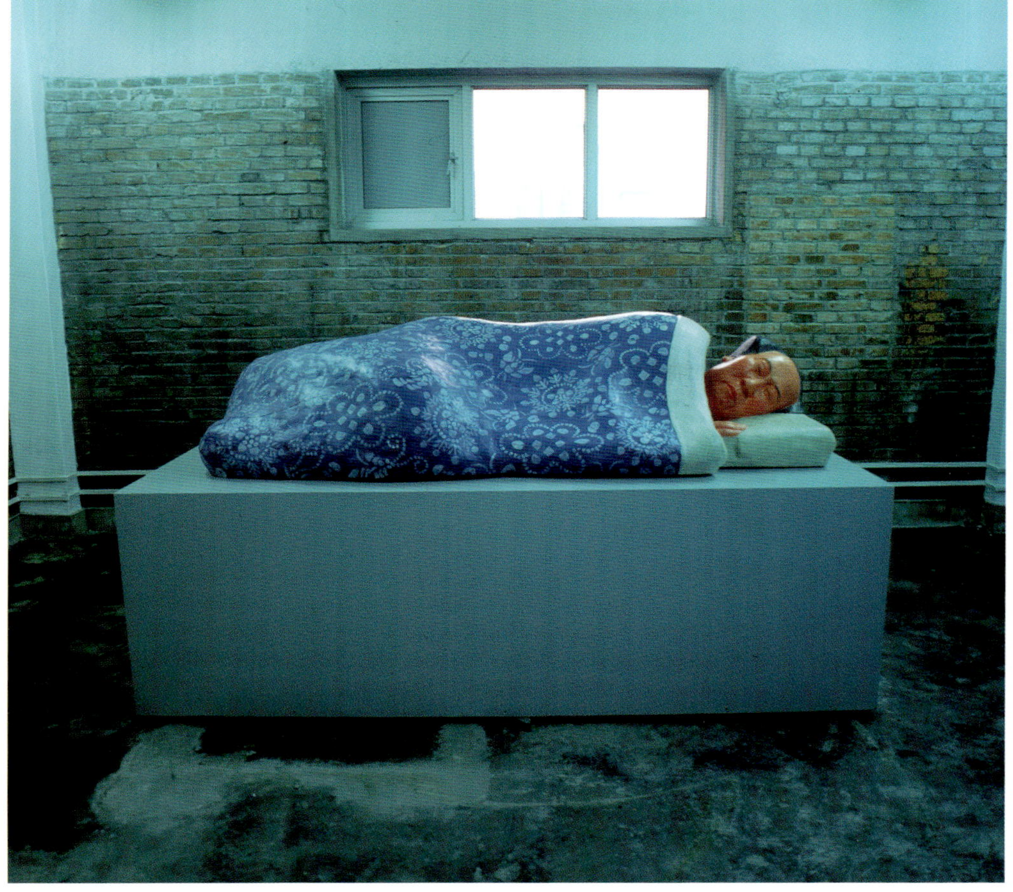

11 Sui Jianguo, *Sleeping Chairman Mao*, 2003

sleeping Mao was initially declined, as the artisan found it
'extremely inappropriate' with regard to Mao's revolutionary
image. The collaboration was only confirmed, after a lengthy
period of reflection, when Wang decided to re-consider the
image of a resting Mao as reflecting the state of entering
Nirvana, an enlightenment whereby the spiritual self is
detached from worldly existence.[11] According to the agreement,
Sui Jianguo would only offer the suggestion of the position
of Mao for the sculpture, but his academically trained realist
skills, aesthetic understanding and artistic personality would
deliberately be excluded from the development of the work. As
a consequence, it appeared to be an authentic piece of folk art,
shaped naturally by its 'original' author. The countenance of
Mao was faithfully depicted, with no possibility of any artistic
involvement with any disrespectful or ironic meanings. His
uncovered face, painted an almost glowing peach-red, and his
hand, in particular showing a clear reference to traditional
Chinese Buddha statues, define him either as deeply at rest
or as an unearthly being.

If Sui Jianguo's Mao laid horizontal is a metaphor for
sleeping, or at least more asleep than lifeless, then Zhuang
Hui's *Mao* determinedly represents death. Chairman Mao
Memorial Hall, located on the central axis of Tiananmen
Square, south of the Monument to the People's Heroes, was
built within half a year and unveiled in 1977 on the anniversary
of Mao's death to display the body of the Chairman for
public viewing. The construction of Mao's mausoleum not
only closed off Tiananmen Square 'physically'; it also,
both 'ideologically and artistically', as Wu Hung suggests,
in 'representing and glorifying death ... defies any former
idealism and imagination even in constructing a Communist
political space'.[12] The body has been neither conventionally
cremated nor entombed, but has instead been preserved as
an archive manifesting the historical achievement of the
communist revolution. And yet, inevitably, and paradoxically,
it reiterates the 'end' of that time. There are rumours about
the authenticity of the corpse, but it is no longer important
to find out if it really is Mao's preserved body or simply a wax
sculpture. In Zhuang Hui's work, the man looks very much
like Mao – and possibly more so than the one that lies in the
mausoleum. Without being covered by a taut Chinese flag,
the Chairman is more 'transparent' or 'naked'. He is not
asleep or at rest, as is suggested by his impeccable Mao suit
and glossy leather shoes; and the glass coffin only reinforces
the death of the leader, which was never imaginable by the
generation of the collective.

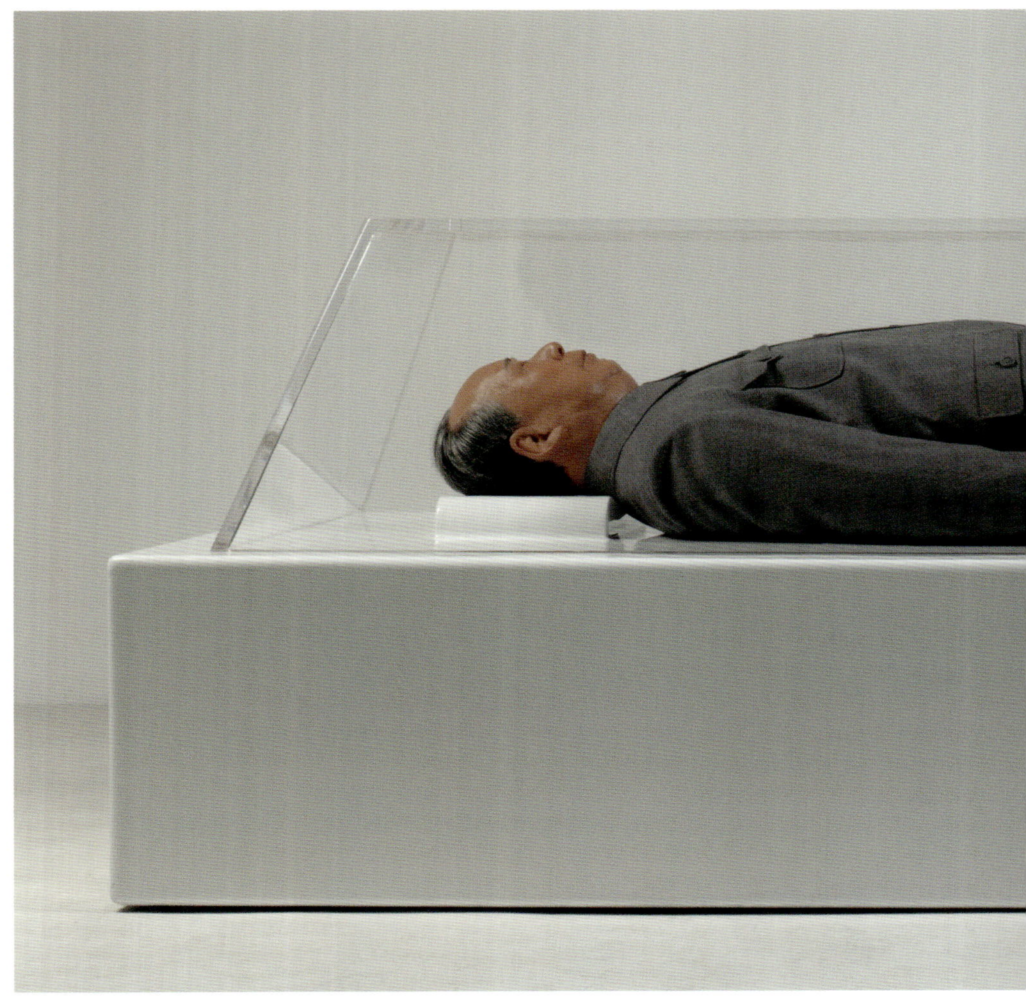

12 Zhuang Hui, *Mao*, 2007

The Tamed

Prior to discussing the representation of the collective, we shall first observe the mechanisms that work on the individuals who have made up that collective. For example, how can we identify a person, when people's appearance changes over time? There are various ways in China to ensure a convincing process of identification. In his early work *People Do Exist*, Geng Jianyi presents a number of pictures of a male, including portraits of him alone as well as photographs taken with

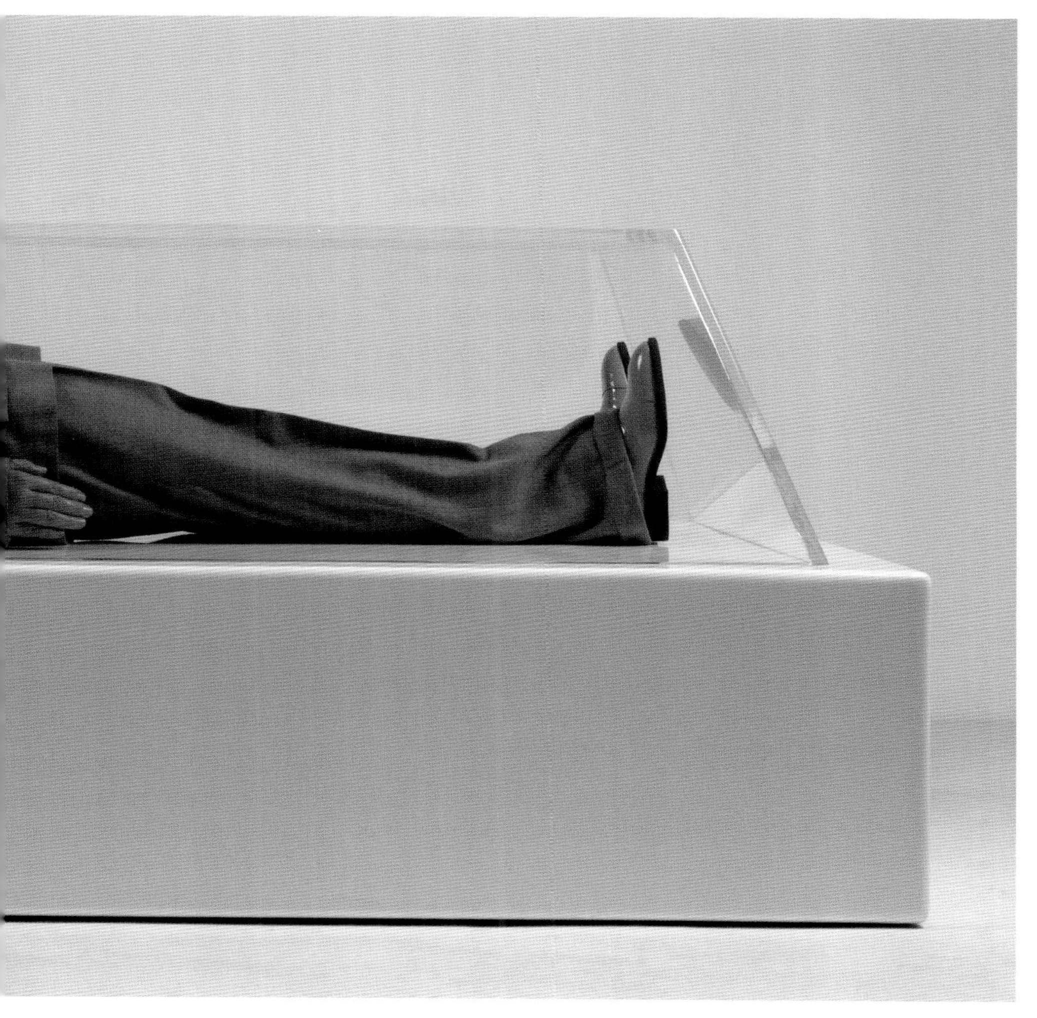

family and friends. This visual aspect is then supported by
a set of documents, which consist of his ID card as well as
character references provided by his family members, his
school classmates, and colleagues from his *danwei* to evidence
the existence of this ordinary person. Similarly, in the series
Definitely Him and *Definitely Her*, Geng manipulates the logic
of the collective life nourished and scrutinized by the system
of *danwei*. In order to verify a series of photographs of men and
women, the artist began in 1998 gradually to collect all kinds

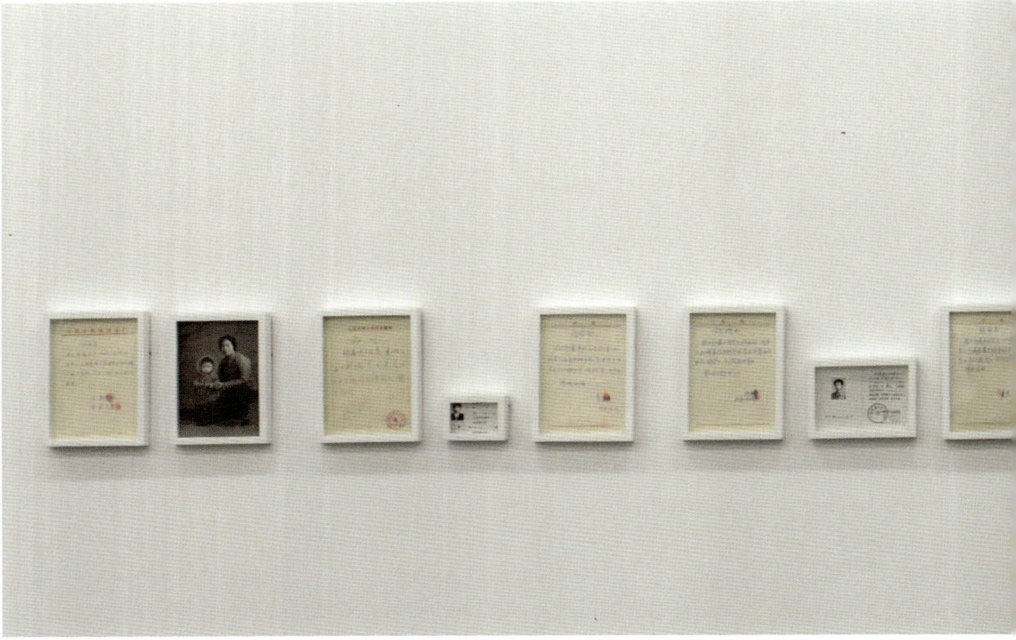

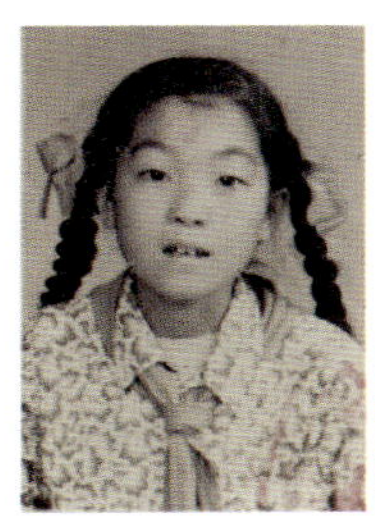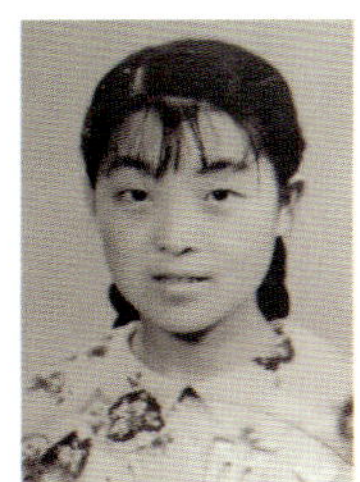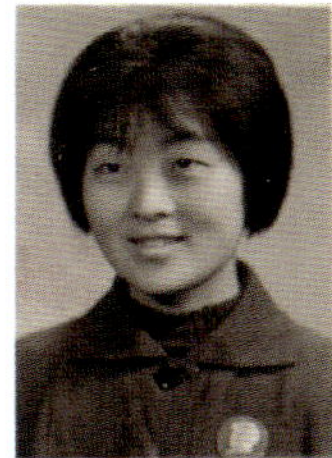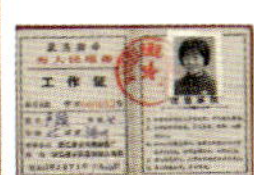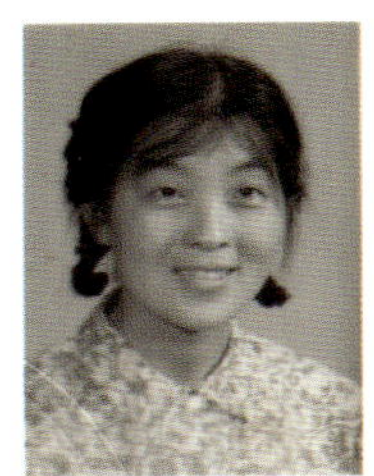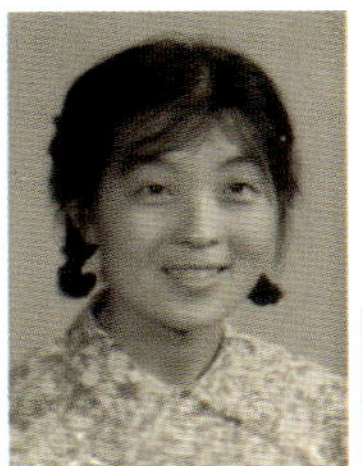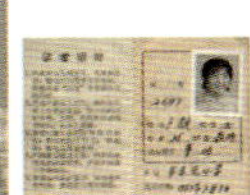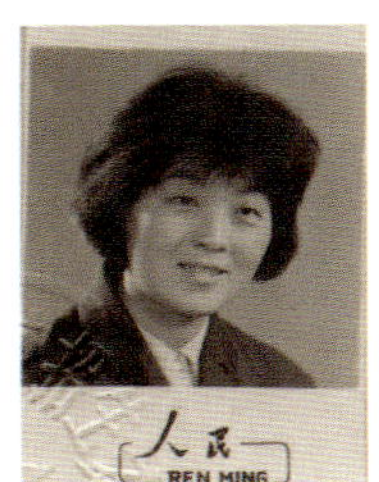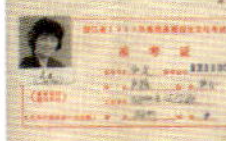

13 TOP Geng Jianyi, *People Do Exist*, 1994
14 ABOVE Geng Jianyi, *Definitely Her*, 1998

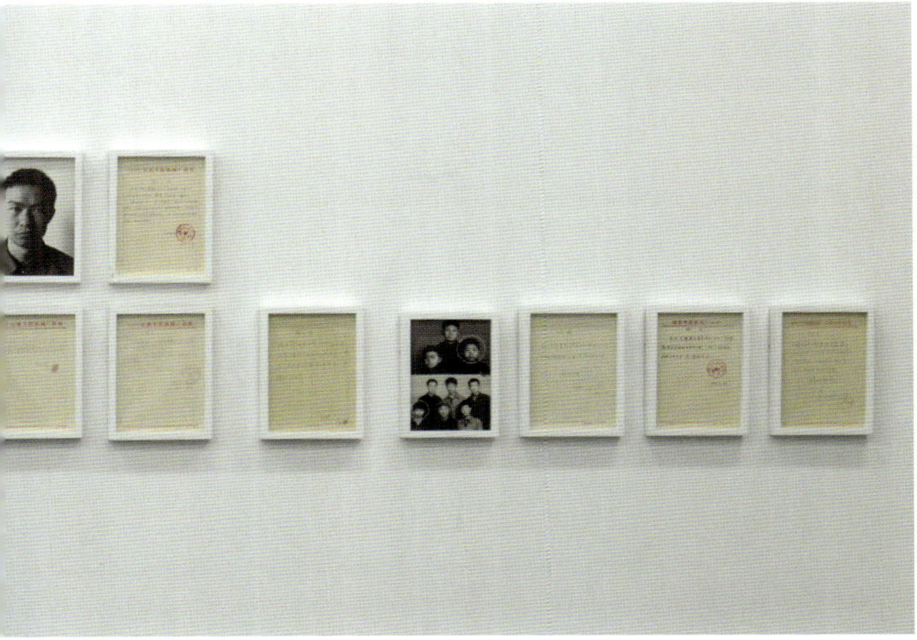

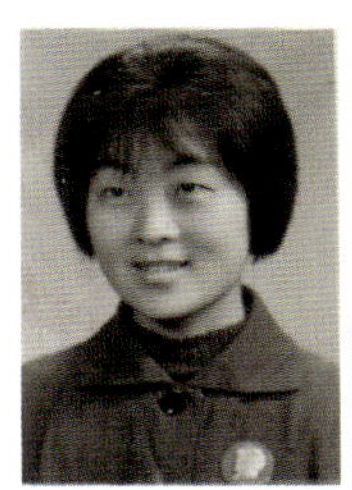
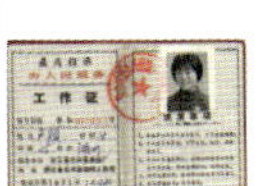
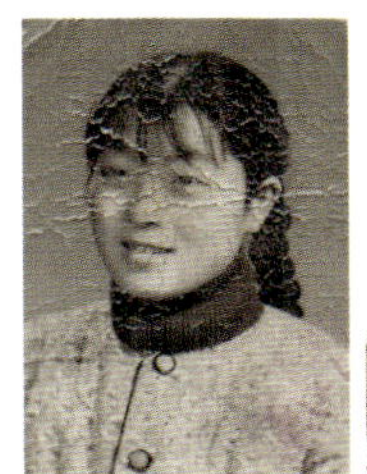

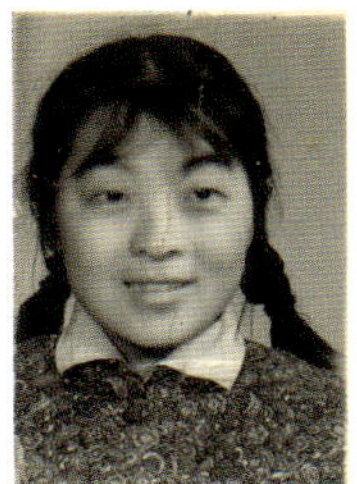
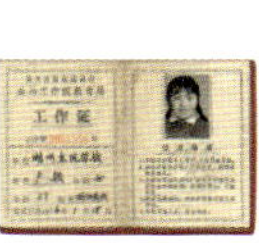
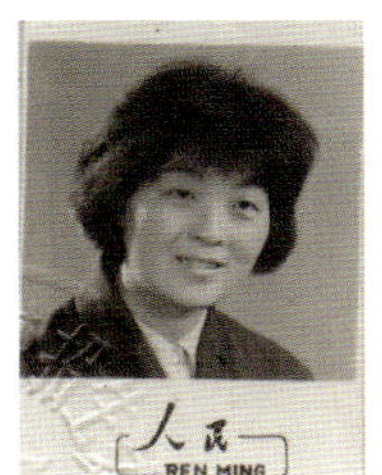
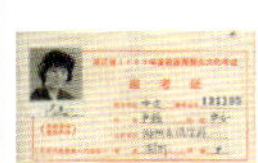
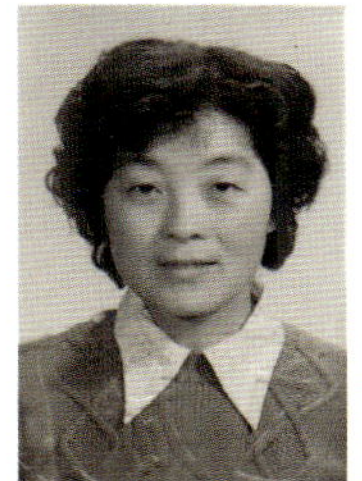
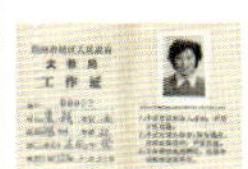
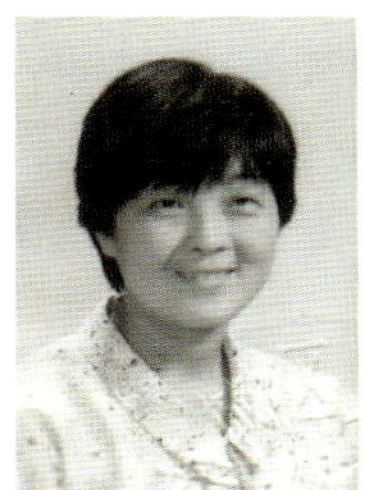
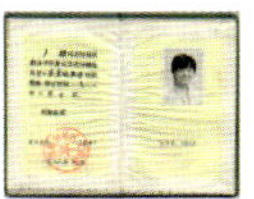

of original certificates and ID cards that had once belonged to his chosen individuals, including work permit, residential card, library card, swimming card, medical card or teaching licence, all of which would include a photograph of the subject taken at a different age. The work seemed to prove the identity of just one individual or two, at a time when Internet search engines or any forms of social media were yet to arrive. In fact, the work revealed the reality that had been enveloped by an unbounded network, or, in Foucault's words, 'power at its extremities, in its ultimate destinations, with those points where it becomes capillary, this is, in its more regional and local forms and institutions'.[13] Each identification not only represents the person, and his/her qualifications or entitlements, but, more importantly, it also demonstrates the social relationships and the affiliation of the collective for any normal daily practices.

Responding to the social framework of collectivism, Geng Jianyi also explored the ways in which each individual had been disciplined to conform their body to the collective movement, such as partaking in broadcast calisthenics (*guangbo cao*) in schools and work units. David Bray elaborates further: 'in socialist China [as compared to Western institutional settings] ... the various micro-level knowledges, disciplinary practices, and biotechnical strategies deployed within the *danwei*, while no less exacting or comprehensive, produced quite a different mode of subjectivity, namely a collective subjectivity focused around production and political participation'.[14] In a sarcastic form of collage as wall chart, Geng's *The Second Series of Eight Steps*, for example, teaches the standard way to smile, with visual and detailed textual instructions. The text in Chinese reads, 'step one, contract the risible muscle on both sides to pull the corners of the mouth, lift the zygomaticus and musculi quadratus labii superioris (inclined top), and open the mouth and close the eyes slightly; step two, drop the jaw and close the eyes; step three, drop the jaw to the lowest position ... lift the corrugator to compress the frontalis, open the mouth wide and lean the head backwards slightly', and so on, with a note of caution to 'avoid subtle movements between each step' and an admonishment to 'act precisely and sufficiently'. In the same vein, to teach people how to practice daily behaviours, the artist even provides instructions on clapping hands and wearing clothes. Geng goes on to reassess yet more common practices in everyday life. In *To Be Your Correct Self*, he filmed

15 OPPOSITE ABOVE Geng Jianyi, *The Second Series of Eight Steps*, 1991
16 OPPOSITE BELOW Geng Jianyi, *Two Series of Five Steps of Wearing Clothes*, 1991

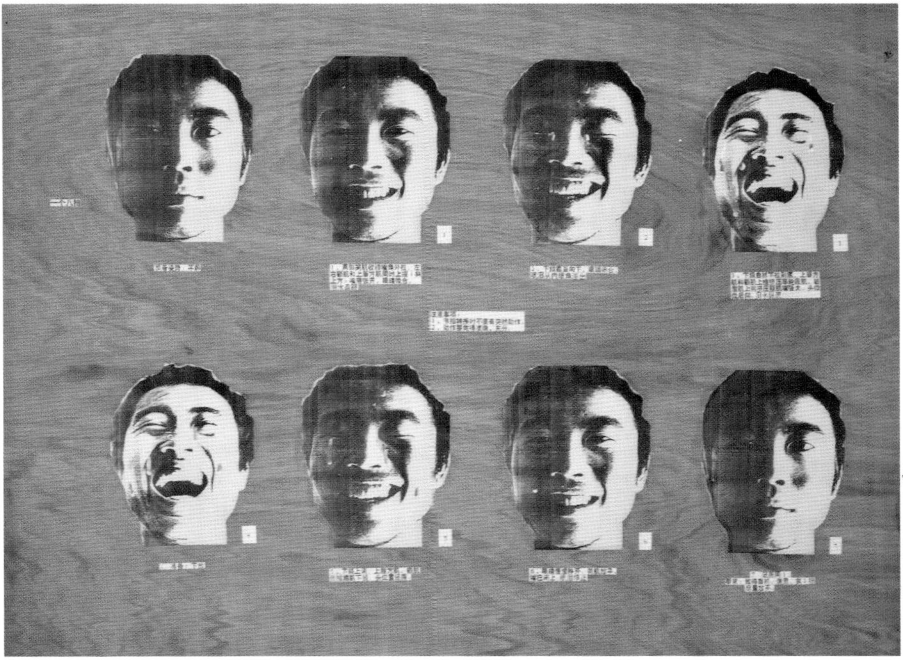

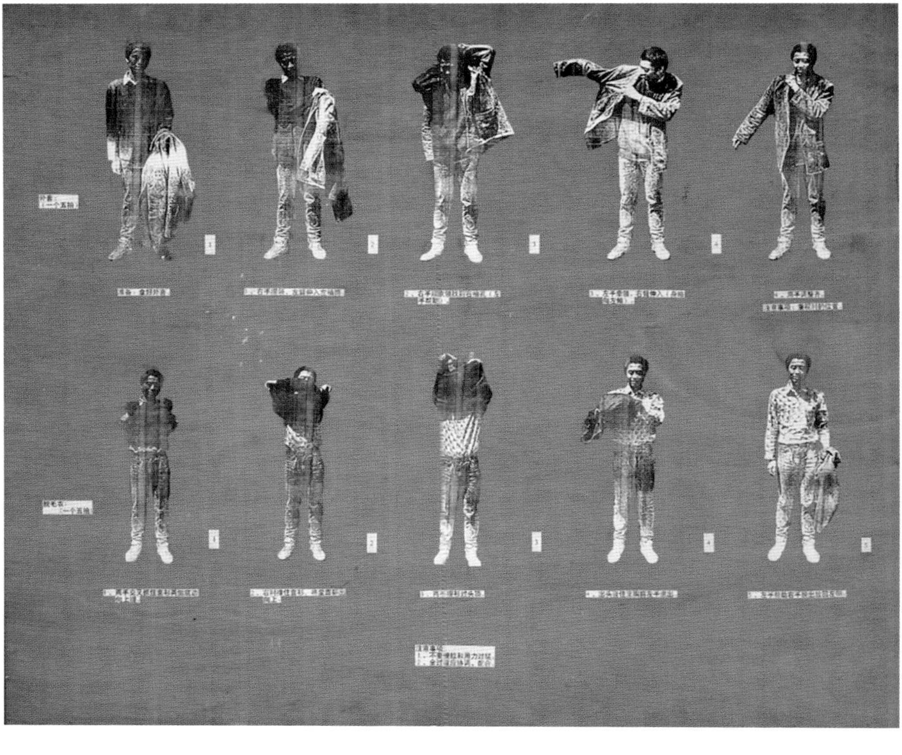

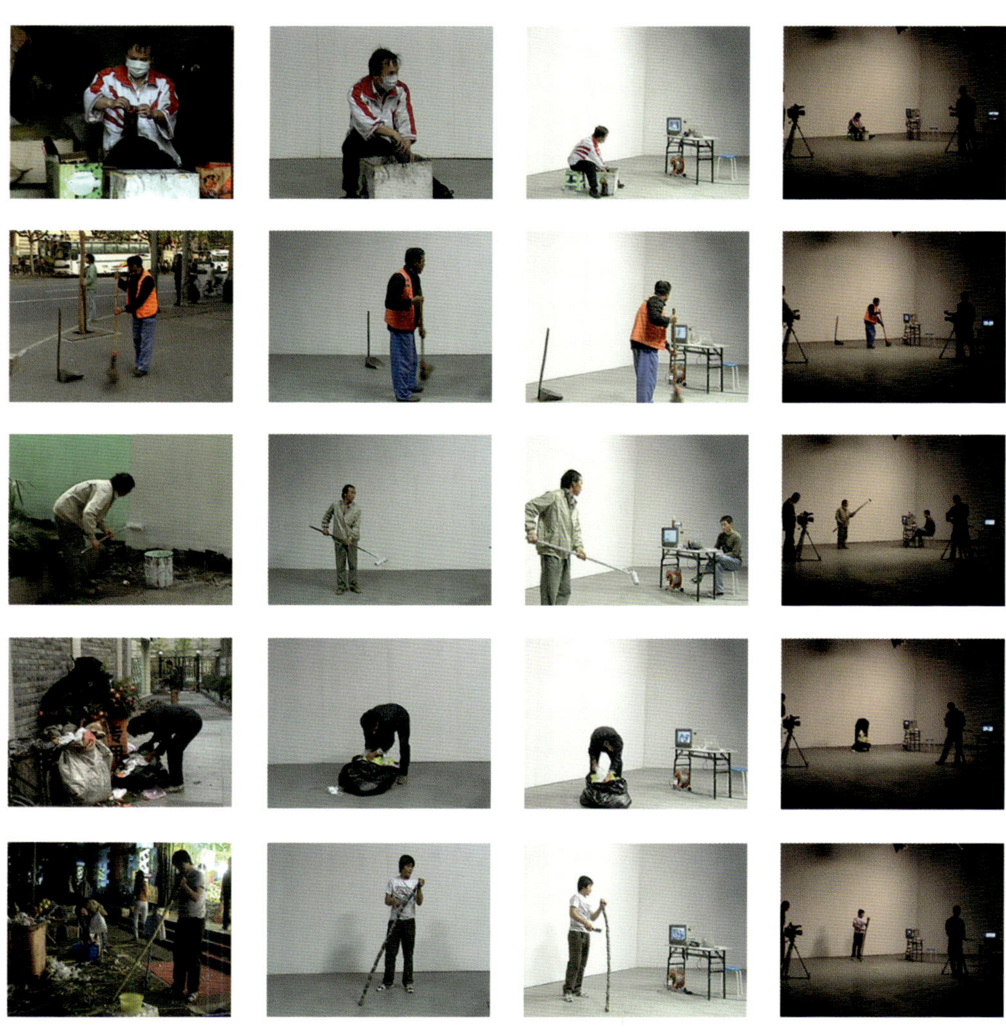

17 Geng Jianyi, *To Be Your Correct Self*, 2005 (video stills)

the movements of labourers on the street: a cleaner sweeping
the floor, a decorator painting a wall, a vendor peeling
sugarcane. The participants were then invited to a professional
photography studio to imitate what they had been doing on
a daily basis, but trying to repeat their actions exactly as per
the original. The work may not have changed or 'corrected'
any of those actions that people make; however, what it does
shift is the psychological perception towards conformity

when one goes through procedures to complete them. It turns the most ordinary action into the extraordinary; the most unconscious behaviour into a 'performance' – something dramatic – through multiple rehearsals, or into a form of ritual, following the orthodoxy of the collective for everyday details.

In artistic representations, the image of the collective sometimes appears as 'tamed' within a solemn atmosphere, but sometimes, instead, it is presented as 'wild', with a liveliness and boisterousness consistent with traditional Chinese celebrations. In other words, the collective can sometimes be seen as a group of earnestly disciplined bodies, and sometimes as a carnival-like troupe that exhibits nationalistic excitement representing a liberation from a confined environment. Conflicts between the individual and the collective, the private and the public, and between family and society can be explored and discussed through visual interpretations of collective identity, with a pair of different, or almost contrasting, approaches towards its hybrid nature.

When Zhuang Hui was growing up in a small town, Yumen, in Henan Province, at the commencement of the Cultural Revolution, he often travelled around with his photographer father. He found it extraordinary to understand that the camera could capture a large number of people with a single click, or, in other words, it could encapsulate the very image of assemblies, themselves a significant visual presentation of the era.[15] Zhuang first chose typical examples of any civil society's institutional framework – organizations of school, work, public security and village residence – in order to preserve this disappearing visual legacy of conformity against the double backdrops of Mao's ideology and China's ongoing economic reformation. In the 1995–96 series *The One and Thirty*, Zhuang invited ordinary people to join him in a portrait. In each set of work – positioned next to the artist, who always wears the same clothing and facial expression, lending a uniformity to the sequence – there are thirty individuals from the different categories of *danwei*: workers, peasants, soldiers and students in China's socialist society. As Karen Smith observes, 'the works are a poignant mechanism for capturing the sense of the masses, those who inhabit the broad backdrop of the Chinese stage, but are recognised only in the wider context of their community group or socially defined status'.[16] The concept of conformability is reflected explicitly not only by the photographic work itself, but also by the execution of Zhuang's practice. The process of the work suggests a dimension of performance art. This became more critical in a later photographic series, *Group Portraits*.

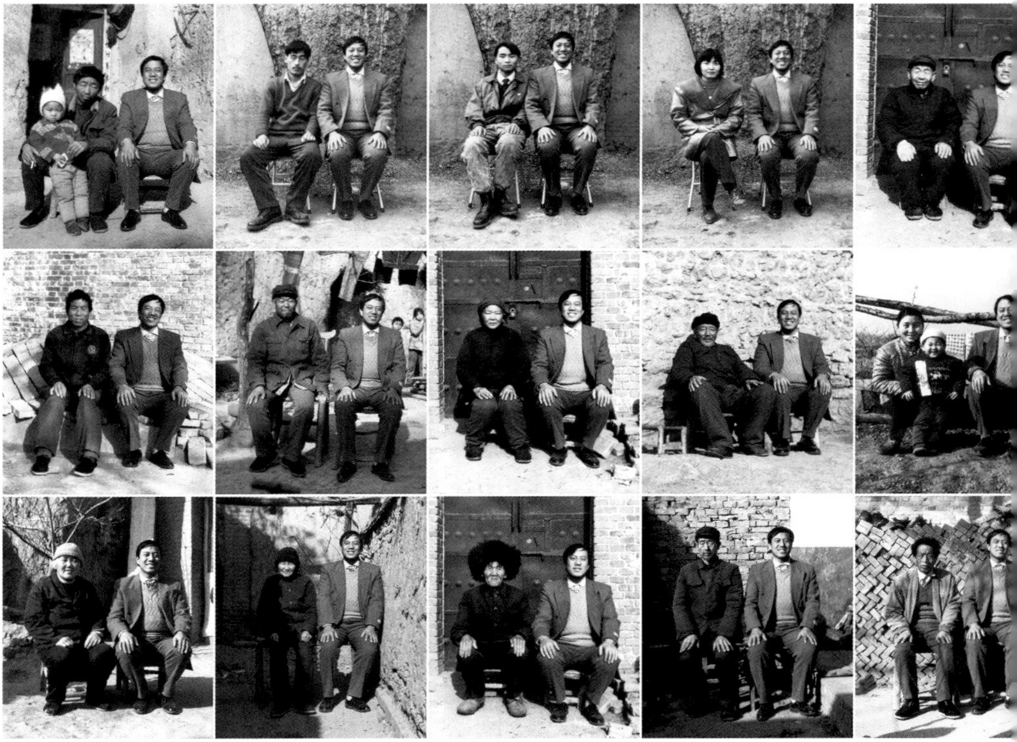

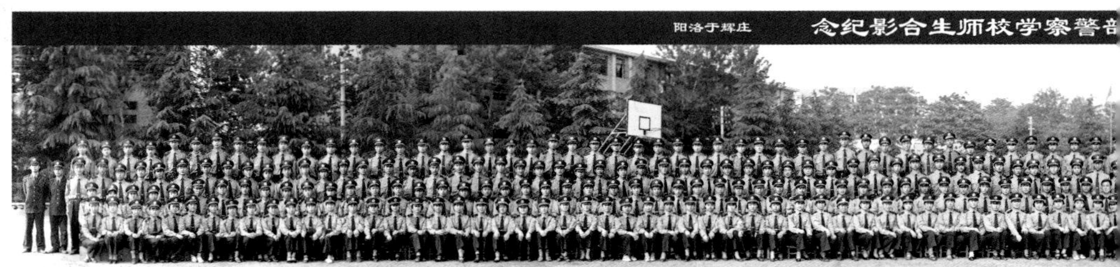

18 TOP Zhuang Hui, *The One and Thirty*, 1995–96
19 ABOVE Zhuang Hui, *Group Portraits: Luoyang Cadre Police Academy Students and Staff, Henan Province, May 13, 1997*, 1997

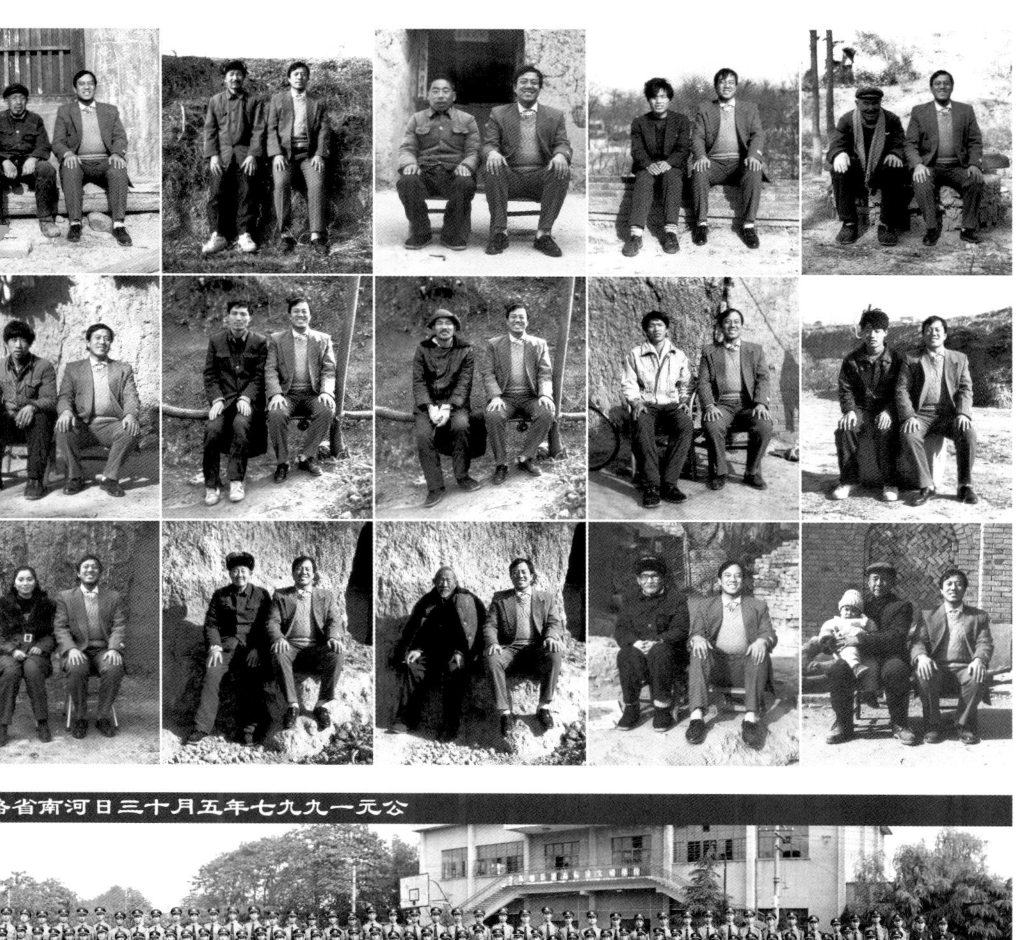

In 1997, Zhuang Hui negotiated with the authorities to organize group assemblies in the 'Chinese way' (typically, this would involve an invitation to a banquet, and the consumption of considerable amounts of Chinese liquor, to form a special 'brotherhood' with the authorities). Several large groups, including over six hundred people, were permitted to be convened and photographed, in one place at one time, through a technique involving a 180-degree rotational lens camera. In the photographs, the artist himself always appeared either at the far left or far right of the assembled group, suggesting that every individual component, including the artist, belongs to the group. The question of 'subject' in the portraits is complicated by his own presence. The answer seems neither to lie in the individuals that comprise the group, nor in the group itself. As curator, critic and artist Mathieu Borysevicz has commented, 'Zhuang Hui's presence mystifies the configuration by leaving the subject a tedious sum of the mass, its component parts, and the artist himself. The disciplines of portraiture, self-portraiture, and group portraiture merge.'[17] The horizontally elongated picture reminds one of the traditional Chinese hand scroll, encouraging spectators to 'read' every single character in the photograph. The presence of the artist serves as a sort of signature seal at the end of the hand scroll – a calculated position of importance, to endorse the validity of each group.

The concept of 'family' is deeply rooted in Chinese culture as a mini version of the 'collective'. When the socialist way of life proposes one big happy national family, however, then the traditional family model can no longer be the same. The

20 Wang Jinsong, *Standard Family*, 1996

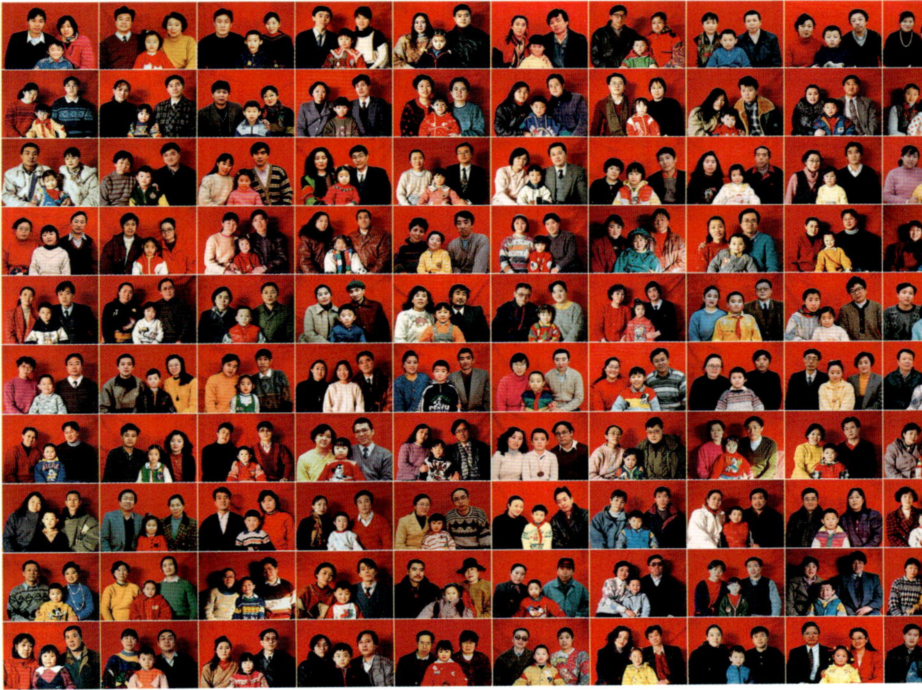

One-Child policy was designed and implemented in the late
1970s as a family-planning programme to control the size of
the population.[18] The policy generated millions of so-called
'standard families' – two parents and a single child. Wang
Jinsong selected two hundred three-person families, and
adopted a straightforward photographic method of direct
observation to portray the most common family archetype
of the period. The artist noted: 'I create theatrical spectacles
beyond what one may have expected and endow them with a
kind of intelligence and distinctive charm.'[19] Each family unit,
with its own appearance and personality, is seen as the most
basic and ordinary element that exists to construct China's
entire society. However, while the repetition of the families in
Wang's monotonic module increases the visual impact of the
work, it also diminishes the significance of the independence
of each family and ignores any individual stories behind the
subjects. 'The reality of China is a great system of unification,'
the artist has explained, 'where the appearance of collective
dominates in the society in the forms of various movements,

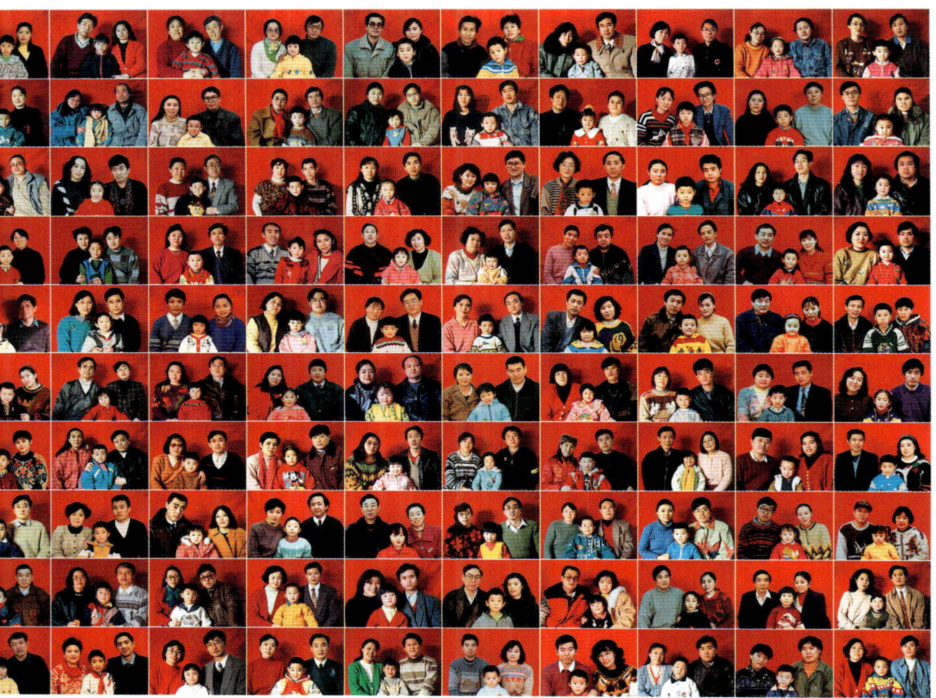

either political or social, and these memories and reflections have become my vocabularies.'[20]

Zhang Xiaogang's interest in old family albums was the starting point for his internationally acclaimed painting series *Big Family*, which first appeared in 1993. There are some common rules for the family photograph in Mao's era. For example, the father is always positioned on the right, the mother on the left, and the child in the middle. The photographer might offer some criteria for the positioning of the body, for gestures and even expressions, offering an idealistic model of society. These family photographs might be further manipulated after the studio shot, being retouched by hand to match the 'standard' aesthetics. During this revision, inevitably, aesthetic and sociological perceptions of the reviser would be added to the photographic image, with or without the subjects' agreement. Touching on the relationship between individual and society, or, in the artist's own words, 'the conflict between *simi hua* [privatization] and *gonggong hua* [publicization]',[21] the family photo, which was originally a private medium, became standardized, or was transformed into something with little obvious individuality or privacy, as a 'public' image.

In the *Big Family* series, typical costumes, such as Mao's suit, the classic military uniform, the 'revolutionary aesthetic' navy-striped top and the red scarf, are appropriated in the works to indicate both the historical background and the Chinese people's ideological pursuance. However, the artist aims not to represent any particular individual or family by depicting personal characteristics, but rather the collective similarity, employing images with a mono-appearance, and portraying the reactions or the situations of individuals who were confronting the public social environment. As Zhang has stated: 'In the beginning I was somewhat faithful to the things I got from the original photographs, including different images of people and details of the apparel. Since 1994, I have realised that I only need to paint "one person" ... a man or a woman...'[22] The light patches falling on the faces like birthmarks emphasize the absurdity of the impersonal expressionlessness behind this generation's revolutionary fervour, while the inevitable colour red links the comrades' spirits and defines them in the context of national collectivization.

Meanwhile, the urban transformation that began to take place following the Open Door policy (see Chapter 3, p. 114) took

21 OPPOSITE ABOVE Zhang Xiaogang, *Big Family No. 1*, 1996
22 OPPOSITE BELOW Zhang Xiaogang, *Big Family: Red Scarf*, 1998

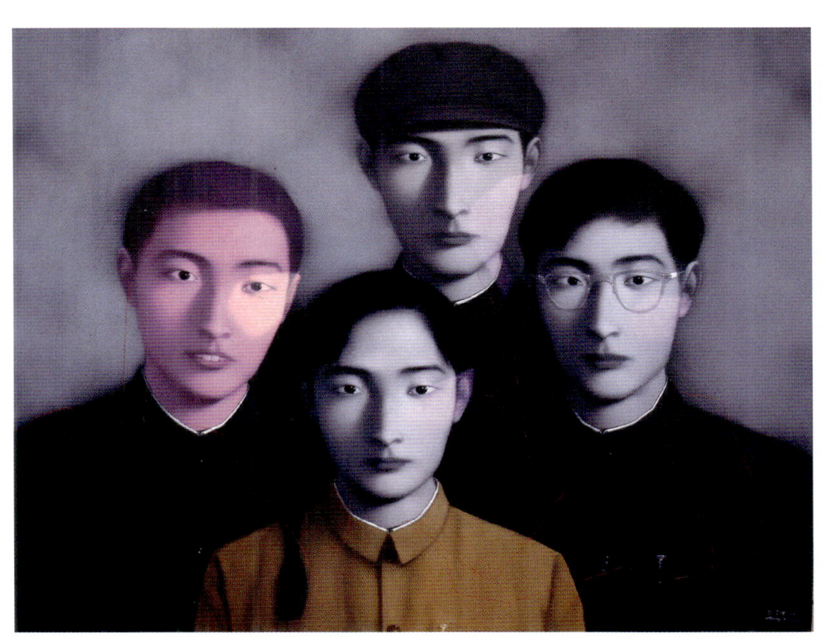

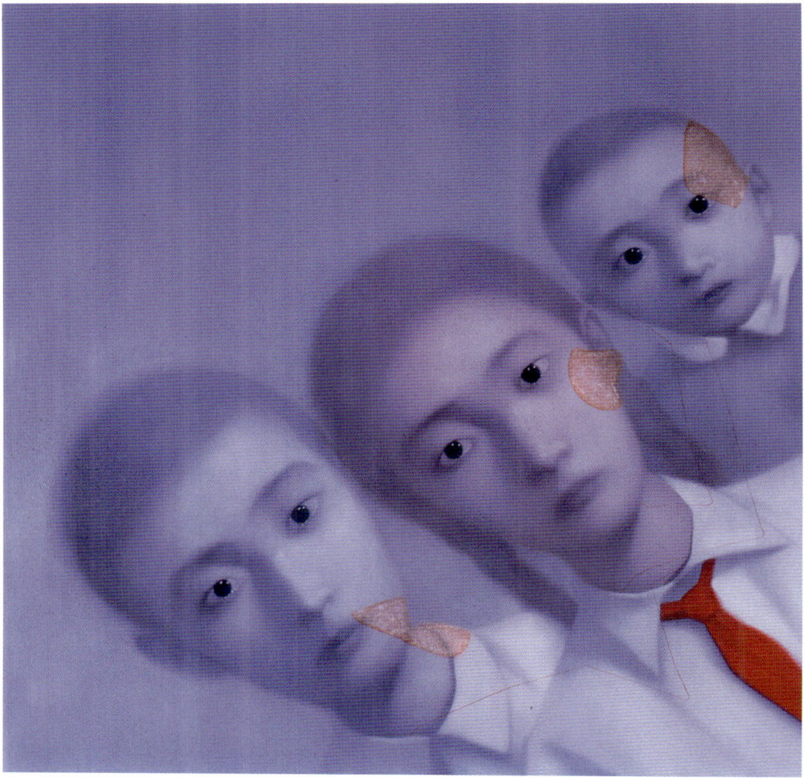

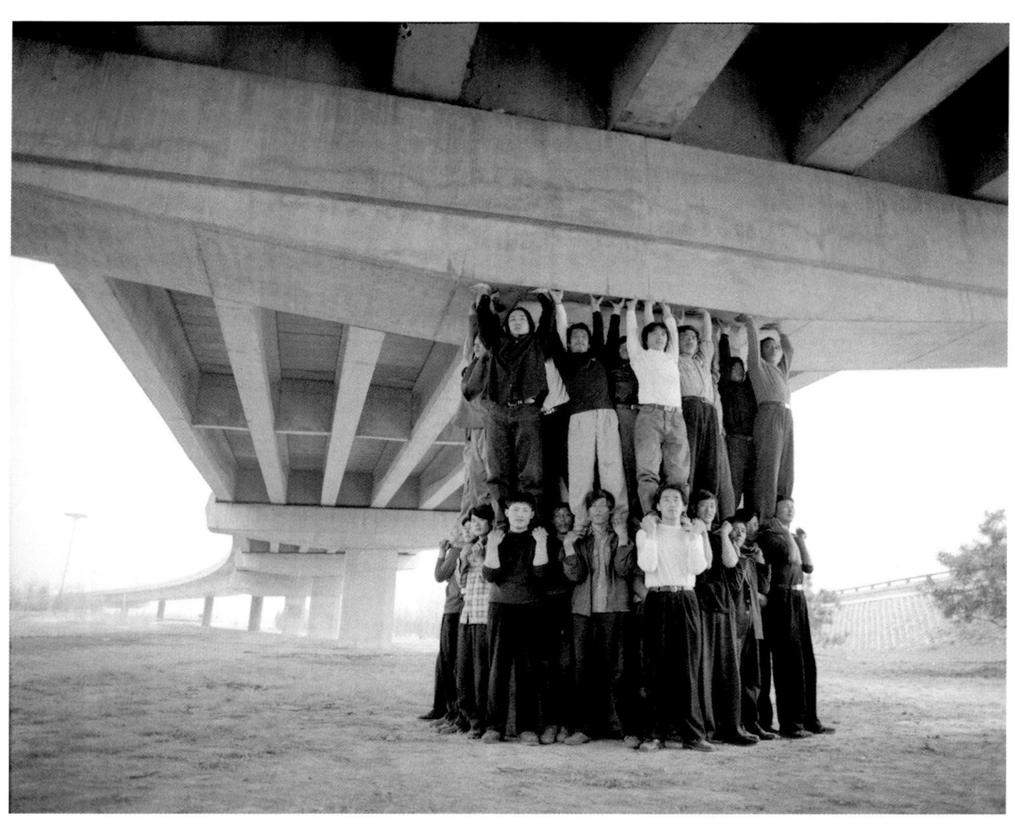

23 Wang Jin, *100%*, 1999

China into an invigorating new era. In order to achieve the planned urban development, a distinctive system of migrant rural labour was initiated from the early 1980s, as a significant social phenomenon, to balance the shortage of farmland and the abundance of household labour, and, more importantly, to power the evolving cities and to turn China into the 'world's factory'. The rural-to-urban migration has had major implications for environmental outcomes, as well as for the corresponding natural-resources management and policy in the areas of origin of rural labourers.[23] This cohort constitutes a new collective, that of migrant workers (*mingong*). From rural areas all over the country, they give up work on their farms and leave home to earn a living on construction sites or in factories in the cities.

Wang Jin's photographic work offers an artistic reflection on the social phenomenon of migrant workers during the process of China's urban development. In *100%*, a group of migrant workers form a circle, lifting another group standing on their shoulders. This group's arms are raised high in order to reach the bottom of a traffic overpass, as if they were supporting the massive urban construction with their bare hands. Metaphorically, in the centre of the image, their bodies are turned into a human pillar, with the same power as reinforced concrete, or else unveiled as a primary force that is able to facilitate and sustain the urban development. And yet, they are *under* the bridge: on the one hand, they are regarded as a 'low-end population'; on the other hand, situated away from the busy traffic that is flying overhead and having no actual involvement in the everyday of urban life, they are literally unseeable.

Responding to the urban changes in Beijing in the late 1990s, Zhang Dali adopted the language of graffiti – in particular, a spray-painted silhouette of a large bald head as his own identity, singular or multiple, which was duplicated and gradually began to appear on construction and demolition sites across the city.[24] These heads became part of the urban landscape, and generated a 'dialogue' between the old and the new, between the artist himself and the makers of all the changes. Having closely observed some migrant workers in Beijing, Zhang then decided to record their existence. First, in 2000, he cast the heads of these workers with gelatine which was mixed with pig-skin jelly and the remains of instant noodles, resembling maggots. The repellent appearance and sickening texture of the heads bring the viewer both physical and psychological discomfort. The moulds were directly copied from real people – the group of migrant workers – and their 'heads' were re-filled with the

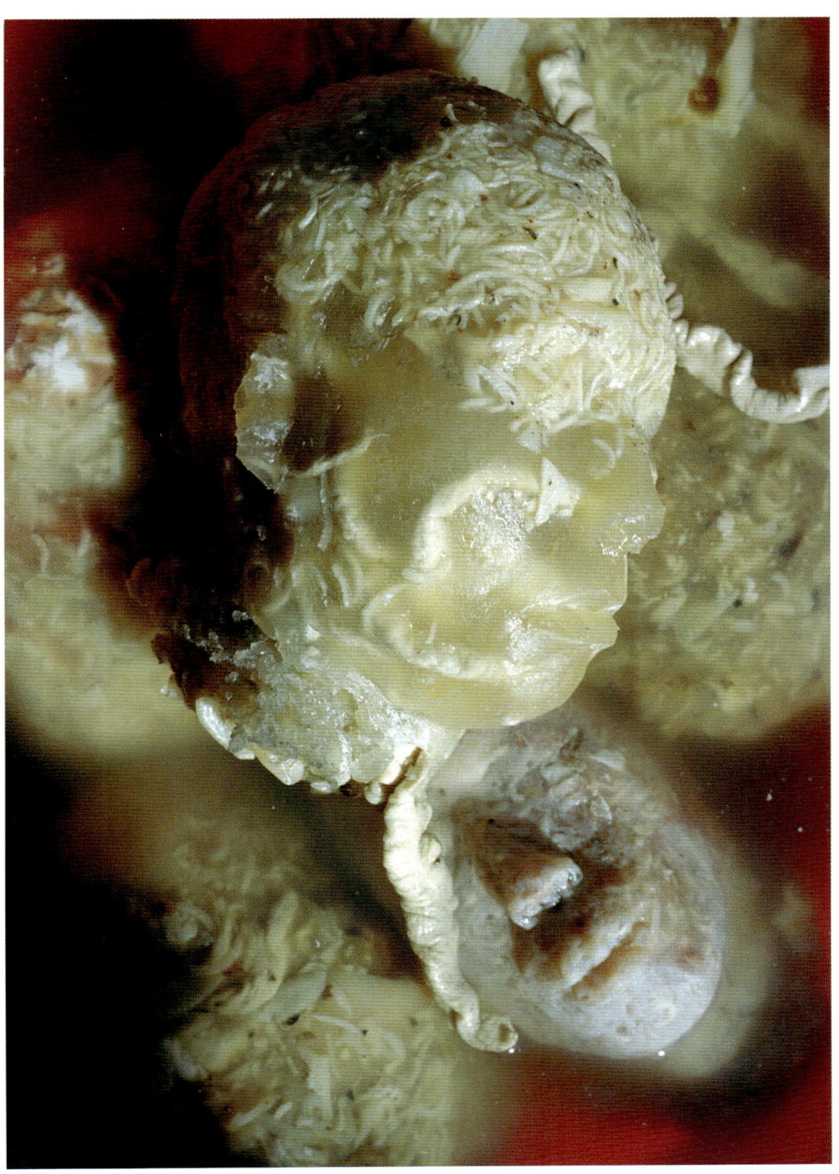

24 ABOVE Zhang Dali, *Migrant Workers*, 2000
25 OPPOSITE Zhang Dali, *One Hundred Chinese No. 56*, 2001

cheap fast food, indicating their lowly and temporary status. The artist then spent two years casting the heads of one hundred immigrant workers in resin. 'These are casts made on the bodies of real people,' he explained. 'These are living examples of our era, true and without revisions... Peeling off the coat of shining varnish, one by one, shows us that we are just like them. We share the same pressures of the collective.'[25]

In his project *Chinese Offspring*, begun in 2003, Zhang portrayed migrant construction workers as life-size sculptures, in various postures, to reveal a vast invisible underclass who in fact contribute to the most visible processes of urbanization. These figures are suspended upside down, emphasizing the uncertainty and vulnerability of their lives, their lack of control over their destiny, and their submission to the power of the Chinese social structure.

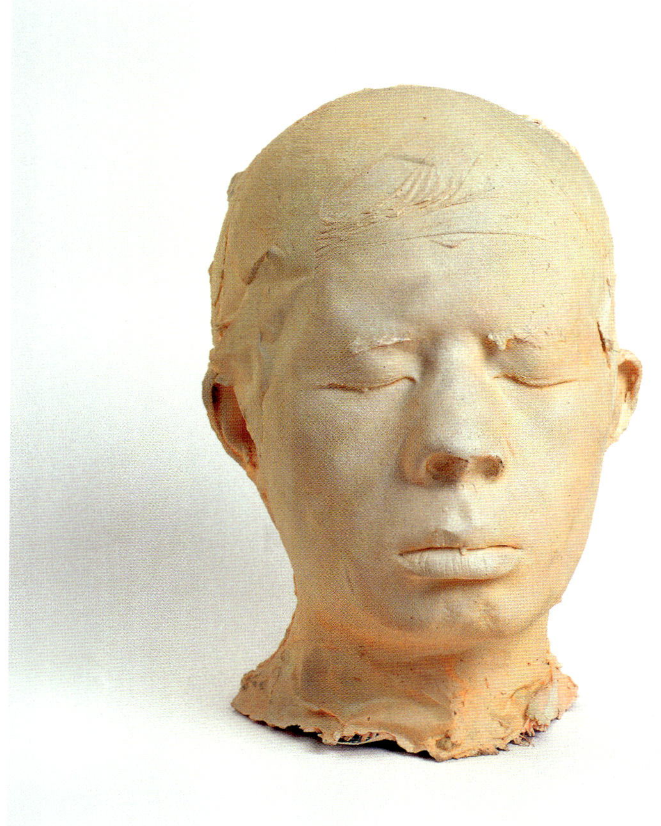

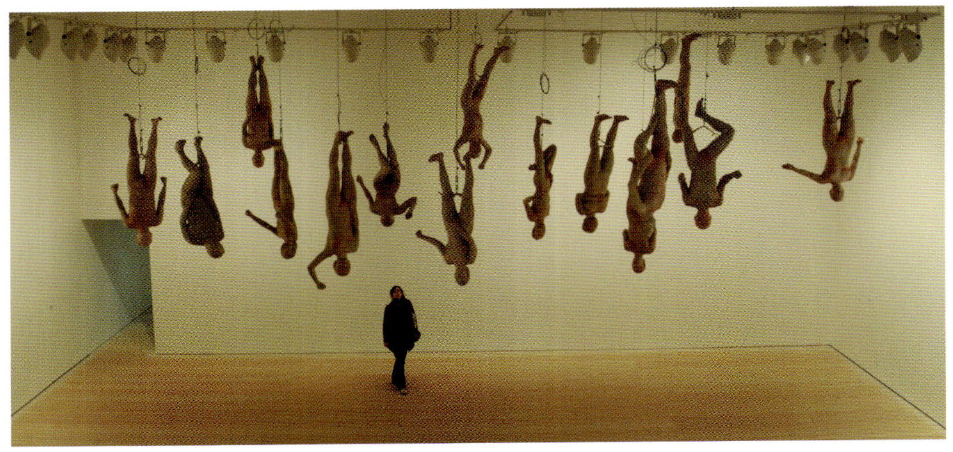

26 Zhang Dali, *Chinese Offspring*, 2003–5 (installation view)

In the 2015–16 work *Monuments*, again, through copies of the appearance of *mingong*, Zhang made a series of statues in white marble, which evokes the classical sculptures in art museums, and which, seemingly, turns the 'lowly' into the 'noble'. If the earlier works focusing on this particular group of people, including *One Hundred Chinese* and *Chinese Offspring*, with their realistic forms and colours, attempt to provide a direct link between the copied and the original, between the sculptured and the actual human bodies, then here the marble material has distanced the two. Wu Hung comments further:

[The sculptures'] relationship to their corporal models recedes to a secondary level of perception. Thus, what happened here was more than a simple switching of materials. It was a crucial conceptual shift: the goal of copying appearances was no longer to challenge the distinction between representation and subject, art and reality, but to use their extraction and abstraction to elicit imagination of the sublime and permanent. They therefore mark the introduction of monumentality.[26]

In these series, although the figures are produced in various poses and with different materials, they have one thing in common: they are all naked, with their eyes closed (due to the process of moulding). Their identity is not easily to be told from their appearance, but they clearly belong to the same group. They are frozen in silence, as if they have been isolated from our vibrant and noisy urban life, with nothing to see and nothing to possess.

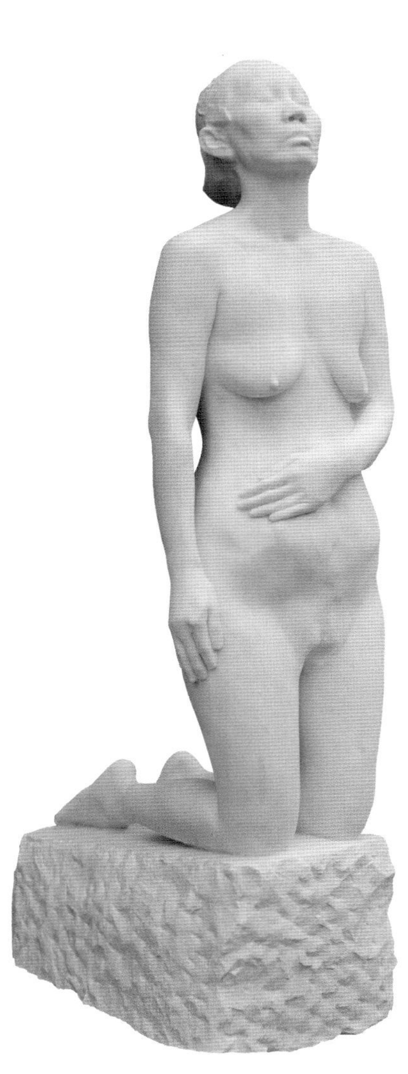
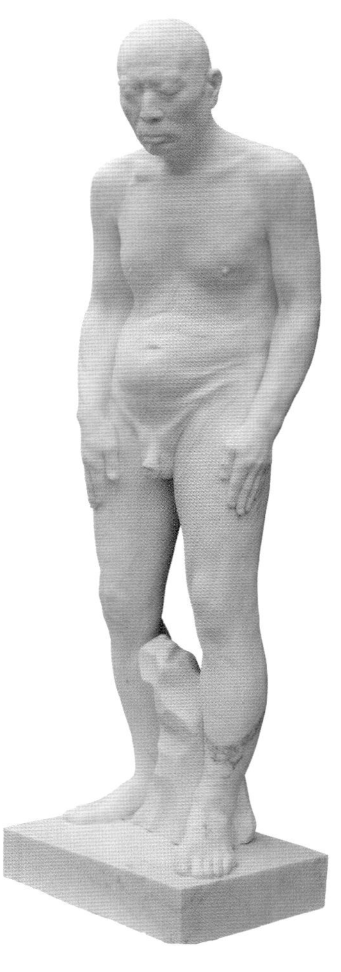

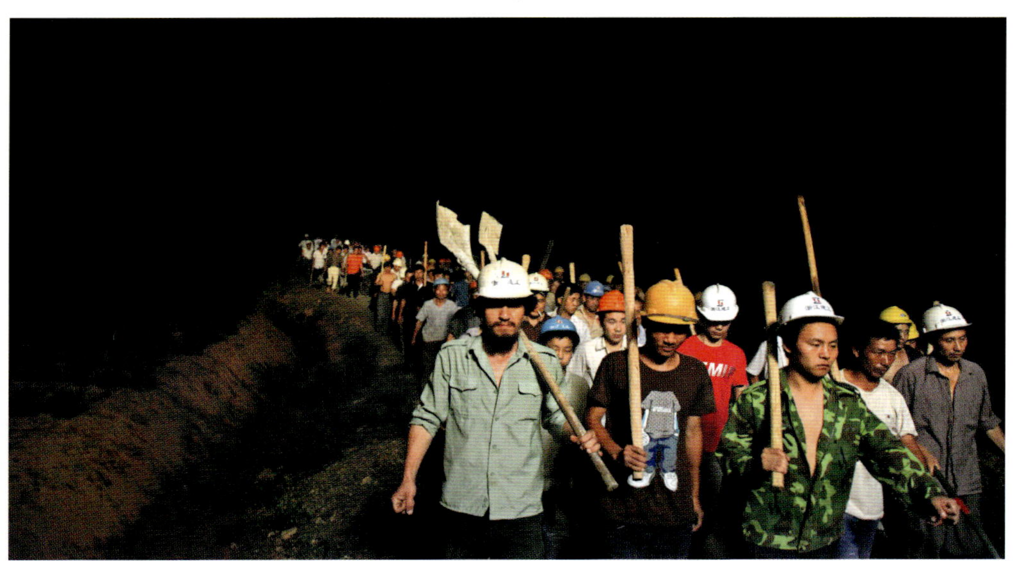

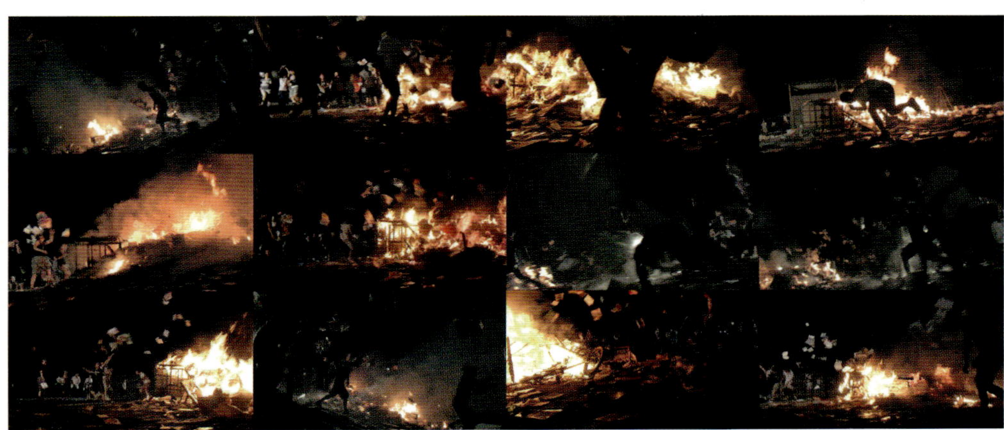

28 TOP Chen Xiaoyun, *Night/2.4KM*, 2009 (video still)
29 ABOVE Chen Xiaoyun, *Fire/3000KG*, 2009 (video stills)

The Wild

The collective is not always restrained, and it does not always appear in inanimate form. Indeed, it can be represented in a quite different manner, or even in the completely opposite manner. In 2009, Chen Xiaoyun developed a pair of video works, each depicting a different scenario. In *Night/2.4KM*, the artist recorded a group of more than one hundred people marching during the night down a single path. They carry different farm tools, such as shovels, hoes and brooms, and yet the safety helmets that many of them wear suggest that they may well have been working on any of the construction sites in the city, again as migrant workers. The march is led by an invisible light, which illuminates the front and leaves the rest in endless darkness. The participants are almost expressionless as they walk, jog, then, getting faster, run. It seems reminiscent of the march scenes in a Chinese revolutionary film – a revolt against an authority. Although the film is silent, the collective movement of the group and each step taken by the individuals – determined and purposeful (or purposeless) – communicates a kind of daunting power. Anything could happen at their destination. If this presents something on the verge of explosion, then Chen's other video work, *Fire/3000KG*, shows how the climax of an uncritical zeal can be achieved through collective actions. In the video, more than a hundred youths are burning thousands of books and documents, with no start or end. One might easily recall the assemblies in Tiananmen Square during the Cultural Revolution, fuelled by a fanatical energy, notably when Mao ascended Tiananmen to inspect his Red Guards in the summer of 1966, and, particularly, the movement of 'Smashing the Four Olds', during which millions of homes were confiscated and innumerable cultural properties were burned to ashes. Here, the participants look exhilarated and energetic, rushing towards the fire and throwing books, whether bags of them or single volumes, into the wild flames. Nothing can hold them back. This is simply an act of burning, or, in the artist's words, 'a rebellious fire, a passionate noise that implies the politics of adolescence, or an aesthetics of revolutionary violence as abreacted by the group of excited youths'.[27]

The wild excitement of former times in Tiananmen Square is depicted in a different way in Yue Minjun's 1992 painting *Great Joy*. Here, smirking frantically, people are lined up in order with the same face, same dress and same posture, while the Tiananmen Tower illuminated by a rainbow is in the near distance, endorsing the apparent happiness. The lines of the collective are intended to present a kind of 'solidified and orderly force', which was a pursuance that is embedded in

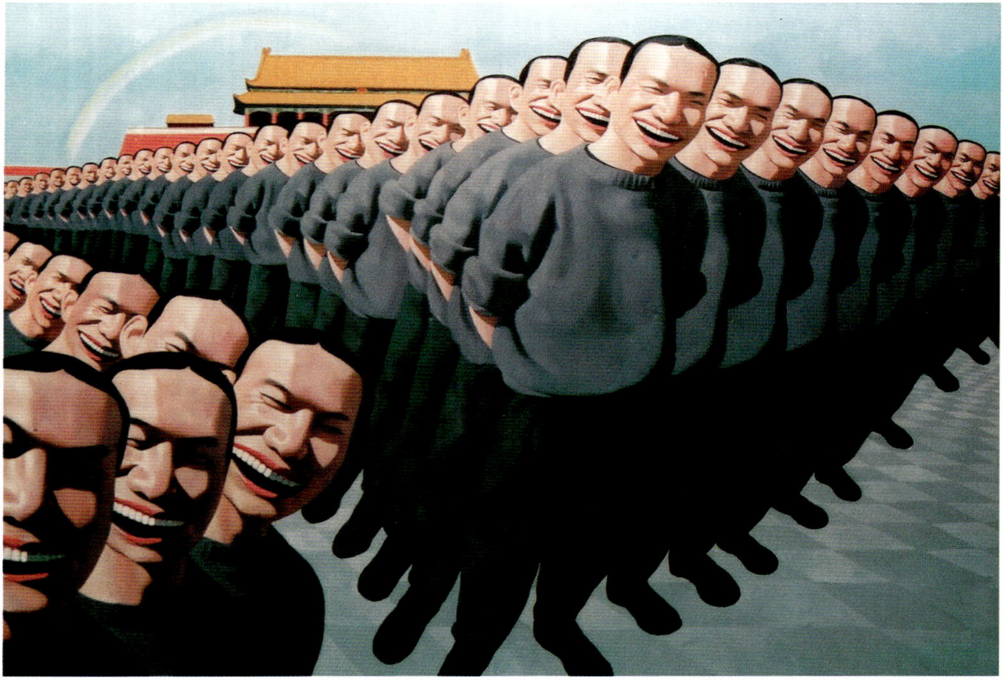

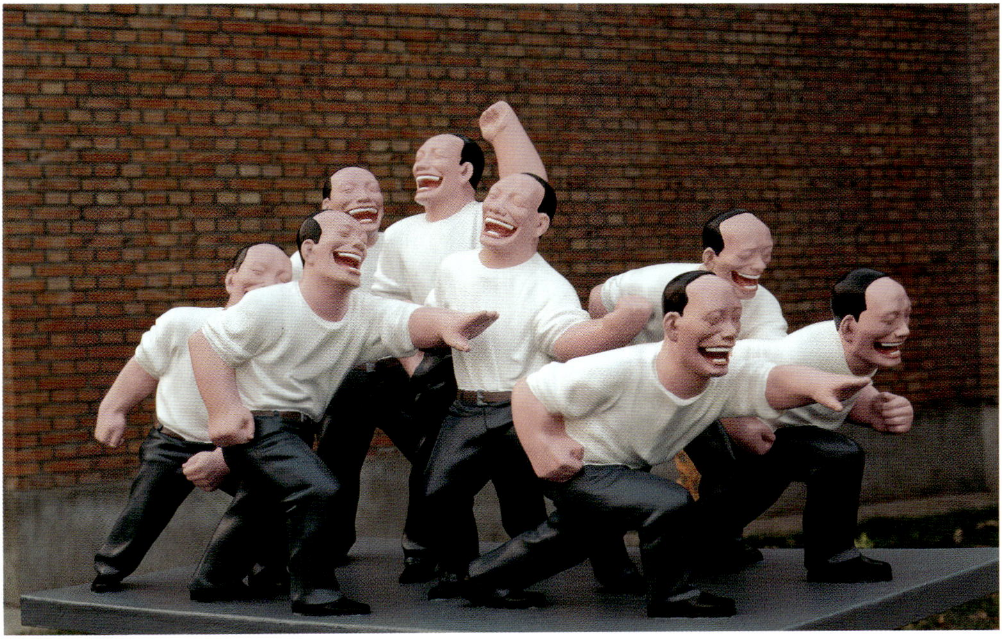

30 TOP Yue Minjun, *Great Joy*, 1992
31 ABOVE Yue Minjun, *Romanticism and Realism Study No. 6*, 2003

the artist's childhood memories of endless collective celebrations and parades.[28] Later in the same year, Yue began to use his own image in his practice, and sometimes replicated this to create a crowd effect. When his self-image is constantly repeated, the power of the individual is exaggerated by the increase in quantity and the generation of the collective. In Yue's 2003 series *Romanticism and Realism Study*, the beaming collective dashes out from the two-dimensional canvas to replace previously encountered Chinese socialist group statues. The more carefully the original positions and poses of the statues were imitated by the artist and 'himself', the more cynically the revolutionary ideology and the power of the heroic collective of worker-peasant-soldier were appropriated, represented and then transformed, or even reverted into a carnival. These images of hysterical individuals, although there are sometimes many of them, seemingly present an attitude of indifference towards reality, or a form of self-mockery, as if to transmit the insignificance of their social position.

A pioneering figure in China, Zhang Peili is generally considered the first Chinese artist to have worked in video. From 2000, however, he began to use 'readymade' videos, which could easily be found on the market. As he has said:

I am concerned with stylised elements of a symbolic nature and with a concept of time, elements that are concentrated in Chinese narrative films of the 1950–70s centred on the heroic and romantic complexes of revolution – these manifest a healthy aesthetic attitude and grammatical habit. I select fragments from these old narrative films and manipulate them in simple ways, releasing them from their original linear structure and temporal background. What I am interested in here are the different possibilities of reading that emerge through this process.[29]

In the video *Happiness*, Zhang appropriates footage from a Cultural Revolution-era propaganda film, *In the Shipyard* (1975), which was a didactic morality tale. The work focuses on a scene in which a crowd heartily applauds a speaker who is orating. Both the audio and the video tracks were edited to play the two segments in an alternating arrangement: the exaggeratedly expressed excitement of the crowd no longer corresponds to what the speaker is saying, but appears instead as irrational, like a mindless craze.

According to academic and writer Katie Hill, in the Western cultural context, 'the hysteric as depicted in art can be seen as descriptive of society on the one hand and on the other, as constituting the artist's own obsession, a cultural critique which nevertheless rebounds onto itself in an act of power and narcissism'.[30] And yet, in contemporary China, hysteria can be represented as a language of discontent. The political and cultural hysteria of the Cultural Revolution has been carried on by the collective, from one generation to the next.

Yang Fudong's 2001 film *Backyard – Hey, Sun is Rising!* depicts a dream-like narrative, in which four young individuals, perhaps representing a larger group of people, dress in the old military uniforms and move – always as a team – to perform a collective carnival. Sometimes they line up and act in unison, and sometimes they chase around, arguing and fighting among themselves. They live in their own ways, with love or hate, but no real agony or pleasure can ever be felt. None of them seems to possess anything but a wooden sword, the only attainable form of property, and their indescribable emotions. The wooden sword plays a vital role in the life of each, not only as a symbolic (functionless) weapon to attack the others, an extension of their body language, but also as a baton to lead their performance, an instrument to initiate dialogues and a guiding tool for their everyday journey. The artist's statement reads: 'when the puppet-like indolence has been punctured by the dancing swords, they communicate within loving indignation, hurt but never with pain ... all the fragments present a discontinuous dream, which might be true, but would only happen within a fleeting moment just before the sun rises'.[31] It seems the revolutionary spirit is still burning in their hearts, while the conformity of the people's collective always threatens a sudden turn to hysteria.

In Yang Zhenzhong's *Disinfect*, a group of eighteen people dressed in various urban styles are projected at life size. They appear to belong to different classes, from low to middle, and are both local and migrant, young and old, male and female; and yet, for some reason, they are all extremely agitated and utterly furious. Their extreme moods erupt, all of a sudden, with no beginning or end. They shout frantically, at each of us, but with no sound. Their fury, anxiety and violence are explicitly delivered through their facial expressions and body language. According to the artist, 'this hysterics, as a kind of urban disease, has been developed behind the scenes of the rapid urban development, and it is the price we pay for the flourishing economic growth'.[32] Discontentment, grievance and anger are all unleashed in the extreme emotions of the generation of an urbanized China. The implementation of silenced slow motion seems to visually maximize the power of their expressions, but, in fact, as a consequence, it only reveals and reinforces the powerlessness of these individuals.

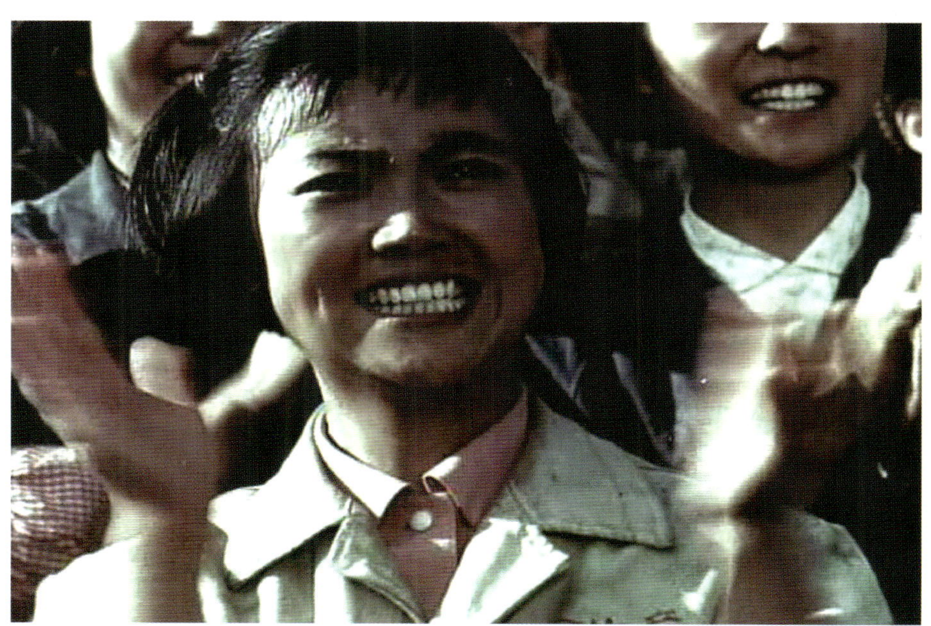

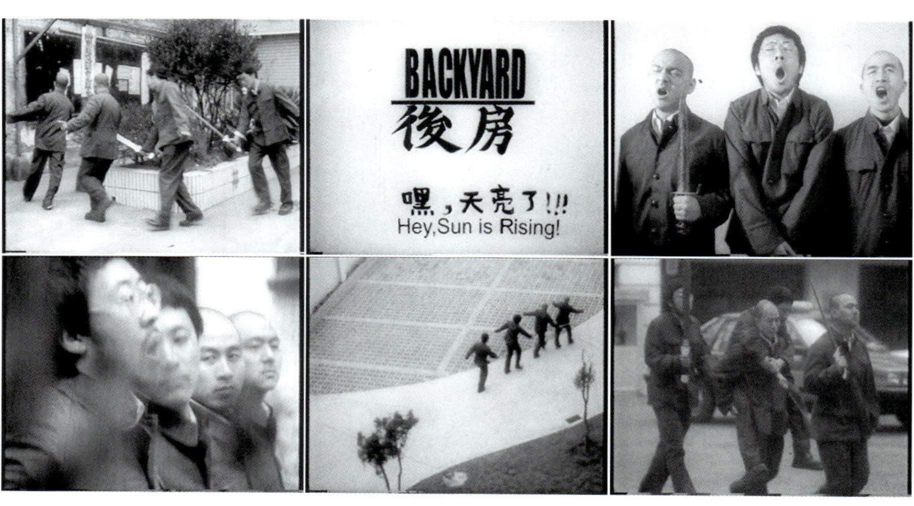

32 TOP Zhang Peili, *Happiness*, 2006 (video still)
33 ABOVE Yang Fudong, *Backyard – Hey, Sun is Rising!*, 2001 (film stills)

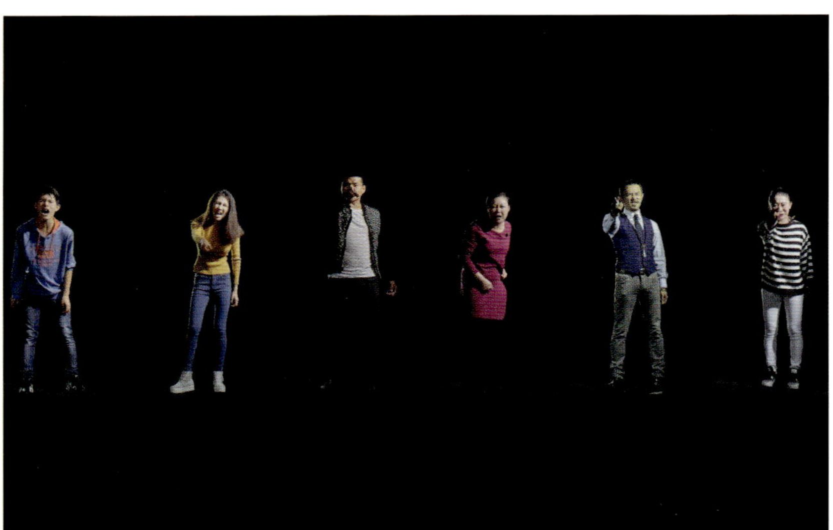

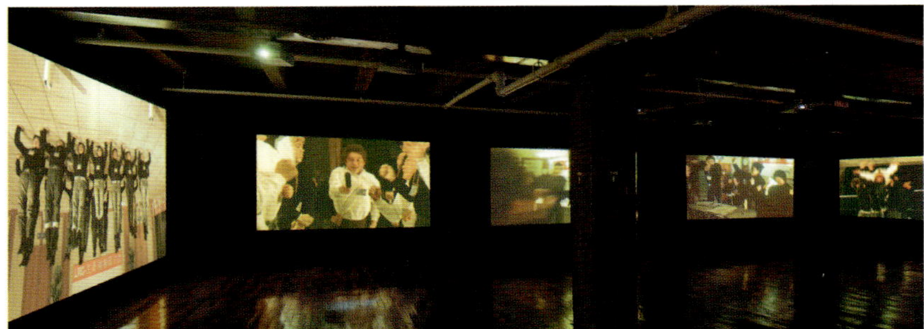

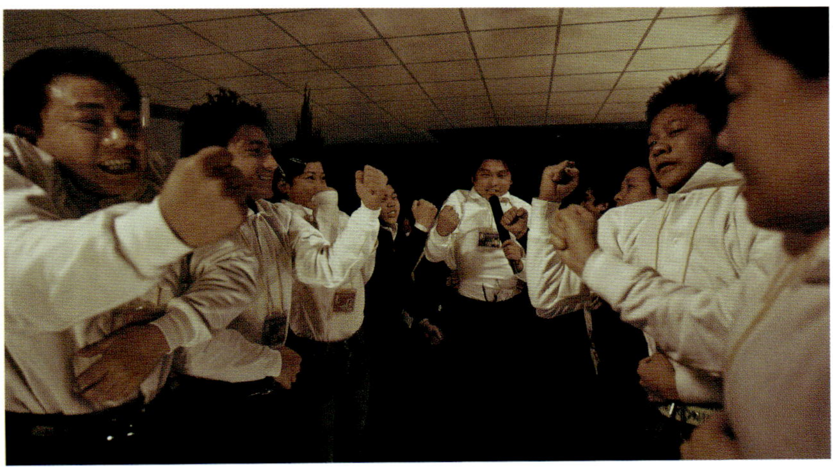

34 TOP Yang Zhenzhong, *Disinfect*, 2015 (video stills)
35 CENTRE Zhou Xiaohu, *Concentration Training Camp*, 2007–8 (installation view)
36 BELOW Zhou Xiaohu, *Concentration Training Camp*, 2007–8 (video still)

Mass hysteria resurfaces in Zhou Xiaohu's eight-channel video installation *Concentration Training Camp*, which depicts a series of employee training sessions at an American-owned and Chinese-based company. Motivational activities include military-like drills, yelling slogans and playing 'games' – for example, sharing individual experiences, from being poor to obtaining success in wealth; revealing personal aspirations and dreams, which mostly sound unrealistic; innovating commercial strategies, which are usually impractical, with collective efforts; and building up a kind of absolute and unconditional trust among team members. The participants look vigorous and stimulated; almost insane. One might suddenly notice that, while undergoing elaborate training practices, they appear disorientated, stiffly upright (including

their hair), and with slightly distorted facial expressions. Zhou Xiaohu comments:

I am interested in this phenomenon of collective madness in sales training in China. How can a particular value or a way of thinking be formed and injected into the muscles of a nation, and how can people's passion be ignited and fermented? What seems to be social and political here must have comprised something frantically poetic, to be unlocked by a subversive act.[33]

In fact, the actors are performing on stage sets, and they are strapped to the ceiling; they are being filmed while hanging upside down from a hidden suspension system. But, in the work, the performances are presented the right way up. Through the subversion of gravity designed into the work, the performed enthusiastic drills, as well as the non-performed participants' excitement, provocatively reflect the nature of propaganda through the mechanism of the collective.

Participation

The collective has been portrayed as a subject – either a silenced group or a wild crowd, two ends of the spectrum – but it can also be used as the method to produce or execute the artwork. In other words, collective participation need not simply supply the content of the work; it can also, more importantly, form the very process of the production, and additionally enable and further extend artistic discussions. Critic and author Claire Bishop notes three concerns – activation, authorship and community – as frequently cited motivations for artistic attempts to encourage participation since the 1960s. The first relates to the desire to create an active subject to be empowered by participation, while an aesthetics of participation 'derives legitimacy from a (desired) casual relationship between experience of a work of art and individual/collective agency'. The second considers the shared production 'to entail the aesthetic benefits of greater risks and unpredictability' when a certain degree of authorial control is ceded. The third 'involves a perceived crisis in community and collective responsibility'.[34] In the works discussed above, for instance, Zhuang Hui and Wang Jin's photographic work, and Chen Xiaoyun and Zhou Xiaohu's video pieces, members of various groups of people participate in the artworks as models and performers. In this section, we will further explore the central role of the collective as an amateur performer in participating in and co-producing an artwork.

The collective unconsciousness is subtly revealed in Yang Zhenzhong's *Spring Story*.[35] In 2003, the artist visited the Siemens factory near Shanghai, where some 1,500 workers were assigned to the production line, manufacturing millions of digital appliances for worldwide distribution. These workers repeat the same action numerous times a day, as part of the process of contributing small puzzle pieces to a larger picture, and yet the very detail of their repetitive and endless practice does not necessarily tell them what is to be produced at the end of the line. Each individual worker's face appears on the screen only for a few seconds, to say two or three words. All these words are extracted from Deng Xiaoping's famous 1992 Southern China tour speeches, which reaffirmed the principle of the reform programme for the country and reassured people of achievement in the foreseeable future. These words are individually captured, edited and reassembled as if on an assembly line to form a meaningful narrative, so that the text of the speech reads as it was originally intended.

Cao Fei's *Whose Utopia* was filmed during her residency at the OSRAM lighting factory in Foshan, a southern Chinese city in the Pearl River Delta. The title of the work seems to question exactly who it is that benefits from the economic boom in early twenty-first-century China, and where the balance might lie between the realization of personal value and the state pursuit of market-driven achievement, especially in the case of those Chinese migrants who have left their home provinces and comprise the majority of workers in large cities. The artist first designed a questionnaire for the employees, enquiring into their feelings about working in the factory, and being away from their home town, and what their hopes for the future were. Some fifty-five of her respondents were invited to plan and participate in the performances and collaborative aspects of the work. According to Cao Fei:

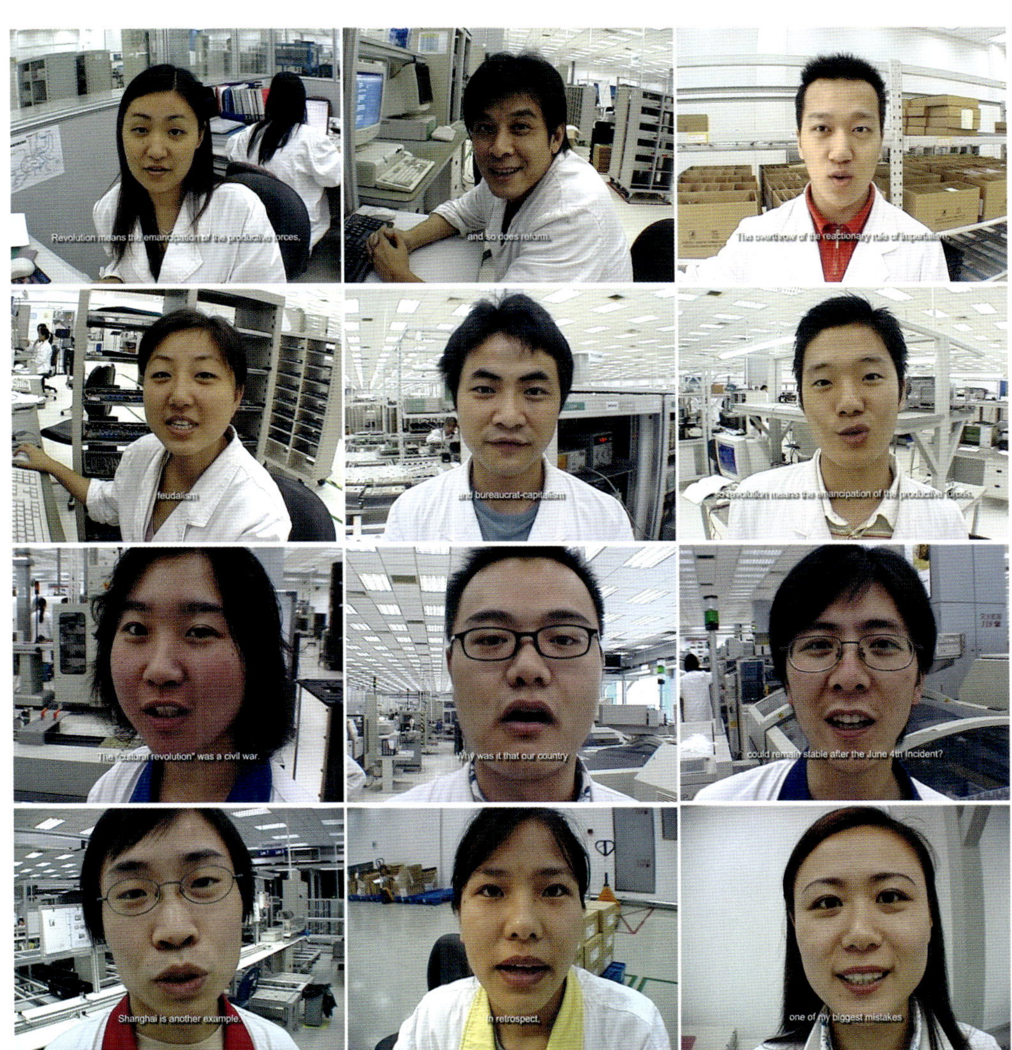

37 Yang Zhenzhong, *Spring Story*, 2003 (video stills)

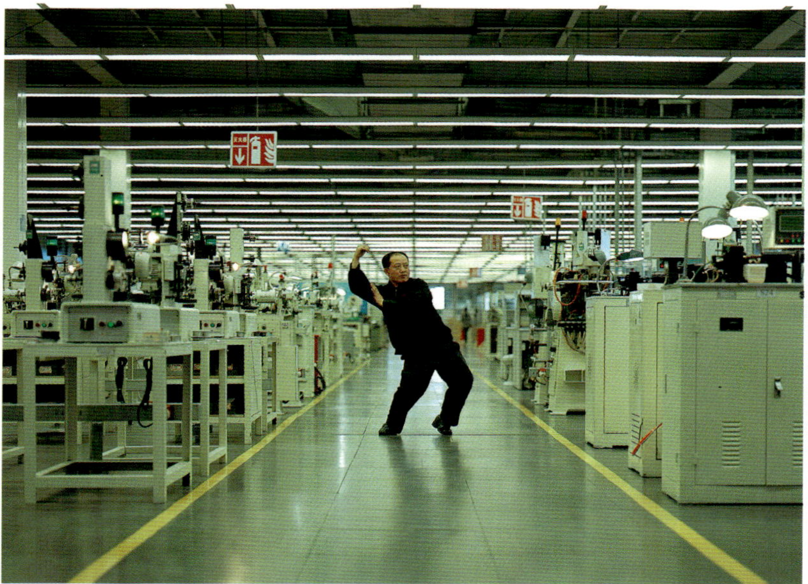

38 ABOVE Cao Fei, *Whose Utopia*, 2006 (video still)
39 OPPOSITE Yang Fudong, *Indeed, the Only Way*, 2018 (installation view)

The 'Utopia' project plans to explore the life of these emigrant factory workers in the Pearl River Delta who represent the 'backup force' for China's competitiveness in a global economy; and how they achieve a totally new experience, new standard and new meaning in the overwhelming trend of globalization. This project therefore allows us to see how they light up their 'Utopia' in a new reality. Their utopia further exemplifies how the wider and wider globalization is reshaping the Pearl [River Delta] area, and even the whole [of] China.[36]

The film consists of three parts. It shows, first, 'Imagination of Product', which focuses on the orderly process of assembling parts on the regimented production line for light bulbs, and the working women and men who toil devotedly at their workstations; second, in 'Factory Fairytale', people dressed either in the working uniform or in costume are dancing and playing musical instruments inside the space of the factory; and third, in 'My Future is Not a Dream', individuals are shown pausing at their work, either standing or sitting completely still, and facing the camera, as living portraits. In the film, the automated machines seem to be animated – their mechanical arms, hands or fingers conducting their endless actions –

as do the light-bulb components, sometimes lit and sometimes dimmed, like many winking eyes. In the meantime, the movements of the workers – those of their bodies, and even just their glances – are repetitive, while all their concentration, meticulousness and accuracy is merged into the picture as parts of the machine. The collective is only broken up by some musical performances by the workers, or by individuals dancing in the styles of ballet or street dancing, almost like sleepwalking, as personal expressions of their individual dreams, disregarding the absence of an audience in the factory, or the workshop full of heavy machinery, and the ongoing work being carried out in the background.

Elsewhere, in a museum space, an immense flight of stairs is covered with a seemingly endless red carpet, which is further extended by the reflective walls on either side. To Yang Fudong, the space could be seen as a square, or a grand theatre. For this situational installation, the artist organized a performance by approximately five hundred people, possibly university students from the same institution, over the first two days of the 2018 Shanghai Biennale.[37] In the work, *Indeed, the Only Way*, the participants are lined up as a large cohort; they then descend from the top of the staircase, to present a moving landscape, like the flow of an orderly force. As soon as they have reached their designated positions, they all stand still in rows and

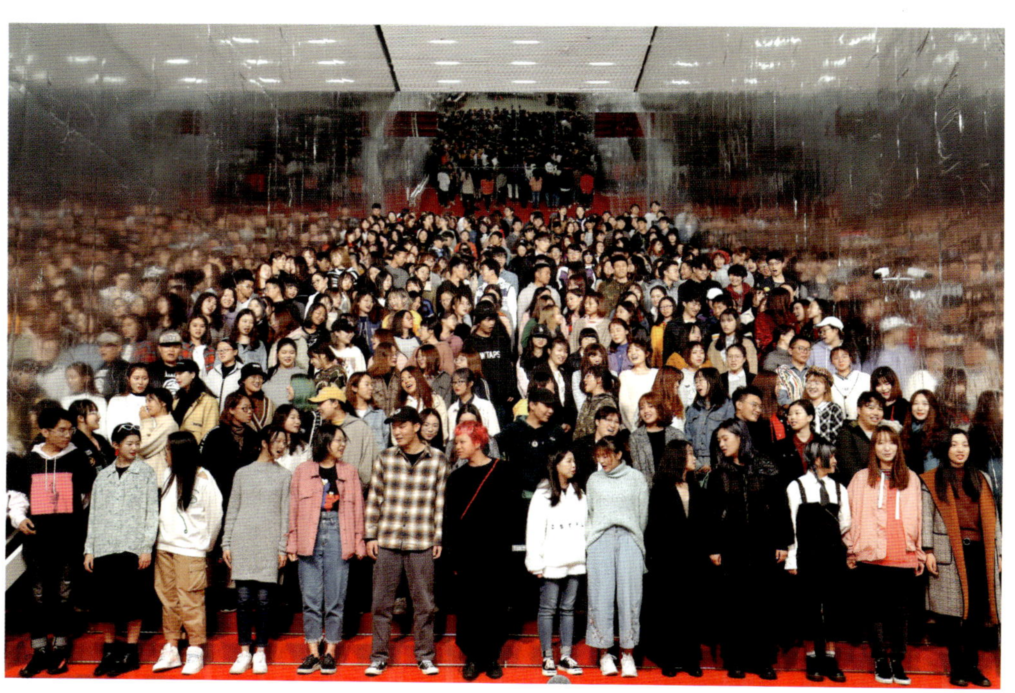

remain silent. Then, one of the participants starts to whisper to their neighbour, at first almost imperceptibly; and then all the voices gradually get louder and louder, until the performers start cheering, clapping, shouting and screaming, and yet the contents of their conversations are still inaudible – too noisy to make out. At a precise point, all of a sudden, they stop talking, leaving the audience in absolute silence; and then, by the same route, they return backstage out of our sight. But what happened backstage, and by what disciplinary practices were these participants trained? For this work, in fact, there is no backstage as such for rehearsals. Or, rather, perhaps one should say that it is a much larger backstage, beyond the museum space: the whole of Chinese society cultivates a specific mode of subjectivity that would prepare any participant for such a collective production.

In China today, urban residents exercise collectively and publicly at various venues. These exercises include traditional tai chi and broadcast calisthenics, and they are performed as a daily routine that is an important extension of cultural and political legacies. Initiated by Xu Zhen, *Physique of Consciousness* was produced by MadeIn Company as 'the first cultural fitness exercise ever made ... [which] reflects the diversity of human ideologies'.[38] It comprises over two hundred movements derived from spiritual rituals carried out in different religions and cultures around the world. *Physique of Consciousness* consists of ten exercises, in ten chapters, with a progression of different levels. It attempts to transform the collected ideologies in human history into actions and gestures. Vital to the work, this exercise is open to the public, and everyone – of all ages – is invited to join in.

40 Xu Zhen, *Physique of Consciousness,* 2013 (video still)

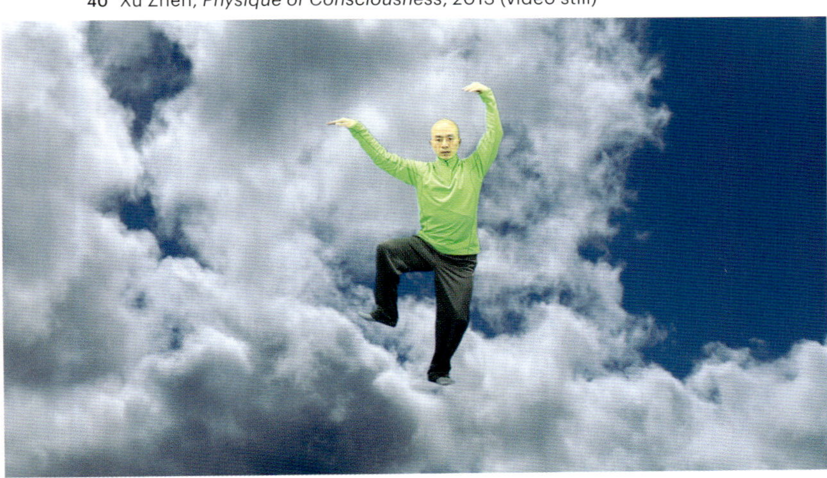

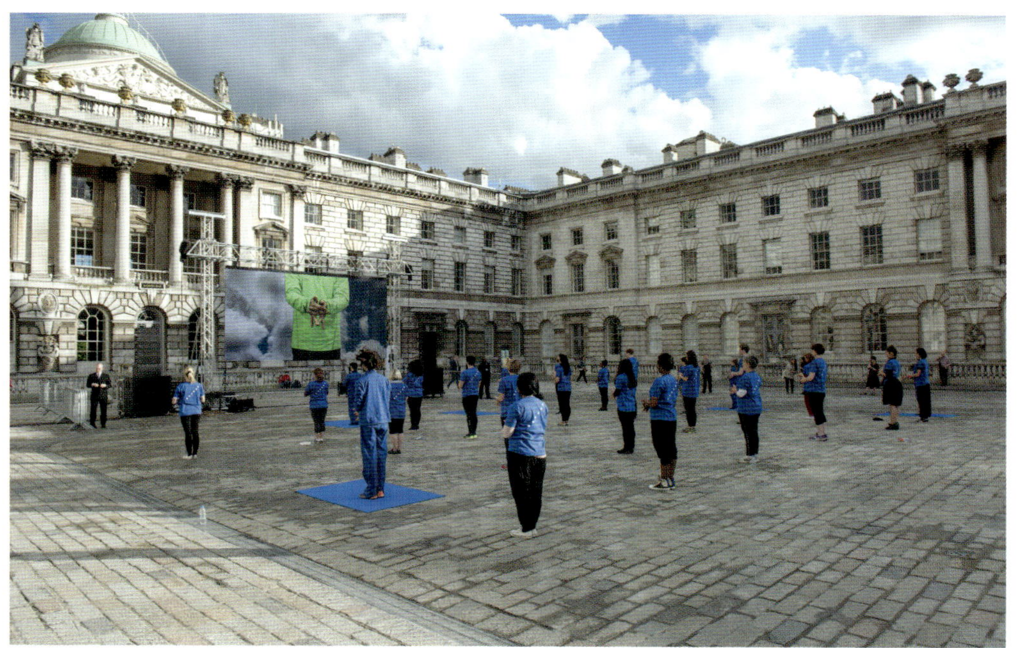

41 Xu Zhen, *Physique of Consciousness*, performance, 2016

According to the briefing, it will be able to benefit both mind and body, including 'maintaining a healthy physical condition, strengthening muscles, joint mobility, and improving the immune system', as well as 'relieving stress ... enhancement of memory capacity' and 'providing a feeling of wellness', and so on. The projected video leads and encourages participation. Every depicted participant looks conscientious, following the instructions, which are provided in detail, and each becomes an inseparable part of the work on their spread-out yoga mats. This project has taken place in public spaces in different cities around the world, including Shanghai, Berlin, London and Liverpool. Whatever one's cultural, religious or political background, one may or may not choose to believe in the ability of the exercises to bring about well-being – a kind of harmonious life, if not eternity. The accuracy of the physical movements performed does not, in fact, matter; it is the participation – in particular, the seriousness or devoutness of individuals – that becomes the centre of the piece. The work reveals how movements of ceremonial worship can be transformed into physical exercise, and vice versa; how bodily training can be turned back into ritual.

Coda

Anyone who grew up in China between the late 1950s and the early 1980s was part of a collective. Small children might have attended a kindergarten with a name like 'New China' or 'Red Star' (many such buildings, which would have formed part of Chinese memory and heritage, were demolished during the country's massive urban development programme; see Chapter 3, p. 114). City dwellers often lived in small apartments with a shared kitchen and a shared bathroom. If a parent worked in a different city, away from the family home, they might be permitted by their *danwei* to return only during certain holidays, such as the Spring Festival. In these cases, children were often in effect raised by a single parent, though they would be reminded constantly that the collective cared for them, too. Before China's opening-up at the end of the 1970s, the 'uniform' for people was a faded grey or navy-blue coat, and the same simple haircuts were seen everywhere. The collective had its own aesthetics.

The first lesson at school might involve learning how to draw a shining red sun, the symbol of the Chairman. Students would aspire to be named on the red board, the place of honour, and to join the Communist Young Pioneers, who, with their dazzling red scarves, were understood to be a superior cohort. However, all students were reminded of a promising life that awaited: the red national flag was hoisted at the centre of the playground every morning, while a league song such as 'We Are the Communist Successors' was proudly sung. During the school day, a pet phrase was repeated determinedly and enthusiastically through loudspeakers – 'Chairman Mao teaches us...' – at the beginning of every session of radio calisthenics or ocular gymnastics. Above all, there was Mao's unavoidable gaze staring out from his portraits hung high on the walls of classrooms, assembly halls and elsewhere, scrutinizing every action and thought. Only by being cultivated systematically by the words of Mao, and being disciplined by his ubiquitous gaze, could one ensure the self to be part of the collective.

Still today, members of collectives, including students and teachers, security guards, waitresses and chefs, and city sanitation workers, perform morning exercises together or read aloud classic texts, regulations or the constitution. They line up in uniform, ensuring that they complete each exercise accurately and in unison. Such group practices are carried out in a public space, such as the pavement in front of a workplace. These are not just exercises; they are performances. Whereas the former is normally executed for the practitioner's own

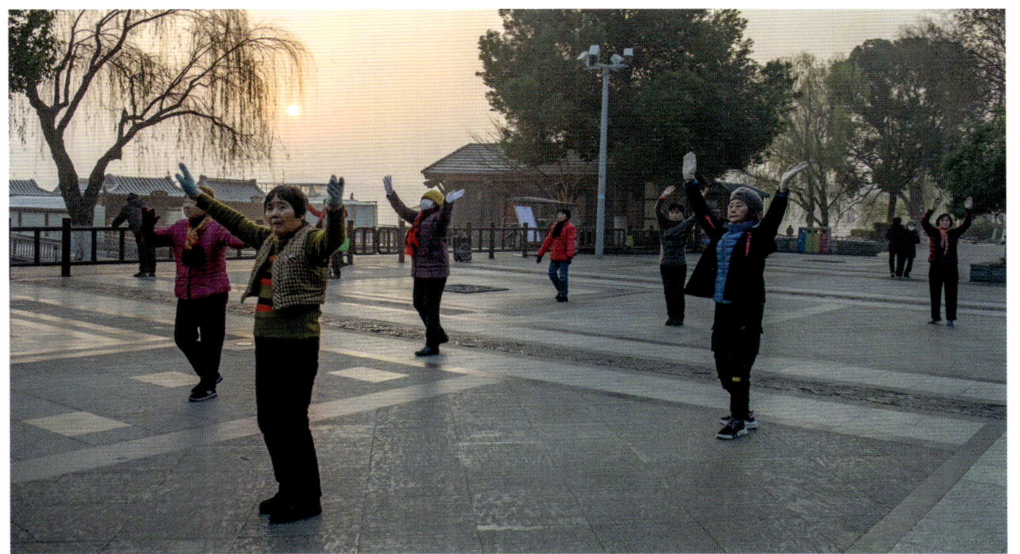

42 Square dancing in Xuanwuhu Park, Nanjing, 2020

benefit, whether physical or mental, the latter anticipates an audience. Every movement to the beat, every unified intonation, becomes the performative statement of the collective, in both body and spirit.

42   Square dancing (*guangchang wu*) has also become an increasingly popular phenomenon in contemporary urban China. Cheerful high-decibel music with a strong sense of rhythm pours out from portable and often out-of-date speakers, to the evident enjoyment of participants and onlookers alike. This dancing seems to constitute a kind of fitness movement, and is popularly accessible, being performed nationwide. The fundamental contrast to the morning exercises and readings mentioned above is the fact that, essentially, square dancing is spontaneous, from organization to practice.

Anyone who has been to a large city like Beijing or Shanghai will understand the notion of a 'square' in China (such as Tiananmen, or the People's Square). They are vast. However, square dancing does not necessarily take place in an actual square. Similarly, participants, who are likely to be middle-aged community residents and predominantly women, may be dressed in a variety of ways, from casual attire to festive costume. They carry out their square dancing in actual squares of the town or district, in parks, courtyards, open areas of the neighbourhood, or even basement car parks on rainy days.

The term 'square' here is not necessarily literal in relation to its rich cultural and political context in China, but rather conceptual. There is no need for a suitable 'square' to accommodate the dance; on the contrary, the dancing practice itself defines the space as 'square' – the 'square' is simply where the dance is performed.

It may seem as if square dancing is primarily carried out for physical fitness. However, unlike exercising in a gym or jogging on a quiet morning as people do in the West, square dancing in China is much more visible and audible – as choreographed performance – creating a new landscape and soundscape, as well as contributing to the image of the 'Harmonious Society' (*Hexie shehui*). In addition, the expectation is not just that it will be viewed; participation is also expected beyond the initial dance group, thus breaking the boundary of performer and audience, and further expanding the collective.

The concept of 'Harmonious Society' was first introduced by the Chinese government during the National People's Congress of 2005 in order to switch China's focus from economic growth to overall societal balance and harmony. It seemed to be an attempt to resolve or dilute the problem of social inequality and injustice, or, officially, 'to build China into a prosperous, powerful, democratic, civilized and harmonious modern country ... continually making new contributions to human progress with China's own development'.[39] Nothing could be more apt than square dancing to demonstrate and celebrate such harmony. To watch a display, such as that staged in the evening on the bank of the West Lake in Hangzhou, next to the Nanshan campus of the China Academy of Art, is to witness through lyrics, music and performance the re-making of a poetic and peaceful space, and the affirmation of a thriving collective synergy.

Chapter 2
Reinventing Tradition

Tradition travels, from one generation to the next, and from one place to another. Through the journey, it evolves, transforms and mutates; it can be reinterpreted, reinvented, or completely reborn through alternative, created paths.

During the twentieth century, China experienced dramatic social, political and cultural shifts. Since the early development of the People's Republic in the 1950s, major cities have been industrialized, and historical architecture and cultural heritage severely neglected. In the late 1960s, the Cultural Revolution provided an extraordinary example of political mobilization directed against the material and cultural vestiges of the past: public properties and cultural relics were attacked, and numerous art treasures and artefacts were destroyed. Soon after, the Open Door policy instigated economic reform, and the world witnessed China's rapid emergence in the Far East, almost overnight becoming the second-largest economy on the planet. In the meantime, fundamental changes were inevitable alongside the development.

In 1860, the Italian-British commercial photographer Felice Beato[1] accompanied Anglo-French forces into China for eight months. He returned with 102 black-and-white photographs – some of the earliest photographic images of the Middle Kingdom (*Zhongguo*, the literal Chinese name for China). These images provide a strikingly beautiful glimpse of nineteenth-century China – original city walls, stone bridges, archways, pagodas, residences and courtyards – but hardly anything is left today. In addition to what has been changed or lost in the physical living environment, calligraphic writing and traditional theatre are fading from people's daily lives, replaced by computer keyboards and karaoke; embroidery, cloth dyeing, lacquer ware, stone carving, paper cutting and other forms of traditional craftsmanship are also declining, because they either lack the avenues of future inheritance and transmission or they have been replaced by the cursory processes of batch production for tourists. The pace of globalization and the force of its reshaping influences have posed a serious threat to the sustainability of tradition within Chinese arts and culture, as Western architecture, furniture, fashion and products have permeated Chinese cities, which have seen a gradual transformation into an 'internationalized' style of living. Urbanization and tourism have collaborated in turning traditional Chinese arts and crafts from indigenous artefacts into touristic and commercial merchandise, from the 'local' to the 'global'.

Traditions have been interrupted, fragmented or distorted. And yet, according to scholar and critical theorist Homi Bhabha, 'The recognition that tradition bestows is a partial form of identification. In re-staging the past it introduces other, incommensurable cultural temporalities into the invention of tradition.'[2] Today, in China, much of what is described as 'traditional' is no longer part of an everyday reality, but is instead an item of material culture, ranging from discrete displays of museum cases to monumental structures of national and historical significance. The consequence of this unique situation, based on these prevailing conditions, has been a state of anxiety – an anxiety related to the search for cultural roots. This may involve a certain degree of disorientation, confusion and frustration, but, at the same time, it offers opportunities and challenges, particularly in the field of art.

To reflect critically upon this anxiety: will a new form of tradition reinvent the past for the future and translate from China to the rest of the world? What is the role of contemporary art in leading critical responses to the situation? On the one hand, contemporary artists manifest the marginalized position – or even the absence – of traditional arts and culture in our daily life, and thereby call up the cultural legacy against the current background of expanding globalization. On the other hand, they are afforded space for imagination, as China's unique circumstances mean that traditions can be constantly reassessed and reinvented, and can continue in unexpected categories and in new forms of expression. Envisaging the fragmented traditions in China, contemporary artists stand in various positions favourable to appropriating, subverting and reimagining the traditional arts and crafts, including techniques, forms, materials and processes of making, as well as more intangible aspects of heritage, harnessing their symbolic potentials and exploiting their cultural and historical resonances. Rather than discussing the ways in which tradition can be inherited, this chapter focuses on the ways in which tradition can be reinvented in art. Reinvention does not attempt to contradict tradition; rather, through contemporary art practice, it reveals and challenges the fault line that has split open in the succeeding Chinese culture, to retrieve what has been lost, and to reassess the cultural and creative values of traditional arts and crafts, as a generative process of speculative knowledge production.

The artworks discussed here reflect the above concerns through a range of perspectives and, naturally, through various levels of engagement with particular traditions. These do not simply encompass the exploration of experimental forms for traditional arts such as Chinese painting and calligraphy; they refer, more broadly, to works of installation, photography and video, which are developed through various kinds of appropriation, interpretation and extension of visual forms, materials and techniques of art and cultural legacies. These approaches of practice are not just about drawing information and inspiration from traditions; they are also about developing artists' cultural understandings and new strategies of visual exploration. For example, according to Wu Hung, contemporary Chinese artists have negotiated with various traditions through the means of 'distilling materiality', 'translating visuality' and 'refiguration'.[3] Curator and writer Pi Li goes further to include a more recent approach whereby artists manipulate traditional *narratives* using a visual method.[4] This chapter highlights artistic and critical reflections on traditions from three different and connecting angles, which are explored in the following three sections.

Things

Through the lens of materiality, contemporary artists have been exploring the aesthetic quality and conceptual value of 'Chinese materials' that are fundamental to literati art (art of the scholar-gentlemen of dynastic China; see p. 88), as well as representative and symbolic in Chinese or oriental culture; for example, gunpowder (Cai Guo-Qiang), silk (Liang Shaoji), bamboo (Xiao Yu), porcelain (Liu Jianhua) and jade (Zhao Zhao). On the one hand, these materials can automatically establish cultural meanings, connotations and implications, which might assist in the development and reception of the artwork; on the other hand, the meanings and connotations behind the materials are further extended by artists through their interests in materiality, and through a renewed understanding and translation in the contemporary context.

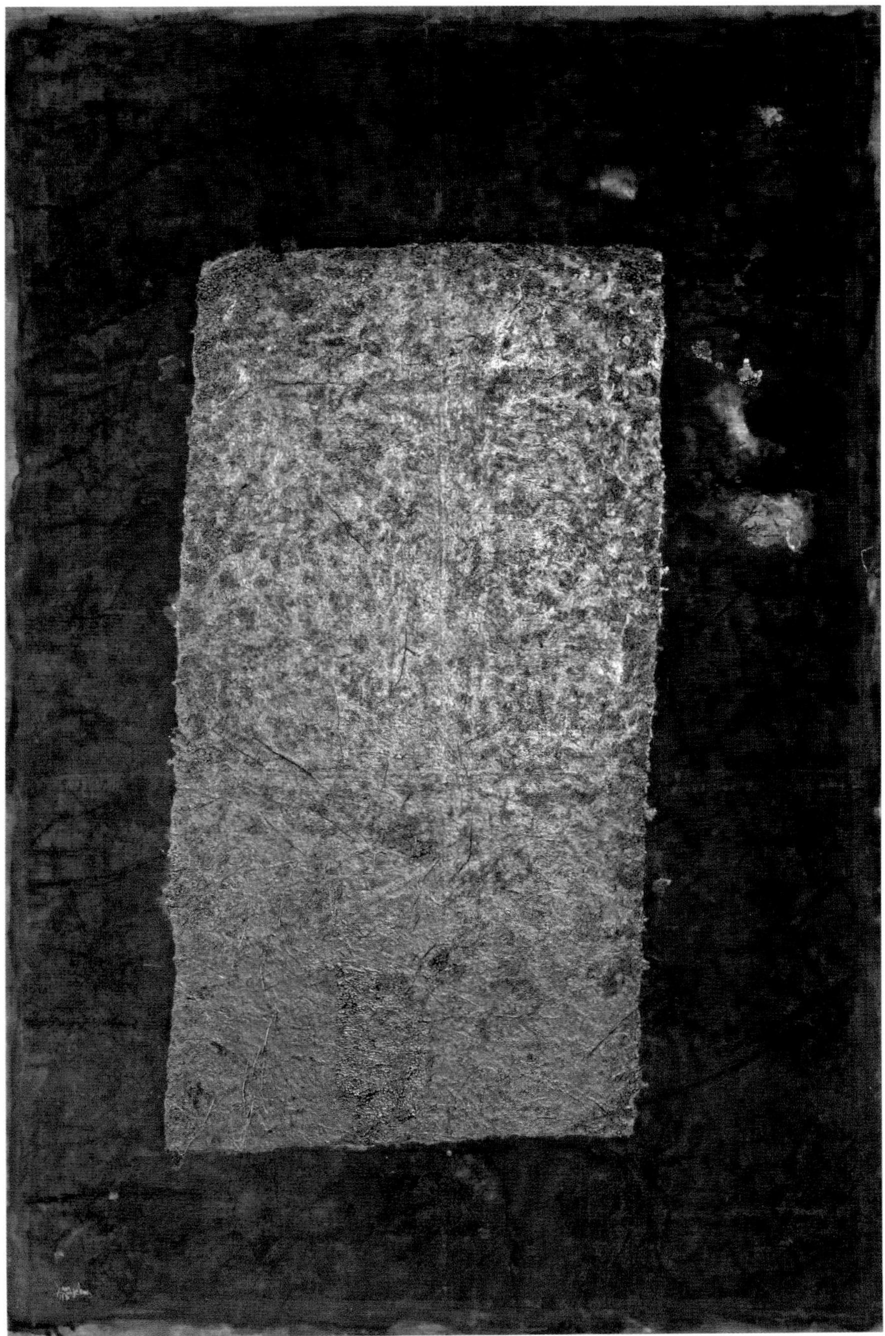

We shall first look at the materials of Chinese ink and *xuan* paper and related brushwork, and explore how these thousand-year-long legacies can be re-introduced in contemporary practice. Yang Jiechang began to create experimental ink work in the late 1980s, his artistic practices being intimately connected to his study of Zen Buddhism and Taoism. Over a decade (1989–99), he developed his first sustained body of work, *100 Layers of Ink*. While the primary materials – ink, paper and water – remain the same as those used by literati artists, Yang obsessively applied layers upon layers of ink, day after day, forming a series of abstract shapes. These are monochromatic, but, more than simply conveying a black colour, they present a kind of aged texture with a luminescent quality, as well as a quality of silence. The process of the production (the repetition of applying ink layers) eliminated any skills that the artist had obtained through years of training in Chinese traditional art, as well as any meaningful imagery or any personalized artistic gestures. It became a daily routine, or a form of ritual, whereby Yang could use dark ink to cover and seal off, or metaphorically negate, what had been achieved, over and over again, and start anew. The layers expanded the artwork from a two-dimensional surface to a three-dimensional object, the whole becoming, according to the artist, akin to a 'room', a space, and an archive of his own history.[5]

An artist of a younger generation, Hu Xiaoyuan, also makes use of ink, as well as *xiao* – raw silk sheets. Her signature work, the installation *Wood*, consists of nothing but pieces of wood, 31 in total, both short and long, leaning against a wall. In fact, they are not natural; they have all been meticulously painted. These battens are first coloured in white and covered with the translucent silk fabric. Using ink, the artist then copies onto the

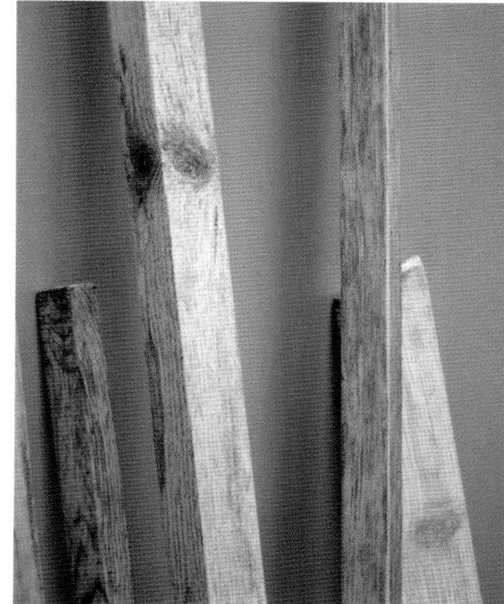

43 OPPOSITE Yang Jiechang,
100 Layers of Ink, No. 1, 1990
44 RIGHT Hu Xiaoyuan,
Wood, 2009–10 (detail)

surface of the *xiao* the grain and texture of the wood; or, in her own words, she makes 'new "skins" for these wood pieces', and discovers 'their original limitation, as well as their infinity' in the long process of the work.[6] Through this process, the natural lines of the wood are extracted, replaced and transformed, and this alters the original properties of the material itself. The artist uses *xiao* as a medium to make her work, but simultaneously it is the intervention of this specific material that enables her reflection to acquire its full depth. The artist's understanding and the transformation summoned by the material come to form a new object, something natural and yet unnatural. As critic and curator Nicolas Bourriaud has stated, Hu's choice of materials, such as *xiao* and ink, 'attaches her subtly to the Chinese visual space, but it is through means other than those of optical recognition that she manages to construct an oeuvre which expresses a specific *way of thinking*, and one that cannot be reduced to European aesthetic presuppositions'.[7]

Contemporary practice is not, however, restricted to conventional art materials; it embraces all. Returning to the point of origin of oriental textiles, or to their basic constitutive unit, Liang Shaoji chooses silk, which can be equated with the creation of Chinese civilization from ancient times. Since 1989, the artist has committed his life to breeding and training silkworms to produce this organic material for art making. His artistic and philosophical reflections on the topics of traditional culture and contemporary life are solely expressed through his understandings of the texture and physical properties of silk, and through his secret communications with these remarkable larval-stage insects. He views his practice as existing 'at the crossroads of art and science, biology and socio-biology, weaving and sculpture, installation and performance art'.[8] In *Snow Cover*, Liang uses natural silk threads, symbols of life, to shape an urban landscape lying in ruins in the middle of a snowy land. The snow-covered city is dimly discernible; among its contours, there seem to be clusters of modern high-rise buildings and thoroughfares. Computer components, electrical cables and fragments of antique pottery are combined to develop the devastation, redolent of skeletal remains or of an archaeological excavation site in a distant future. In another work, *Chains*, what viewers might perceive first of all is not the materials themselves, nor the form of the installation, but rather a sense of warmth. In this work, chains are wrapped by thick, multiple layers of stretched silk threads from top to bottom. The dialogue taking place between these two materials is so intimate that neither the viewer nor even the artist himself has any possible way of intervening. One is

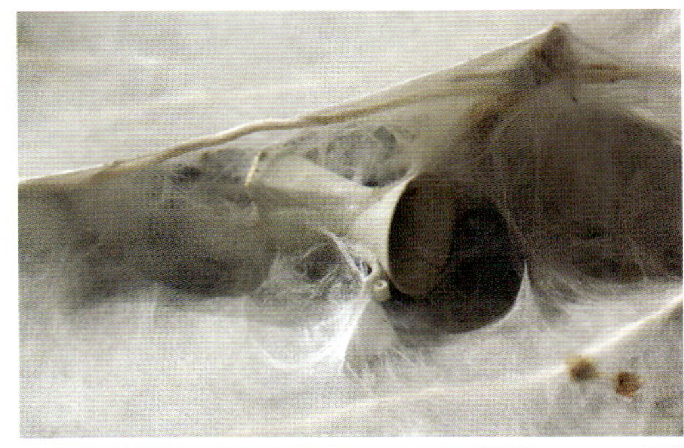
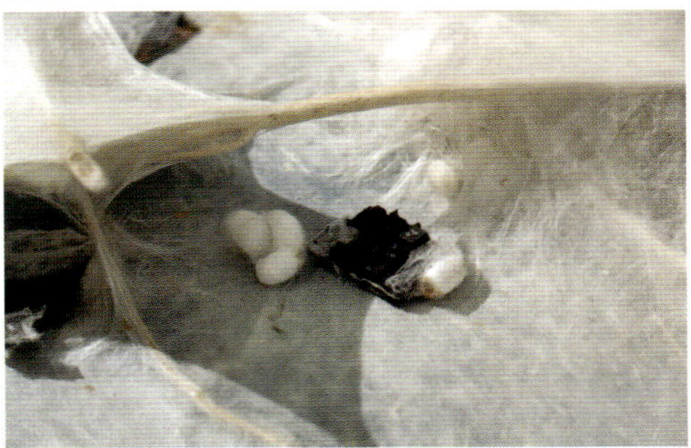
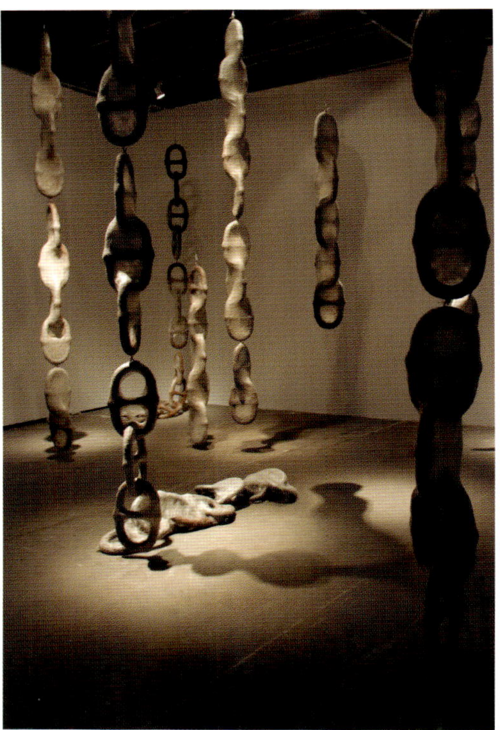

45 ABOVE Liang Shaoji, *Snow Cover Series: Snow in the Woods,* 2016 (details)
46 RIGHT Liang Shaoji, *Chains: The Unbearable Lightness of Being / Nature Series No. 79,* 2003–16 (installation view)

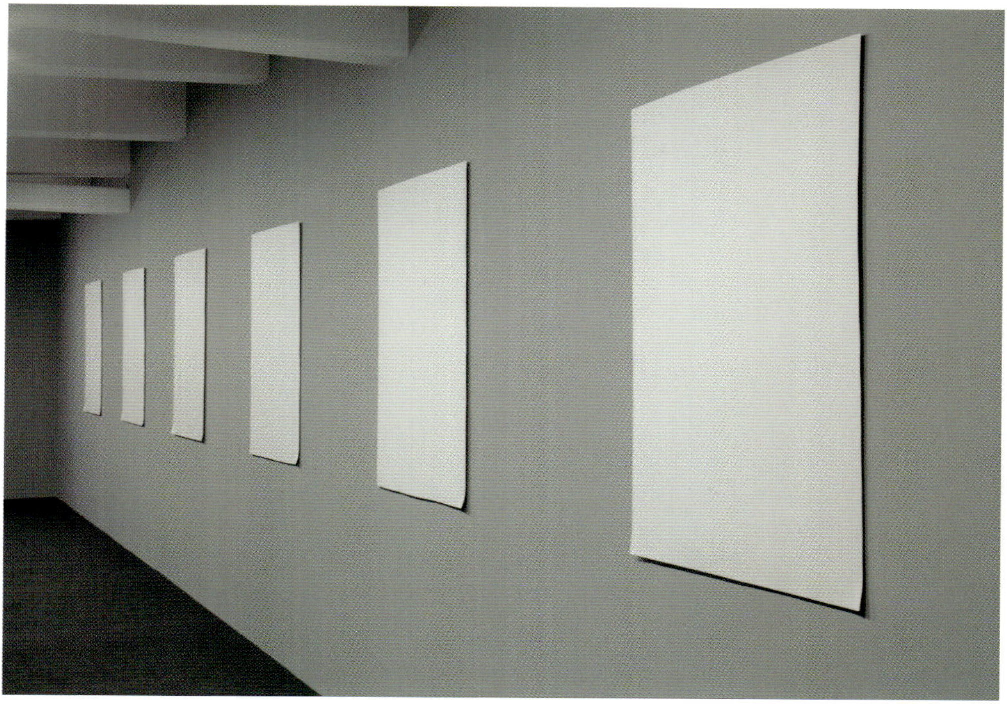

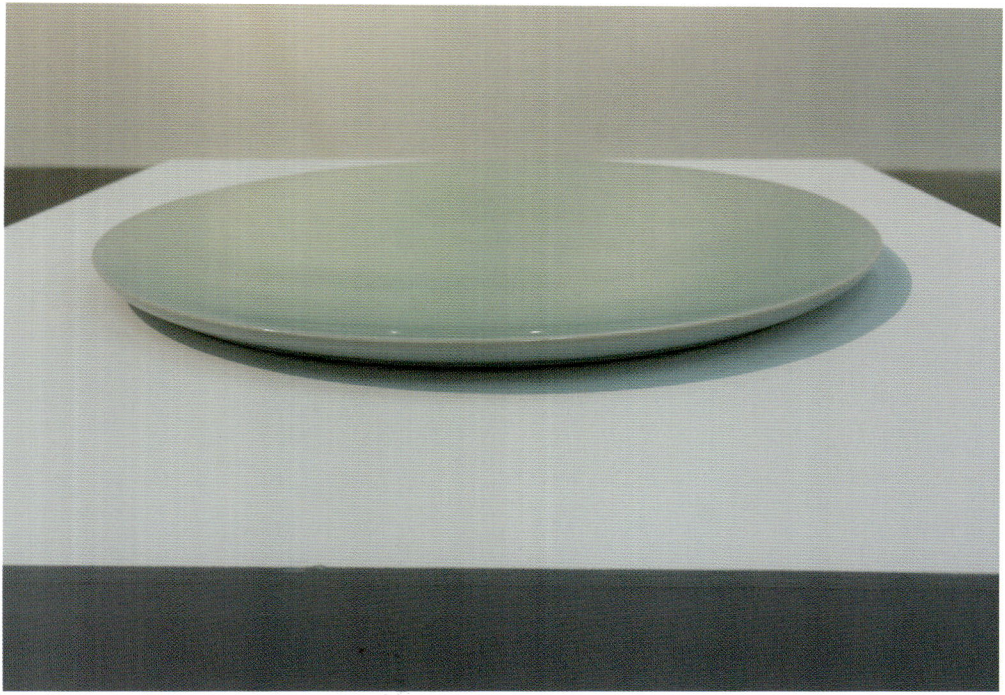

gentle and soft, somewhat 'feminine' and exquisite, abstract
and formless; the other, in contrast, is rough and heavy, rigid
and 'masculine', and made of industrial geometric shapes. The
two are entangled in an impasse. In fact, they form a paradox:
the chains, which should have the authority to bind, are
actually in the grips of a dream-like mist – the thing that has
the power to expropriate freedom has lost its own freedom.
In other words, the wild is tamed by the domesticated; hatred
is appeased by patience.

In China, porcelain is arguably of an equal cultural
significance to silk. Some say the English word 'china' comes
from Changnan, the old name of Jingdezhen town, which, as
part of Jiangxi Province in the Tang dynasty (618–907), was for
thousands of years known as the 'Porcelain Capital'. Through
years of rigorous training during his apprenticeship, which
began at an early age, ceramic and porcelain have become
Liu Jianhua's language, through which he can understand,
interpret and communicate with today's society.[9] When
a certain material becomes part of contemporary artistic
language, this language is built not only with the material
itself, as the 'vocabulary', no matter whether this is dazzling or
ornate, simple or unsophisticated, but also, more importantly,
with the rules governing the intangibles that result from the
particular craft and production process; in other words, what
constitutes the 'grammar' of this language. Liu's works, such
as *Blank Paper*, or more recently *Filled*, all explore the limits
of craft techniques within the domain of a traditional
'grammar', as they convert minute changes observed in the
realms of nature into an aesthetic form, and thereby shape
the artist's personal and specific language system. At first
glance, *Blank Paper* appears to be minimalistic – simple
sheets of paper. This is suggested by the colour, the texture,
the slight flipping at the corners, and the slimness of the
production, which in fact – at the giant size specified by the
artist – represented a new technical challenge, because the
medium is porcelain plate, traditionally made as a ground
for paintings. Similarly, in *Filled*, a large porcelain dish
appears to be filled to the brim with crystal-clear spring
water, and this looks as if it has been disturbed for an instant,
as communicated by its 'vibrating' surface complete with
ripples. Be it via paper or water, through his 'language of
porcelain' – itself a seemingly metamorphosed material –
Liu unfolds his aesthetic narratives.

47

48

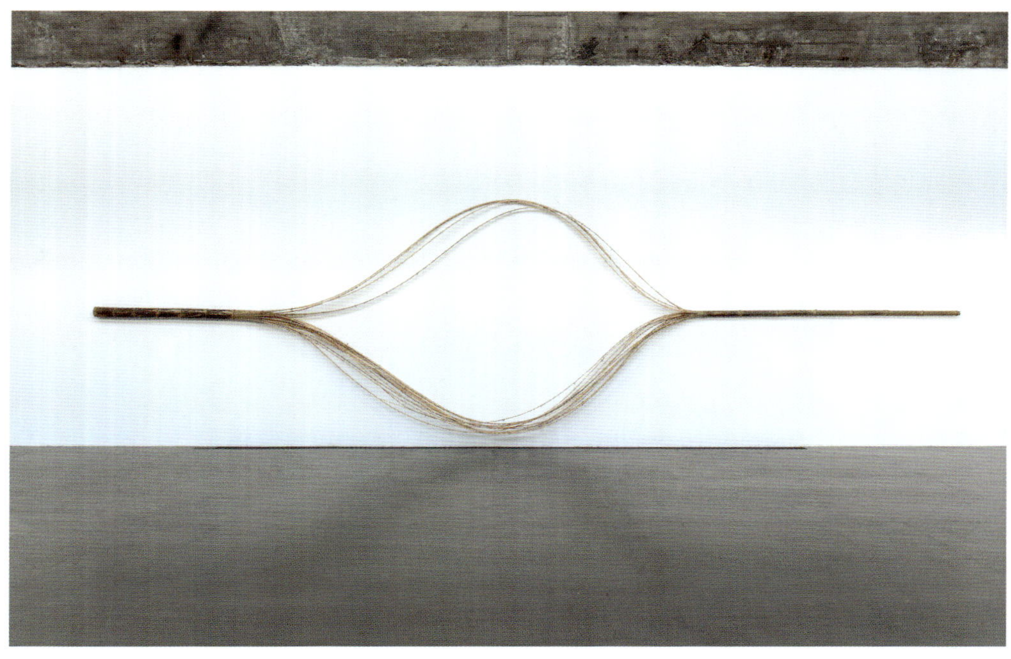

49 ABOVE Xiao Yu, *Translocation, No. 17*, 2017
50 OPPOSITE Xiao Yu, *Infinitive, No. 1*, 2018

Xiao Yu is sceptical about so-called 'conceptual art'. In his view, it seems as if today's art has to depend on both concepts and excessive theoretical interpretations. Sometimes, he feels, it would be enough just to 'hear' the project proposal, without having to trouble to see its realization in materials and space. In his opinion, such art is too keen on its interactions with politics, philosophy and sociology to manifest its modernity and its dynamic and disciplinary potential; at the same time, it seems somehow less confident and lost in identity.[10] Xiao always proceeds from an oriental perspective, whether consciously or subconsciously. Bamboo has been favoured in literati painting and poetry since the Song dynasty (960–1279). From his series *Translocation* onwards, it has played a central role, not only as the subject *per se*, but also as the primary working material to set up a new point of departure for the artist's further explorations of intuitive and bodily perceptions. In his work, this special plant – strong, tough and flexible – has been cut, twisted and inflected by human force to its absolute limits. These rearrangements allow the bamboo to appear somewhat unfamiliar, thereby reinterpreting its original

49

symbolization in Chinese culture, maximizing the spiritual power hidden inside its visual forms, and extending the existing aesthetic imagination. Xiao's canes are fractured and bent into various shapes and configurations, demonstrating their forbearance and elegance, and seemingly conveying the pleasing sound of strings; they also create and accumulate a powerful energy, apparently on the verge of breaking out, ready for war at any minute.

In 2018, as an extension of his work, Xiao Yu conducted a purer visual experiment – by replacing all the bamboo with copper. Through a precise casting process, the form of the work retains or even monumentalizes the symbolic significance of the original material. It is the artist's further attempt to liberate this particular material from its fixed cultural associations, as a new form of vocabulary in the contemporary context. The related video work shows a section of a mature bamboo cane that is almost perfectly straight – the same thickness from end to end, strong and steady. In extreme slow motion, the bamboo perceptibly begins to tremble. It is being twisted. Driven by the unknown source of forcible tension, it cracks and distorts until – crushed, or transformed – it is broken down into fine strips and strings. At a pivotal point, the twist is slowly reversed, the broken is restored and the wounded is recovered, as if the bamboo has regained its strength, ready for a new challenge. In Xiao's work,

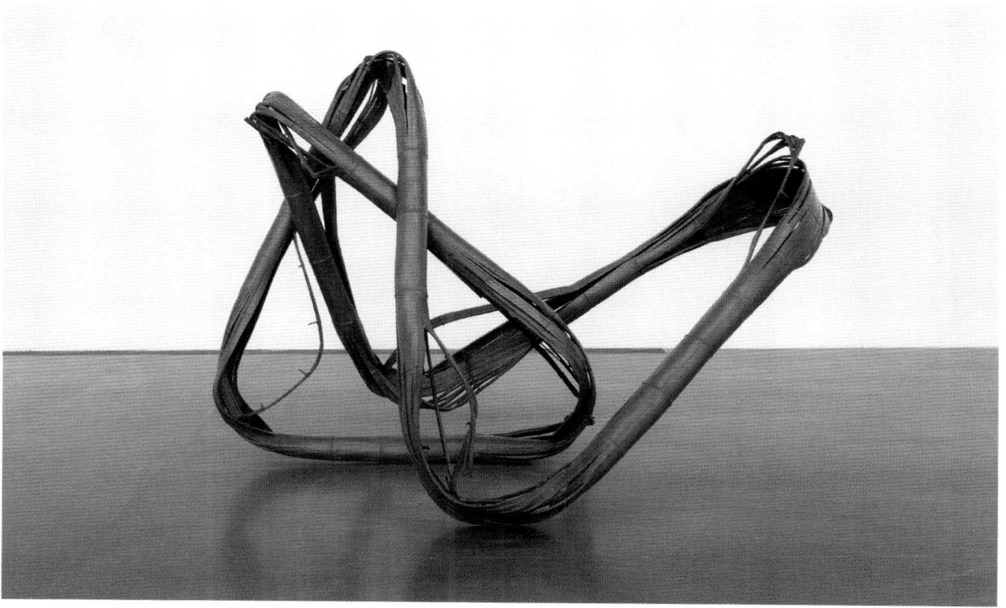

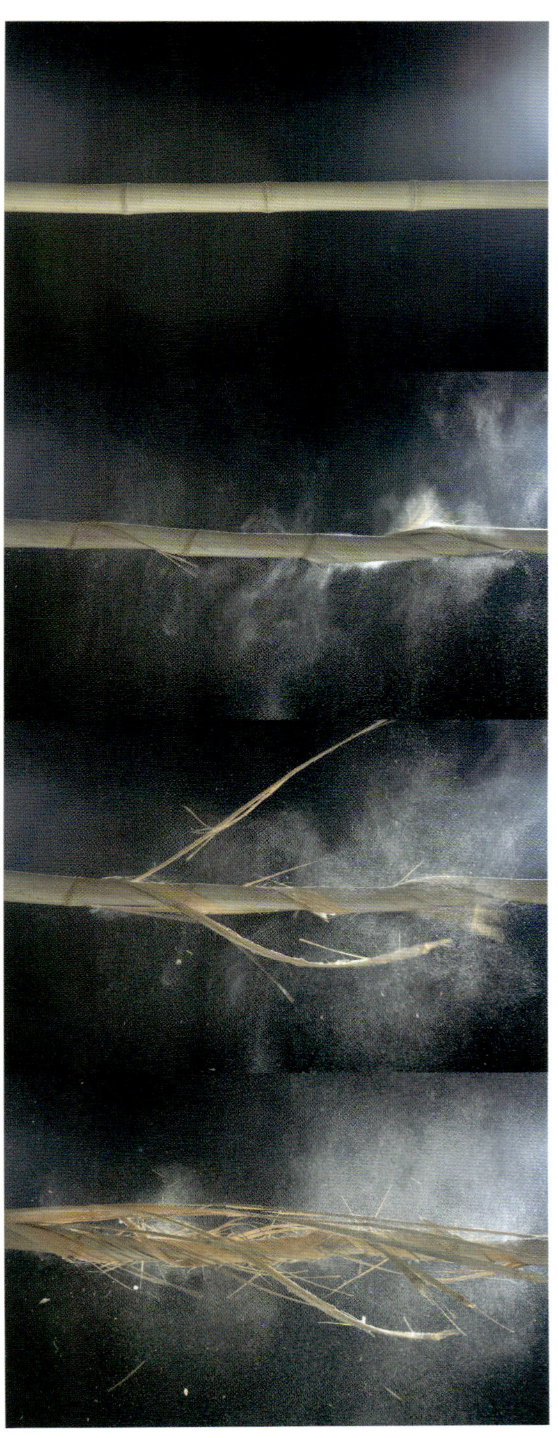

51 Xiao Yu, *Thinking Too Much That... No. 5*, 2015 (video stills)

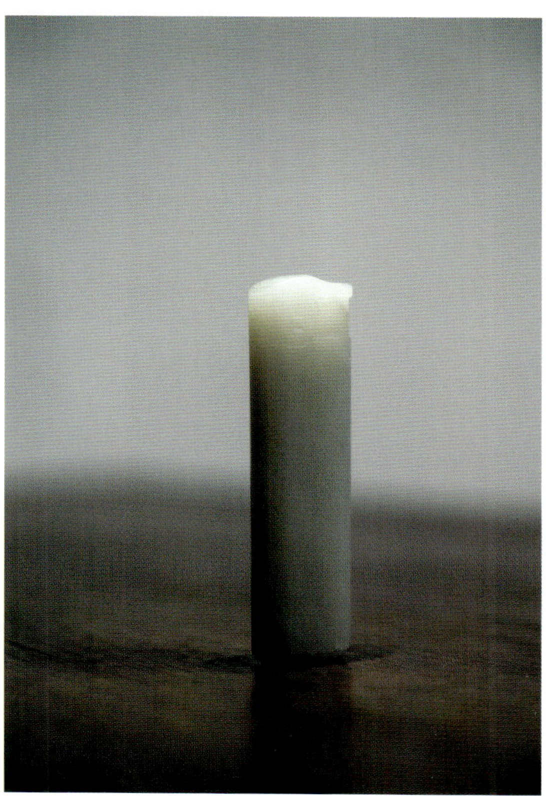

52 Zhao Zhao,
Lighter, 2016

bamboo is not only subject, and not only material; it is
also a readymade channel to imagine 'a shape of power'.[11]

Zhao Zhao chose jade from the 4,000-metre-high (over
13,000 ft) Kunlun Mountains as the medium for a life-
size carving of a cheap, mass-produced, everyday item –
a lighter. This luxurious material, together with the long
and painstaking work of exquisite craftsmanship, was
therefore expended on a daily consumer product that can
be manufactured in the blink of an eye or discarded at any
moment. The work merely preserves the exterior appearance
of the plastic lighter, and therefore is naturally devoid of the
original item's functionality. It creates a strange relationship
between material and object: one is to be fondled lovingly
in the context of elegant traditional culture, while the other
can be consumed in the daily life of our present time; the
translucent and supreme quality of the stone has here
assumed a cheap and low-grade shape.

If *Lighter* demonstrates a process of conscientious craftsmanship, then Zhao Zhao's minimalistic installation *Again* is a result of 'violence'. It appears as a 1.5-metre (nearly 5 ft) cube, comprising hundreds of stone blocks of different sizes, all confined and consolidated within a single set of dimensions. Each block in the geometric shape was, in a previous incarnation, part of an ancient Chinese Buddha statue. Collected by the artist over the years, these Buddha sculptures had already been damaged during periods of Buddhist persecution in dynastic China as well as political campaigns during Mao's Cultural Revolution. The shapes of the original figures, together with their artistic styles and forms and the time of their making, whether actual or estimated, have been eliminated. They are no longer sculptures, or rather they are a new sculpture, abstract and industrial, cut by electronic blades on a cold machine bed. As an extension of the concept, in the work *Countless*, Zhao further divided the stone that the statues were made of into innumerable cubes, each only 1 square centimetre (⅜ sq. in.) in size. These cubes can be displayed as a large mosaic-like floor, or they can be lined up to mark out a 100-metre-long (330 ft) wall. Just like in the fierce revolution that took place in the last century, anything of religious, cultural or political significance has been thoroughly pulverized by the violence of the machine and 220-volt electricity in our modern day. The execution of these works could have immediately raised concerns at different levels. Legally, one might question whether this could be testing the law of cultural-relics protection. Ethically, one could ask how devout Buddhists might receive the work, which was purposely made (or 'damaged'), manipulated and accumulated only with visual considerations, and then presented as art. Other viewers – artists, perhaps – might not view these as sacrilegious acts, but rather as a precise symbolization of a fragmented tradition in China. From a

53 opposite Zhao Zhao, *Again,* 2014
54 below Zhao Zhao, *Countless,* 2014 (detail)

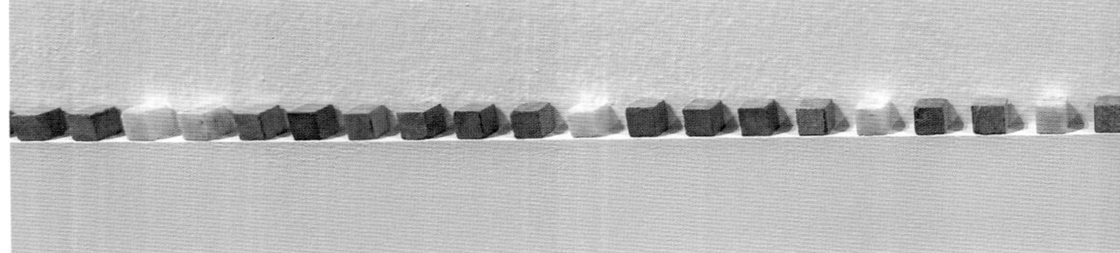

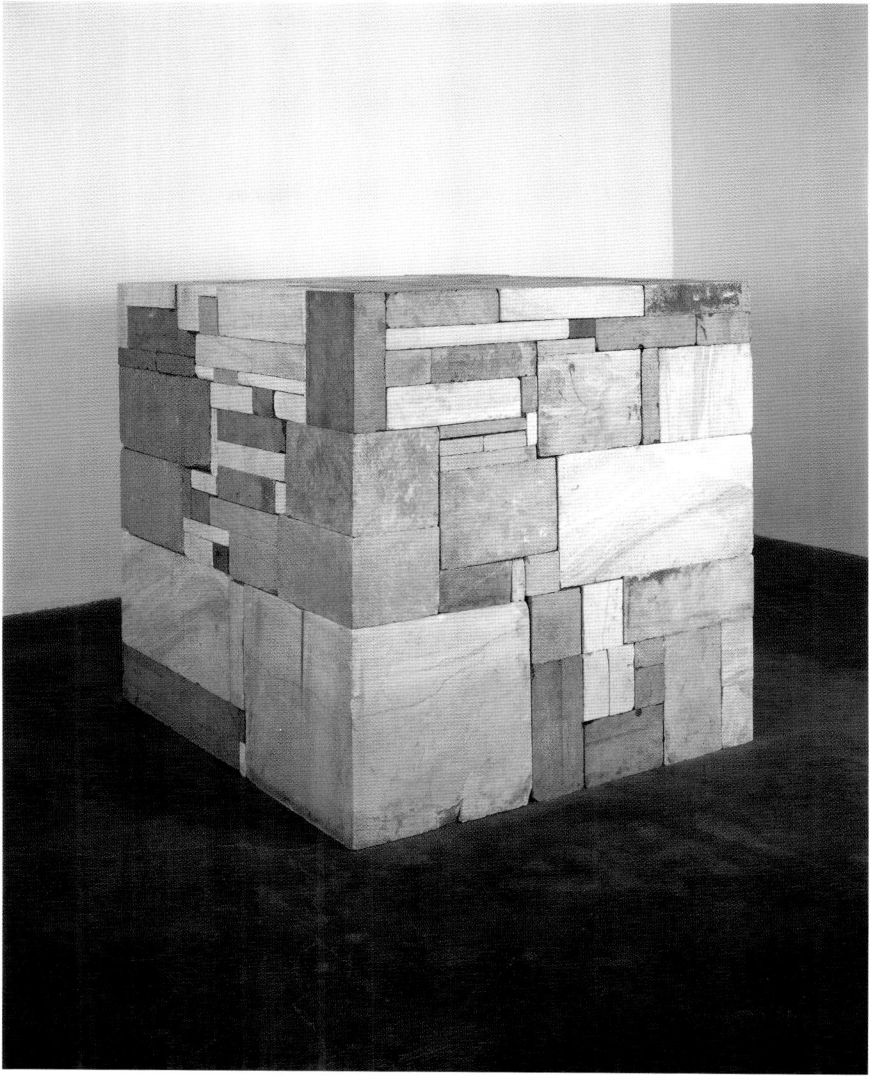

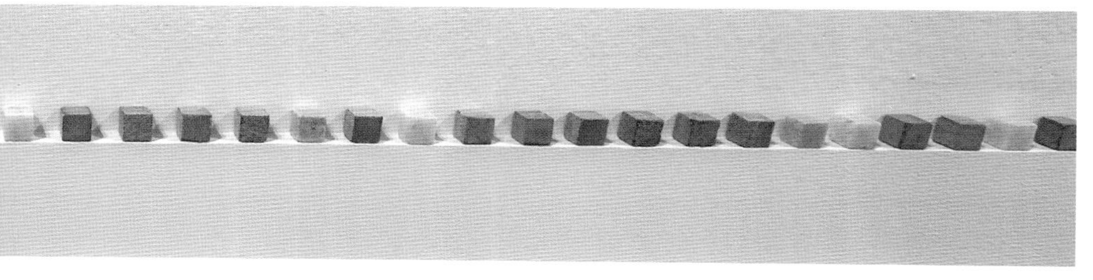

positive point of view, in this way, the past has been preserved, not merely in a glass cabinet, but transformed into a new form of life, to be experienced by future generations.

Returning to Hu Xiaoyuan (see p. 71), similarly, in her 2008 work *Useless*, she deliberately placed herself first of all in a mood to exert all her strength and tear up a large sheet of *xuan* paper randomly into shreds. The quality of the paper remained unchanged, but the form of its existence was improvised from one full piece into multiple individual pieces, of various shapes and sizes, produced by each action of the artist. She then collected all the fragments and spent weeks meticulously restoring the sheet, piece by piece, so that it was as close as possible to its original complete form. This might conjure up one of the earliest video works in China, *30 × 30*, by Zhang Peili, in which the artist carefully smashes a 30 by 30 cm (nearly 12 sq. in.) mirror, then glues the shards back together,

55 BELOW Hu Xiaoyuan, *Useless*, 2008 (detail)
56 OPPOSITE Zhang Peili, *30 × 30*, 1988 (video still)

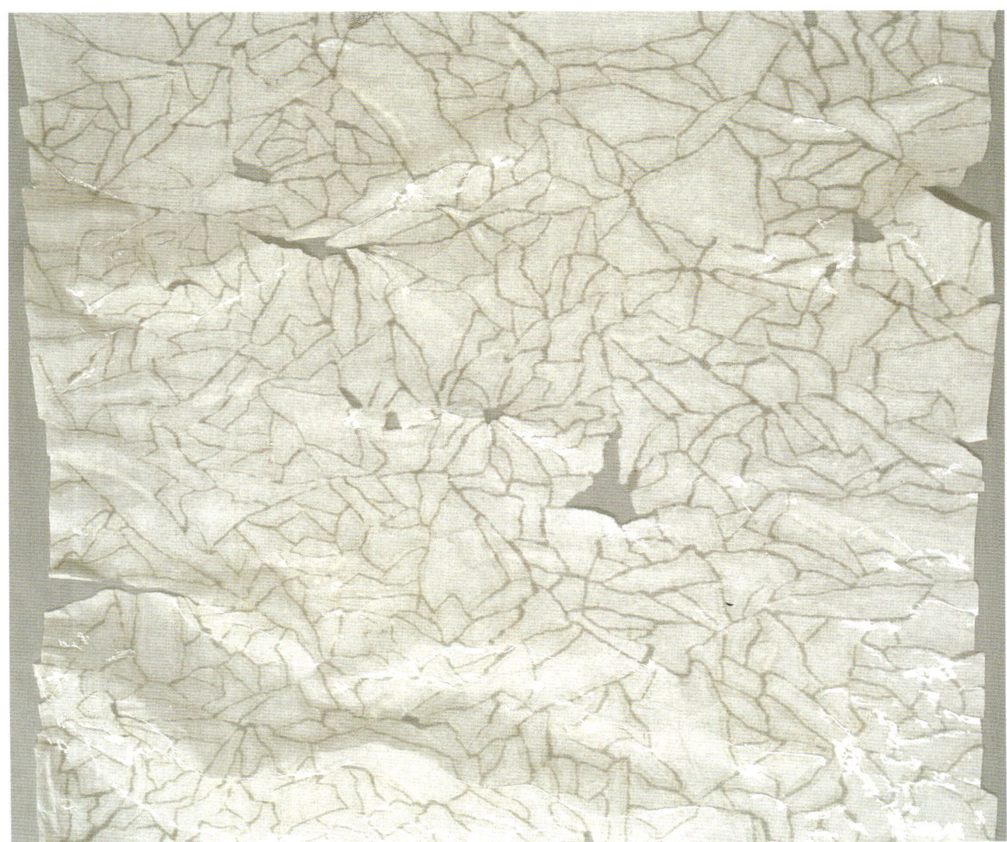

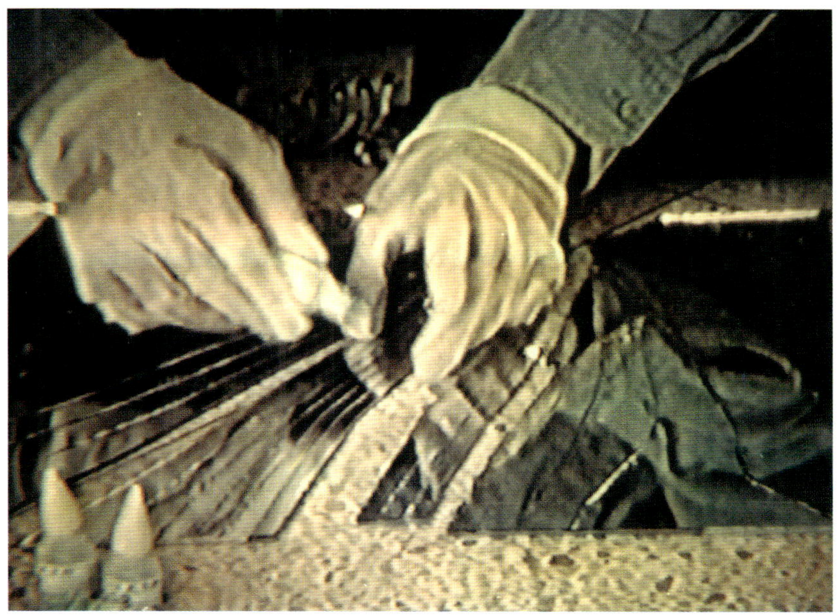

over and over again.[12] Although both these works appear to consist of a similar process of fragmentation and restoration, they in fact have different focuses. Zhang Peili's work employs a limited time frame – the 180-minute duration of the piece is the full length of the videotape – and repeated actions to comment on aesthetics of boredom. Hu Xiaoyuan's actions are presented not on video, but inscribed in the artwork itself, and they are reflective not of boredom but of extreme moods (the violent tearing of the paper, followed by its careful, patient reconstruction). The process is not just an exercise in self-reflection; it demonstrates the artist's understanding of – and ambivalent attitude towards – tradition, as represented by that very sheet of *xuan* paper.

When Ai Weiwei was asked about the relationship between history and his work, he responded: 'in terms of the history of my country, my personal history or the history of those who live around me, all these are fragments, missing many parts and difficult to be reunited. Those remaining fragments provide me with a larger space to imagine their original possible structure, although that is now non-existent.'[13] Or one could, in fact, conclude that the missing pieces are even more important than the remaining pieces: they can turn the tangible into the intangible, and make the factual fictional.

Beauty

If traditions can be reimagined with materials, with 'things',
they can also be reinvented through the appropriation of
aesthetic forms. To appropriate form does not refer here only
to the understanding of traditional shapes; it also includes
a renewed reflection as regards their contemporary value in
the new visual production. Zhan Wang started his *jiashanshi*
(artificial rocks) series in the mid-1990s, with the aim of
engaging in a reinterpretation of traditional Chinese culture
while also hinting at the industrialization process undergone
by modern cities in the country. His works, which make use
of stainless steel to take three-dimensional 'rubbings' of
traditional Chinese rockeries, suggest an alternative object or
space – halfway between garden and city, the natural and the
artificial. These 'rocks' are both real and fake: while they are
faithful reproductions of the originals, of the same height, size
and shape, scrupulously copied right down to every little detail
and texture, they are made of a completely different material.
In this way, they are slightly reminiscent of the cyanotype,
a photographic technique invented in the early nineteenth
century that was used to chemically capture and record actual-
size projections of the concrete shapes of everyday objects,
thus generating faithful reproductions. To some extent, Zhan's
rockeries are like three-dimensional 'shadows' of the original
shapes. Unlike the images captured by the mechanism of
photography, however, these shapes are all born from the
artist's subjective point of view, his own understanding and
personal touch, to form an unadorned yet sophisticated
series. Zhan's works borrow the structure of traditional literati
rocks, but only exist as 'pure form'. They originate from actual
substance, and yet they give short shrift to it; they appear full
and substantial, and yet are actually hollow. On the level of
representation, the form of Zhan's works seems traditional;
however, this traditional appearance is not what motivated
their production. It was instead the method, present within
tradition, of copying an original shape by means of rubbings.
In front of the stainless-steel surface of these 'rocks', one may
gain a renewed experience of the myriad shapes long present in
nature, or observe a different self through the reflections made
by the natural but irregular facets of the lumps and creases in
the surface.

Shao Yinong, too, has always paid great attention to
the question of how to translate his own appreciation of
traditional 'literati aesthetics' into the context of contemporary
practice. In his 2011 work *The Nine Twigs*, several densely
interlocking tree branches hang in mid-air, as if they have

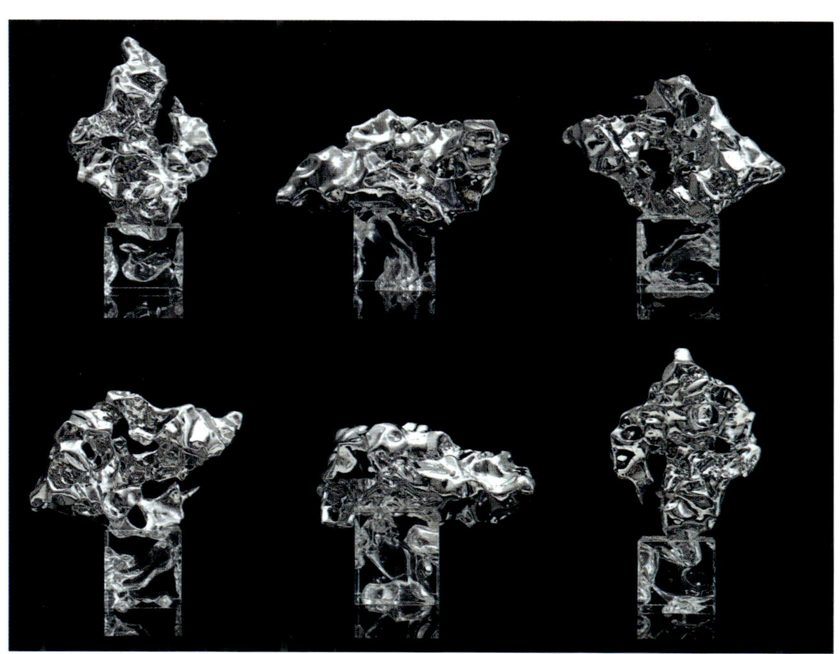

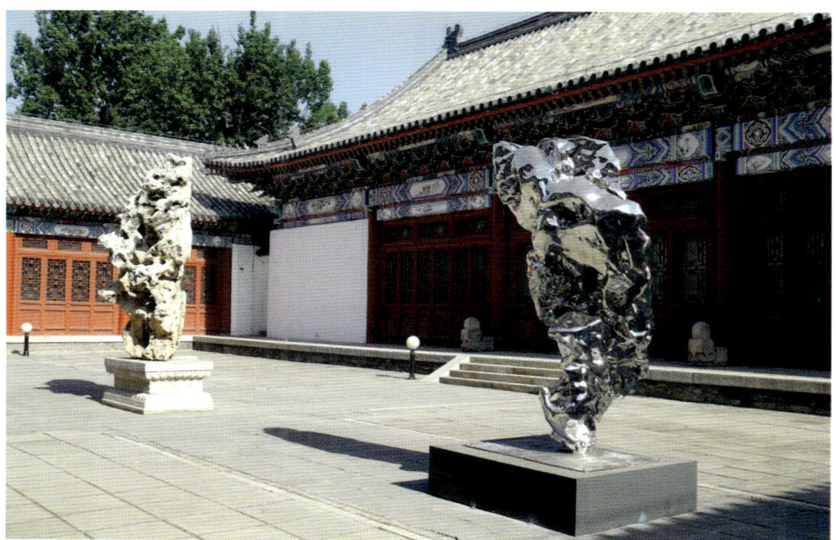

57 TOP Zhan Wang, *Artificial Rocks, No. 164*, 2013
58 ABOVE Zhan Wang, *Artificial Rocks, No. 175*, 2013 (installation view)

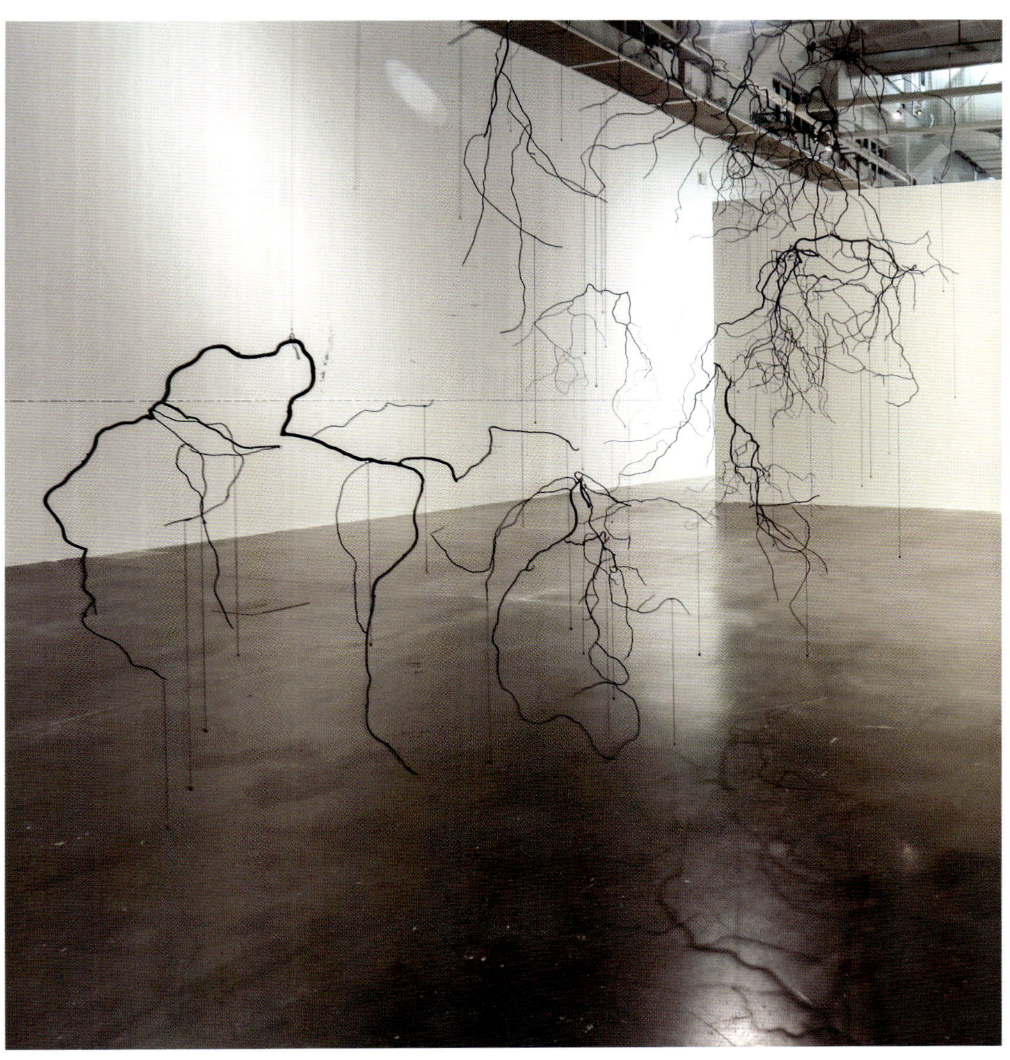

59 Shao Yinong, *The Nine Twigs*, 2011 (installation view)

naturally grown there, some of them restful and compact, others lively and expressive. However, they are anything but natural; they are in fact made from iron rods that were forged, hammered and welded together, inch by inch, through a long process of traditional craftsmanship. To Shao, this work has two main reference points: the first, of course, is the beauty of forms found in nature; the second is the particular mood traditionally registered and inherited by Chinese literati through calligraphic writings. Each branch seems to be inspired by the cadence and modulations of the flowing brush in calligraphy – at times elegant and ethereal, at times involved and abstruse.

Like most artists who have been trained in the art academies in China, Yu Ji spent many years studying realistic techniques of Western sculpture, which allow artists to faithfully depict a subject based on an understanding of the precise structure of human anatomy. In her *Flesh in Stone* series, Yu returned to a Chinese aesthetic system and employed the plastic language of traditional Buddhist sculpture to craft typical oriental bodies. The description of shapes in Chinese language can be literary and, sometimes, poetic; accurate, but never measurable. For example, the so-called 'nail round' is neither a circle nor an oval, let alone being of any specified dimensions, while the 'bean curd square' is never a perfect square. Such shapes refer to a particular radian or rectilinear through images beyond the original object that is being described. The uncertainty, and paradoxically the certainty, of these descriptions is rooted in culture, and they are reflected in the work of Yu Ji. If one studies the surviving Buddhist sculptures in museums and temples, they are a kind of distillation of the human figure based on traditional aesthetics and craftsmanship outside reality, the artist enjoying the journey travelling between the actual and the crafted. Yu Ji's series collects fragments of human bodies – a robust and bent back, or a single leg (with no foot) accompanied by a penis – the surface of which still preserves the rough texture of the artist's medium of cement, as well as traces of mould rims, which appear as slight bulges on the cross-section of each work. They are presented as naked, and mercilessly affixed to the walls with metal brackets, dissociated from the Western systematic categories of 'figurative' or 'abstract' art. One fails to read on these bodies any signs of the cultural, social or political discourse that might otherwise be expected; even sexual features are attenuated. While these bodies might read as fragmentary on the level of physical appearance, in the artist's view, once they are cleared of any identifying symbols, they are in fact more

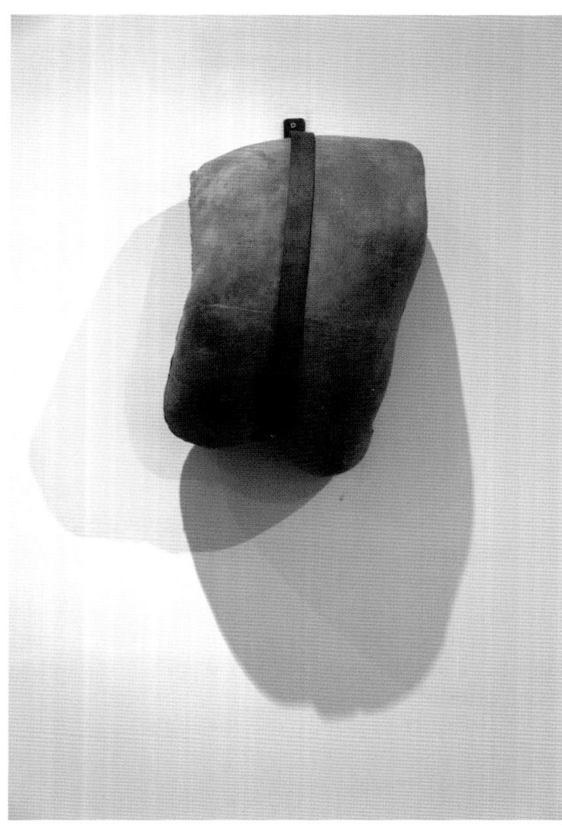

60 LEFT Yu Ji, *Flesh in Stone, No. 6*, 2016
61 OPPOSITE Yu Ji, *Flesh in Stone, Component 1*, 2015

'complete': they simply become 'purer bodies – bodies that have been minutely prepared to exude an oriental essence'.[14] This distinctly elusive form of beauty is different from that which is defined in the West, or fundamentally by Aristotle, based on order, symmetry and clear delineation, and it will continue in its own way.

According to Dong Qichang, the Ming dynasty (1368–1644) politician and artist, Chinese literati adopted the practice of painting as early as the eighth century. The poet Wang Wei has been credited as the initiator of literati painting (*wenren hua*). In the literati tradition, art is neither realistic, nor necessarily critical. Instead, it is seen as a spiritual representation of the individual, and a personal reflection as expressed through a created image of nature. This inclination towards 'reclusion' from a secular world led literati painting to its climax during the Song and Yuan dynasties. Now, plants, such as plum

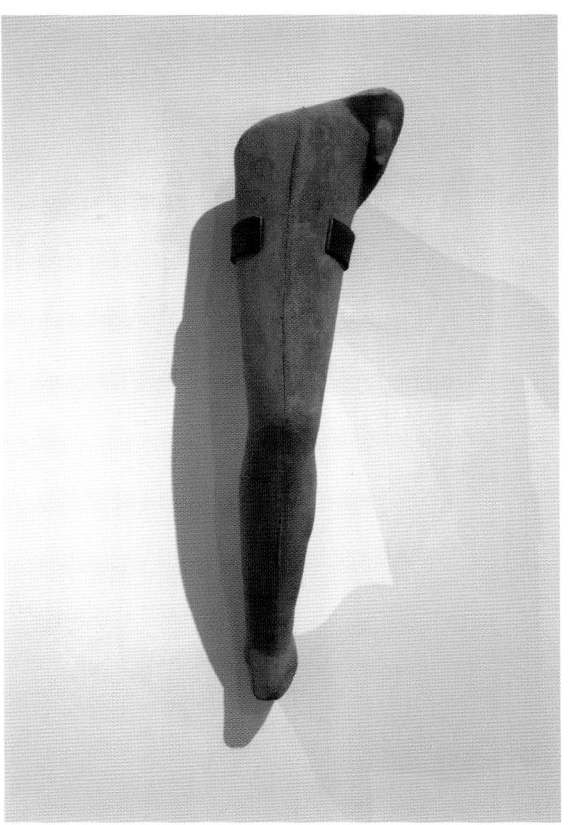

blossom, orchid, bamboo and chrysanthemum, and mountains and water (*shanshui*), became significant motifs, depicting a *shiwai taoyuan* (a land of peach blossoms beyond the world), or an earthly paradise, a notion first conceived by the poet Tao Yuanming in the Eastern Jin dynasty (317–420).

Even today, when art museums are replete with a great diversity of media, the artist Hao Liang remains fascinated by the materiality, techniques and imagery at the heart of traditional art; he is also immersed in the deductive logic of traditional painting theory and literary works. In his own practice, hand scrolls have always been an important form, and have come to constitute a perfect stage for his contemporary narratives. The act of holding a hand scroll, unfurled on one side and rolled up on the other, grants its slow and dignified contemplation a specific temporality. This involvement of time has caused Western scholars to compare reading these scrolls to reciting poetry, or listening to music. Although music and poems may stimulate our visual imagination, they cannot provide the concrete boundaries for imagination, nor the visual references, that are the domain of hand scrolls. This kind of reading implies a process rich with visual expectation and visual memory. A hand scroll is to be perused, from right to left, in the same order as the visual narrative is produced. The reader thereby gains an experience of the artist's creative process, and is able to travel back and forth into an imaginative space. How do this particular medium and its aesthetic experiences inspire the artist's practice within a contemporary context? And how may the artist make use of this visual form to lead the viewer on a new journey across time and space?

In Hao Liang's view, the core of the transformation from the historical to the contemporary is to have a full understanding of the evolution of Chinese art as a whole. To him, tradition is not something to be concluded or distilled; it is everyday life, it is the way in which he understands the world. He does not have anxiety about tradition, and he believes in its vitality over time.[15] In his large horizontal scroll *The Tale of Clouds*, he focuses on depicting spatial transformations between different times and scenes. Through his own imagination and understanding of tradition, Hao continues to give shape to all manner of interrogations, deliberations, and compromises between the body and the world, as well as between past and future.

The proposition of literati art is poetic, and ink-wash (*shuimo*) is its language. The Taipei-based artist Wu Chi-Tsung still speaks the language of ink-wash, but he does not necessarily use ink-wash as his physical material. His acclaimed series *Wire* first appeared in 2003. The initial version of the installation imitates the structure of a slide projector,

62 BELOW Hao Liang, *The Tale of Clouds*, 2013 (detail)
63 OPPOSITE ABOVE Wu Chi-Tsung, *Wire I*, 2003
64 OPPOSITE BELOW Wu Chi-Tsung, *Wire II*, 2003

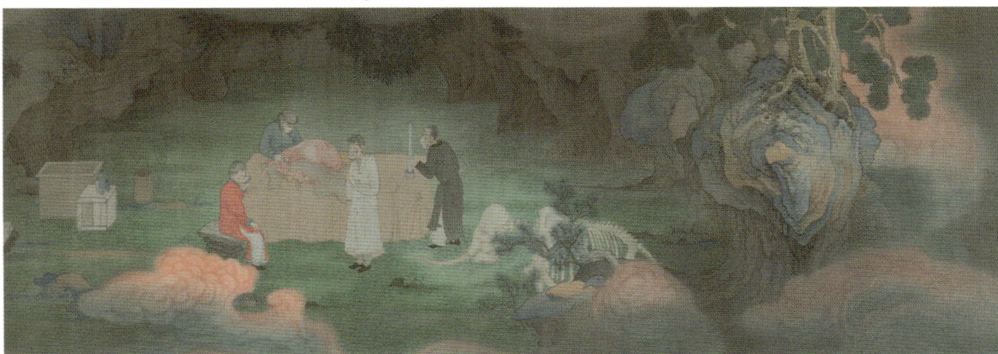

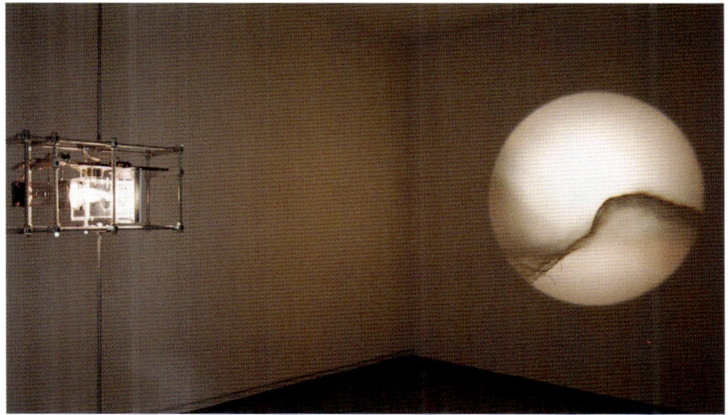

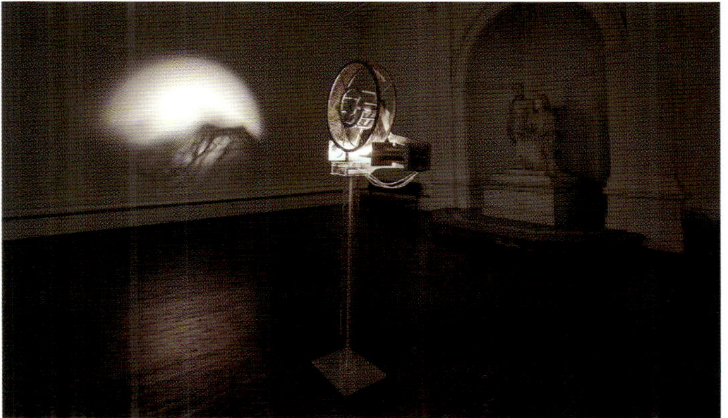

with an additional imaging magnifier at the front, constantly moving back and forth to project the shadow of a piece of wire netting within a certain range of changing focal length. When the projector alters its focus onto different parts of the object, the shadow of the image evolves. In contrast, *Wire II* has a fixed lens, which projects a rotating spool of wire netting. Through the different mechanisms, the images become alternately blurred and focused, disappearing and reappearing, while the cold, industrial wire netting is transformed into visions of humanistic scenery. As the artist has noted, 'If *Wire I* is seen as the misty and heavenly atmosphere in the Southern Song dynasty (1127–1279) landscape painting, then perhaps *Wire II* resembles the magnificent mountains and rivers in the Northern Song (960–1127) style.'[16] In later works in the series, sometimes a restructured projector, with a piece of wire netting placed inside, revolves to project the shadow, or rather

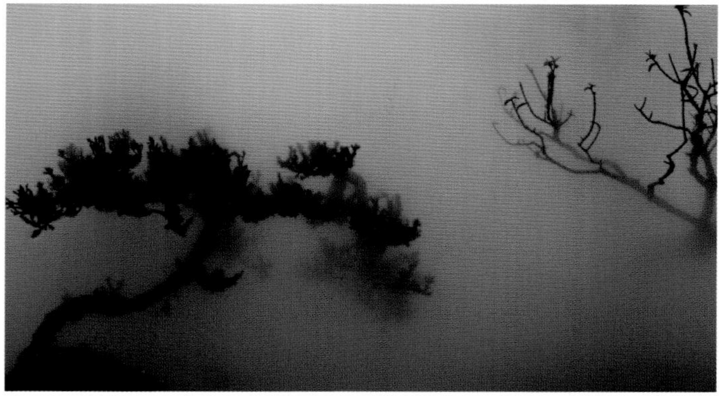

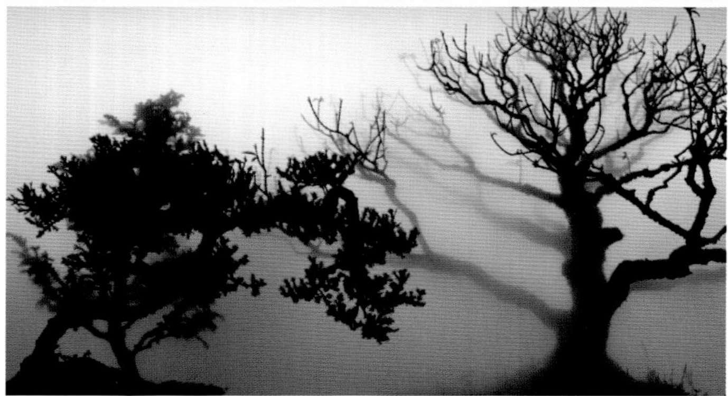

65 LEFT Wu Chi-Tsung, *Landscape in the Mist*, 2012 (video stills)
66 OPPOSITE Lam Tung Pang, *A Day of Two Suns*, 2016

to 'scan' the images that adorn the circular wall; sometimes, an additional zoom lens included in the device changes the projected image, focusing in and out, offering a fictional sense of distance that differs from the ordinary perspective. Regardless of the technical differences in projectors, the poetic qualities that can be found throughout the *Wire* series remain the same, while the artist delineates with shadow the outlines of a literati landscape that would be familiar to viewers who have a traditional vision of *shanshui*. When a hand scroll is understood as a time-based medium, the nature of the moving image can be considered particularly significant in providing not merely a series of individually framed stills, but a prolonged visual tour through a landscape. According to the artist Guo Xi (*c.* 1020–1100), fine *shanshui* painting can offer not only images to view and observe, but also places to travel to and inhabit.[17] When a projection loops, audiences are invited into an infinite space defined by the textures of black and white strokes.

The spirit of ink-wash is also conveyed through Wu Chi-Tsung's *Landscape in the Mist*. At first glance, the bamboos, orchids and pine trees are perceived to be simply photographic images, elegantly quiescent and poised, until one realizes that they are either furtively disappearing into or emerging from the surrounding mist. Following the natural flow of the milky vapour in the installation, a twig may subtly tremble or flip, an unexpected gesture of an animated plant, or indeed a decisive transition in a calligraphic rhythm. To echo the same spirit and the reclusive mood of literati, Hong Kong artist Lam Tung Pang's installation *A Day of Two Suns* projects a charming landscape, in black and white, awakening a reminiscence of ink-wash aesthetics as well as lines of pastoral poetry. Four back-to-back looped projections feature a bird and a shoreline on large paper screens, while additional props – miniature models of mountains and buildings placed in front of the screens – add another dimension to the play through scale and perspective. Everything is bathed in calmness, which can be easily broken even by a birdcall. As soon as the audience enters the space, their shadows are cast onto the landscape to join the journey and become part of the scenes of traditional life depicted.

On the one hand, these works reflect the aesthetic legacy of traditional art; on the other hand, they have also been inspired by ways of seeing, where visual curiosity is led by the literati spirit and through technical experimentation in the areas of photography and moving image. The oriental vision of nature, positioned ambiguously between abstract and realistic, is consequently shaped in the shadow of ink-wash, celebrating, as ever, the transparency, flux and poetic narrative.

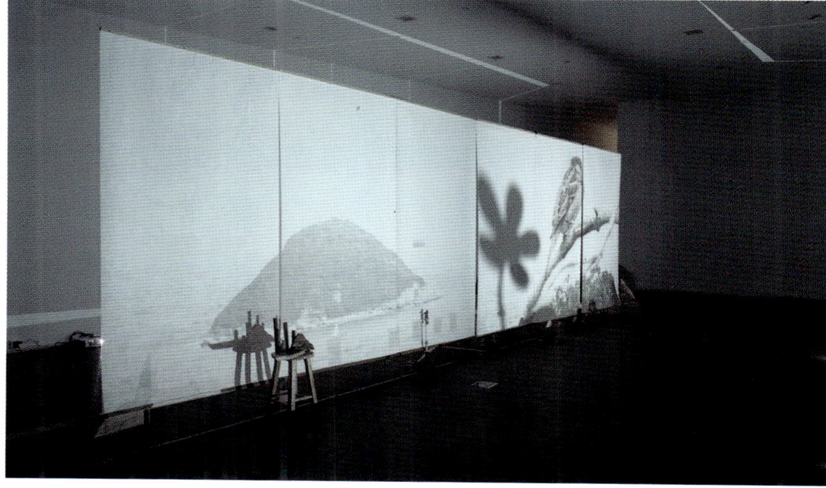

When views of the past have been modified, disrupted or disconnected through radical cultural and political transformations, the Chinese term *chuan tong* (tradition) can become an alternative version of *chuan qi* (legend). In China today, the line that distinguishes what is 'historical' and what is 'traditional' seems to have become very blurred. In fact, most of China's so-called 'traditional' aspects are no longer popularly recognized, understood or practised every day, and are therefore now 'historical'. When the notion of 'legend' can usefully cover the discrepancy and, particularly in art, expand the platform for imagination, contemporary practice acknowledges an irretrievable gap between past and present, and reflects critically upon the current situation with regard to cultural heritage.

How many dynasties and emperors are there in the history of China? Historians, archaeologists and anthropologists all differ on the answer to this question. Starting from Beijing, Kan Xuan travelled nearly 29,000 kilometres (18,000 miles) to seek out and photograph every single surviving imperial tomb, as if these were the evidence of China's dynastic history. Her journey was not necessarily historical, archaeological or anthropological; rather, it was guided visually by these mounds, protruding from the earth, their exposed underground tunnels leading to graves and ancient relics now only faintly discernible. Old folks in the villages call these imperial tombs 'Millet Mounds', from which the artist takes the title of her work.

Millet Mounds consists of 171 stop-motion videos, each of which presents the moment when Kan encounters an imperial tomb site. Each video is composed of many photographs of each searchable grave, taken on the artist's iPhone and looped into short narratives, ranging in length from thirty seconds to a few minutes. Any imperial tomb, of whichever emperor or dynasty, whether prominent or hidden, grand or humble, records the peak of each dynastic power and the personality, wisdom and fate of one individual, as well as the affairs of the imperial family and of the state. Viewed in their current condition, some of the tombs are merely crumbling towers of dirt in the middle of fields, and some have been encroached by nearby villages or tourist infrastructures. These raised shapes seem like hills, but they are not hills; they look natural, but they are man-made. Representing almost two thousand years of dynastic rule, they rest in the distance, in the centres of tourist sites or beyond wastelands, and invite travellers to share the same space and to revisit the same time frame as the legends of the past. Kan Xuan's work with animated

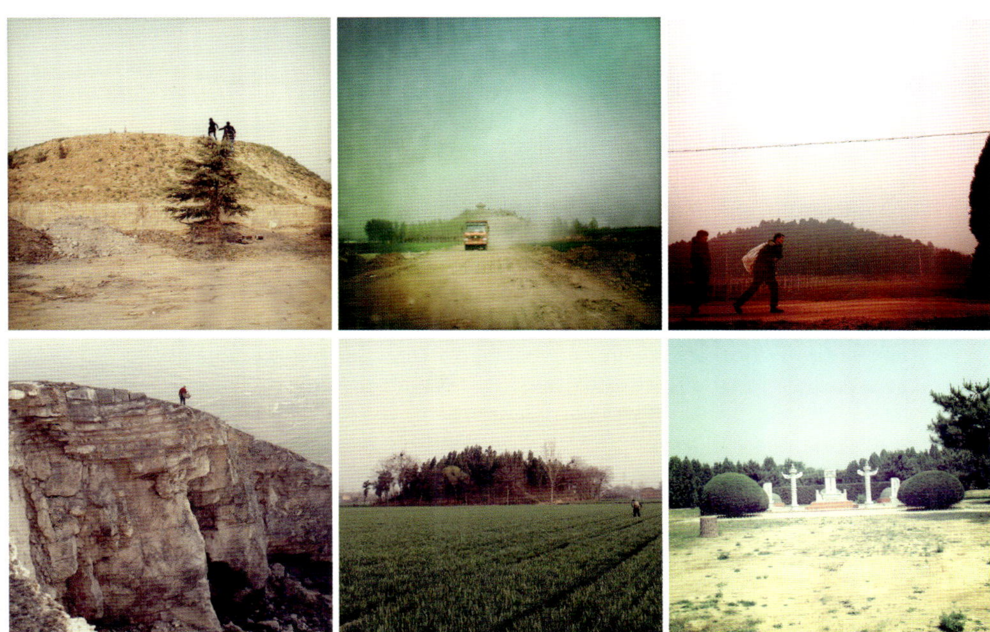

67 Kan Xuan, *Millet Mounds*, 2012 (video stills)

photographs seems to be the start of an exploration of the
unknown, but paradoxically it is the end of it. The remains
of imperial burial grounds over the years represent a distance,
untraversable, between life and death, the high and the
low, the experienced and the unworldly, and the known and
the unknown.

Zhao Zhao has always been fascinated by traditional Chinese
craftsmanship and objects, such as jade carvings (see p. 79),
which in his view are more aesthetically 'reliable' than those
that are produced in contemporary China. However, these
original objects are either lost or locked in museum cabinets
as specimens waiting for a small number of visitors. Although
in many cases the legacy of fine craftsmanship has been
discontinued, the artist believes that contemporary art can still
engage with early culture and reinterpret the old with the tools
and skills that are available today. Based on their authenticity,
cultural significance and an oblique sense of mystery, these
objects can then be reborn to materialize contemporary artistic
concepts and reflections, and to generate greater impact for
the historical objects. In his work *Waterfall*, Zhao Zhao gained
access to an original throne belonging to the Kangxi Emperor

68

of the Qing dynasty (1644–1912), located in one of the most important oriental collections, at the Museum of Asian Art in Berlin. With permission, the artist covered the throne with thick layers of wax, as if it had experienced an endless red snowfall over the centuries. The emperor's throne and its unique rosewood screen complete with exquisite craftwork of rich pearl inlays, gold decorations and lacquer work – symbolizing the highest position in China (if not, then, the world) – are completely veiled and can only be conjectured through the overall shape of the wax piles. The wax seems to protect, or perhaps to overprotect, the historical objects, suggesting an impassable estrangement between the lively everyday of the past and the limited perceptions of what we see through the remains today.

Calligraphy once played a prominent role in China, both as a prestigious art form and as an essential way to understand and inherit culture from the past. It can be a pertinent example today of how the 'traditional' turns into the 'historical'. The venerable tradition of the written word in China started to become widespread from the fifth century BCE all the way through the dynastic history, and was then reinvented by and for China's post-imperial leaders, as an indispensable instrument of the modern political culture and power structure. Today, however, when calligraphic writing with ink and brush is no longer everyday practice, is it still a 'tradition', with the same (or indeed any surviving) cultural significance in contemporary society?

Chinese characters (*hanzi*) were once seen as a divine form, and Chinese culture was perceived, inherited and sanctified through calligraphic writings, which were traditionally presented as the most prestigious form of the visual arts. Both the originals of masterpieces and their paper copies, or those engraved on wood or stone, were treasured, and creating accurate imitations of them, both in shape and in rhythm of practice, aesthetically and spiritually, was regarded as one of the ultimate ways to be considered cultured. Since the early twentieth century, the simplification of many traditional Chinese characters, as one of the government-enforced curriculum changes, has been a debatable issue in cultural and political circles. It aimed to reform and popularize the Chinese language, or rather to prepare an educational platform for cultivating the new ideology. This change shook the very foundation of Chinese culture and paved the way for its modernization.

Responding to such a transformation, Gu Wenda used traditional calligraphic techniques first to compose pseudo and miswritten words. These contain components that are wrongly

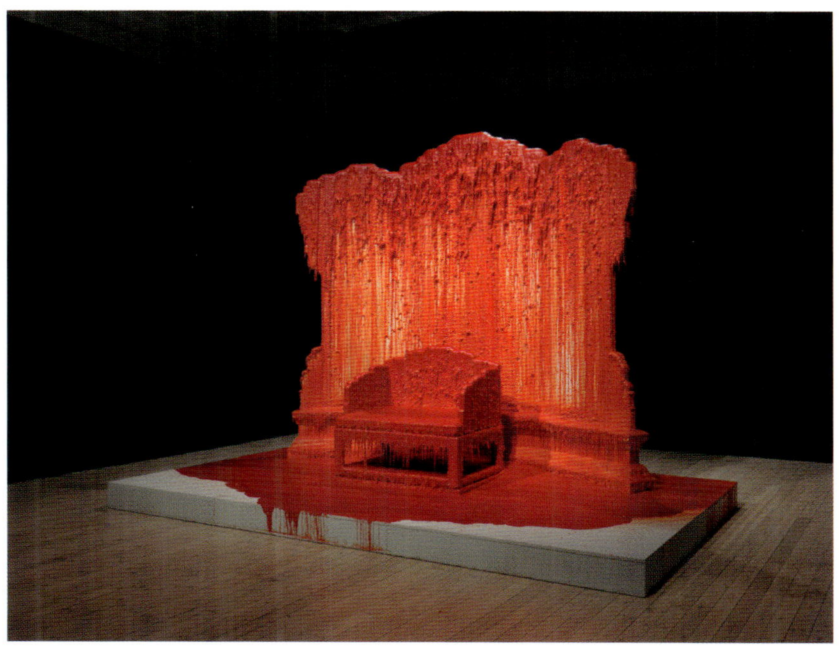

68 Zhao Zhao, *Waterfall*, 2013

written or misplaced, upside down or reversed, detached or
overlapping, leading to an uninterpretable world of literature,
and challenging the dignity of Chinese calligraphy. These
deconstructed and reconstructed characters turn the text into
images, inhibiting and yet, at the same time, stimulating the
viewer's attempts to interpret the meanings. They are both
calligraphic works and paintings of Chinese written words as
pure imagery. As curator and gallerist Chang Tsong-zung has
pointed out, the artist releases a powerful disruptive energy
to elevate his calligraphic writing to a level of monumentality,
while the incorrectness of Chinese written words becomes an
offence to the orthodoxy of Chinese culture and recalls the
power of Mao's revolution.[18]

Since 2003, Gu Wenda has taken this approach further,
extending the simplification of traditional form, to synthesize
Chinese characters in his own way of simplifying Chinese
phrases. In actual fact, for thousands of years, the Chinese
language has never adopted a single character for phrase use;
in other words, all the existing phrases are composed of two or
more characters, and conventionally a single character cannot
make up a phrase. This time, rather than creating incorrect

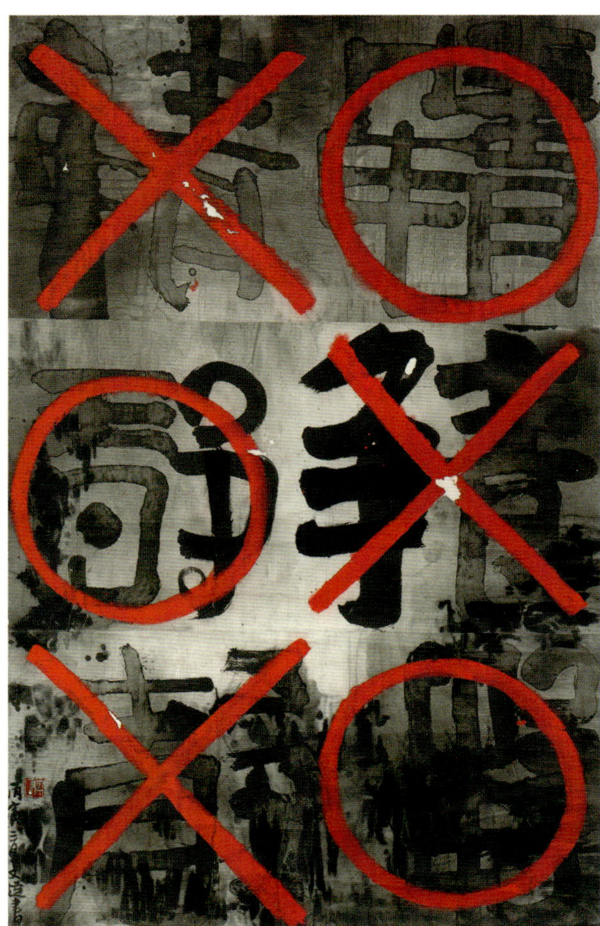

words, the artist conceived the development of a new series
that 'has never been tried in the history of Chinese language
and character development'; a series that 'must be practical,
applicable ... easy and understandable [and] which facilitates
memorizing and application, [and] demands no in-advance
training for learning...'.[19] For example, as a basic method
for phrase composition, the artist combines two characters
together, integrating two into one, and these originally
independent characters now serve as radical components of
the newly shaped character (phrase). In Gu's *Forest of Stone
Steles series 5 – Orientalism*, the four characters in each chosen
phrase – such as *qian kun chen fu* (the ebb and flow of the

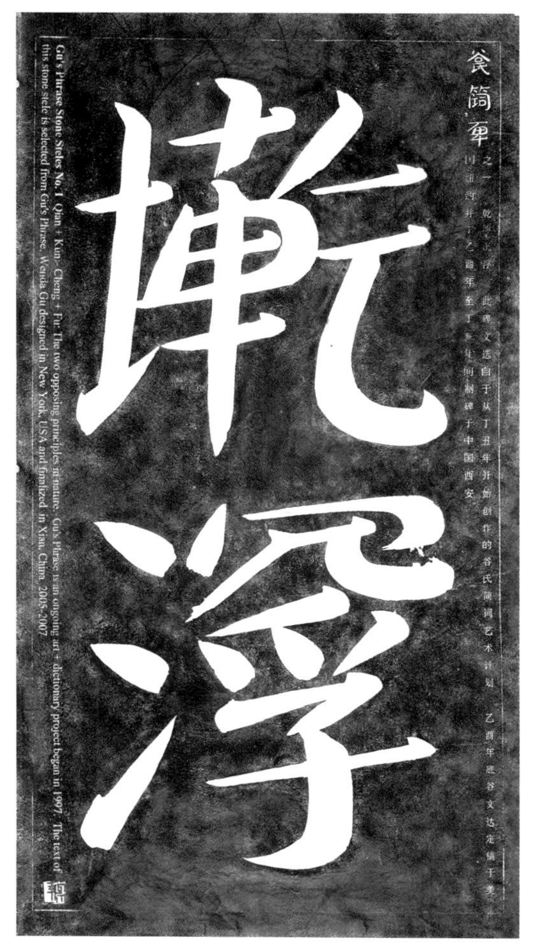

universe) – are reconstructed as two, represented through traditional processes from stone carving to ink rubbing.

Xu Bing argues that Mao's revolution of culture infringed upon the most deeply rooted aspect of society – language – 'because the Chinese language directly influences the methods of thinking and understanding of all Chinese people. To strike at the written word is to strike at the very essence of the culture.'[20] Trained as a woodcut printmaker, Xu spent many years of intensive work hand-carving more than two thousand movable wooden print-types to finally accomplish his *Book from the Sky* in 1988. As it happens, the characters invented individually for the *Book from the Sky* cannot be understood by Chinese readers,

71

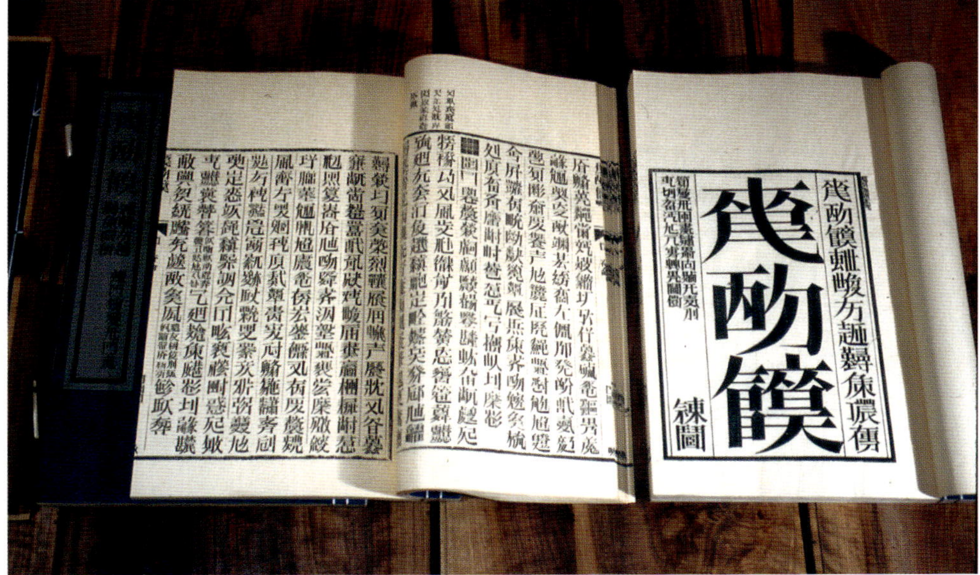

71 ABOVE Xu Bing, *Book from the Sky*, 1987–91 (detail)
72 OPPOSITE Xu Bing, *Book from the Sky*, 1987–91 (installation view)

or by Westerners. The artist's exquisite workmanship becomes vital in the deliberate composition of a 'lie'. It seems that the harder Xu worked on his fake writings, the more fully the semantic significance of Chinese characters could be removed, and the better the intended 'meaninglessness' could be achieved. The complete installation consists of hand scrolls, books in the traditional thread-bound format and large panels that cover the entire wall, echoing the big-character posters of the Cultural Revolution for people's daily reading. Art critic Alice Yang has observed the central paradox in Xu's *Book from the Sky*:

While it speaks in a national syntax, it disarticulates such syntax and renders it completely garbled. While it constructs a symbolic national text, it evacuates all meaning from such a crisis, which might be afforded by simple allegiance to culture and tradition. In 'A book from the sky', Language – a symbolic system fundamental to the integrity and perpetuation of a national culture – is endlessly reproduced but vitiated of any functional value and thus made curiously unproductive.[21]

The original version of the *Lantingji Xu* (*Orchid Pavilion Preface*) was written in the fourth century by Wang Xizhi at the Lanting Pavilion in Shaoxing, Zhejiang Province. During a *yaji* (literally, an elegant gathering) at the pavilion, which was attended by 42 literati, 37 poems were composed and a preface to the collection was improvised by Wang, it is said, in a state of insobriety. The original script of the *Lantingji Xu* was lost in the seventh century, when the Emperor Taizong of Tang (r. 626–49) ordered it to be entombed with him in the Zhao Mausoleum in Xi'an. Numerous copies in ink on paper were made, and stone inscriptions have survived to the present day. The so-called Shenlong version by Feng Chengsu was widely regarded as bearing the closest resemblance to the original, which has been celebrated as the climax of the 'running style' in the history of Chinese calligraphy. This masterpiece demonstrates Wang's extraordinary calligraphic skill, with elegant and fluent strokes in a coherent spirit throughout, while Feng's authoritative copy has been set as an unsurpassable model for all calligraphers to learn, admire and revere. For three years, from 1992 to 1995, in his work *Copying Orchid Pavilion Preface One Thousand Times*, the artist Qiu Zhijie repeatedly copied the *Preface* onto a single

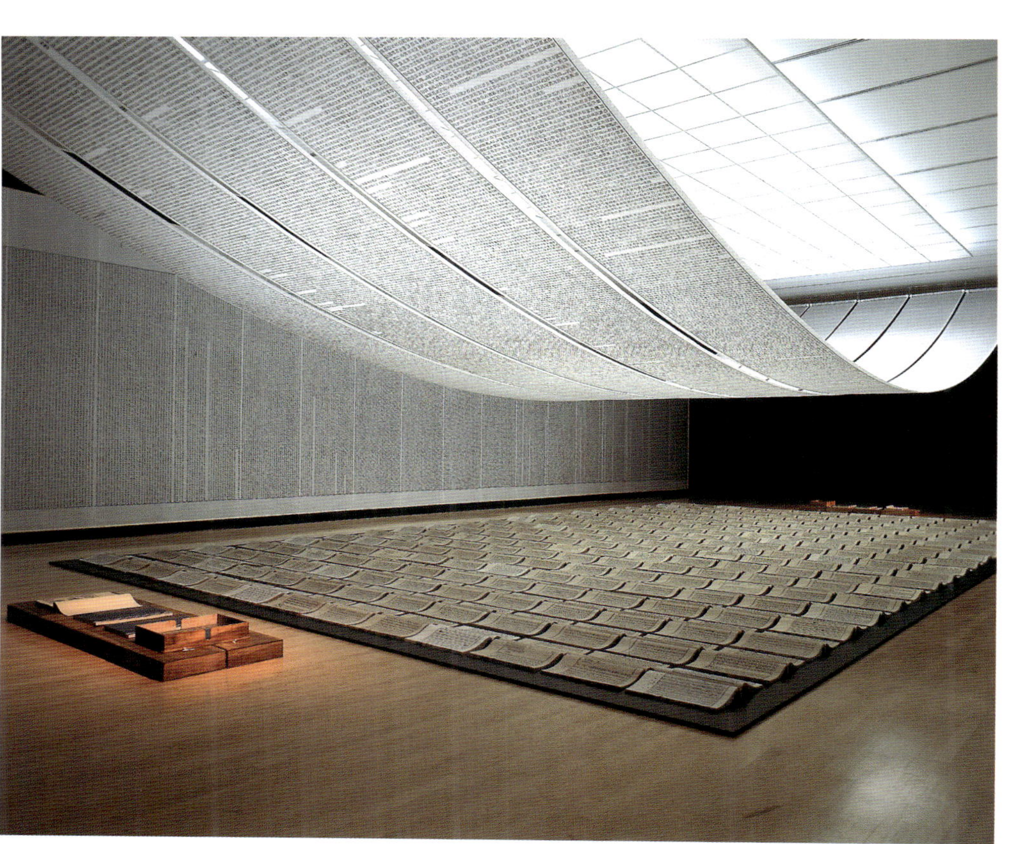

sheet of paper, which by the end of the process had become a mass of black ink. As art historian Norman Bryson has noted:

If in Qiu Zhijie's work orthography is a metaphor for social orthodoxy or cultural reproduction, the basis of the text's power is not to be found in its contents – in what its author said – but in the sheer force of cultural repetition, especially through the internalization of social authority that is performed within the calligrapher's body as he attempts to incorporate the text inside his own musculature and gestural reflexes.[22]

The performance challenges not only the aesthetic and literary value of the *Preface* by turning the script into something completely illegible, but also, more critically, the way in which culture has been inherited and extended in China. The artist's own statement reads:

The first item to eliminate was the literary nature of calligraphy in order to return calligraphy to its original activity of modelling or, specifically, composing ink traces, to arrive at pure visual abstraction. The second step was to return writing to the original act of writing itself without producing the formal traces of the brush. In abandoning these formal traces, one listens attentively to how the activity of writing is guided by the subject: writing is the excuse for the writer's tiny dances of the brush; the primary value of the subject is ultimately achieved in the disappearance of its formal traces. Repetitive writing on an ink background strictly observes the classical standards of Chinese calligraphy and strengthens its innate meaning as a form of 'written meditation'. The daily repetition of this activity turns part of the calligrapher's life into play. The insipid re-creation of playing further stimulates the transformation of the individual state of the writer. Thus, the act of writing the Orchid Pavilion Preface (Lanting xu) a thousand times, in terms of its medium, is a return to the original mode of Chinese calligraphy and not an innovation in any sense.[23]

The work created a series of interesting paradoxes. First, the addition of meticulous and deliberate strokes over the years onto the same sheet of paper gradually reduced the significance of the text until it became utterly meaningless. Secondly, this most faithful mode of learning – even a daily ritual of worship – actually subverted the authority of a truly classic piece. And thirdly, the repeated act of pursuing authenticity, as a traditional method of studying calligraphy, transformed all the 'copies' of the *Preface* into a new 'original'.

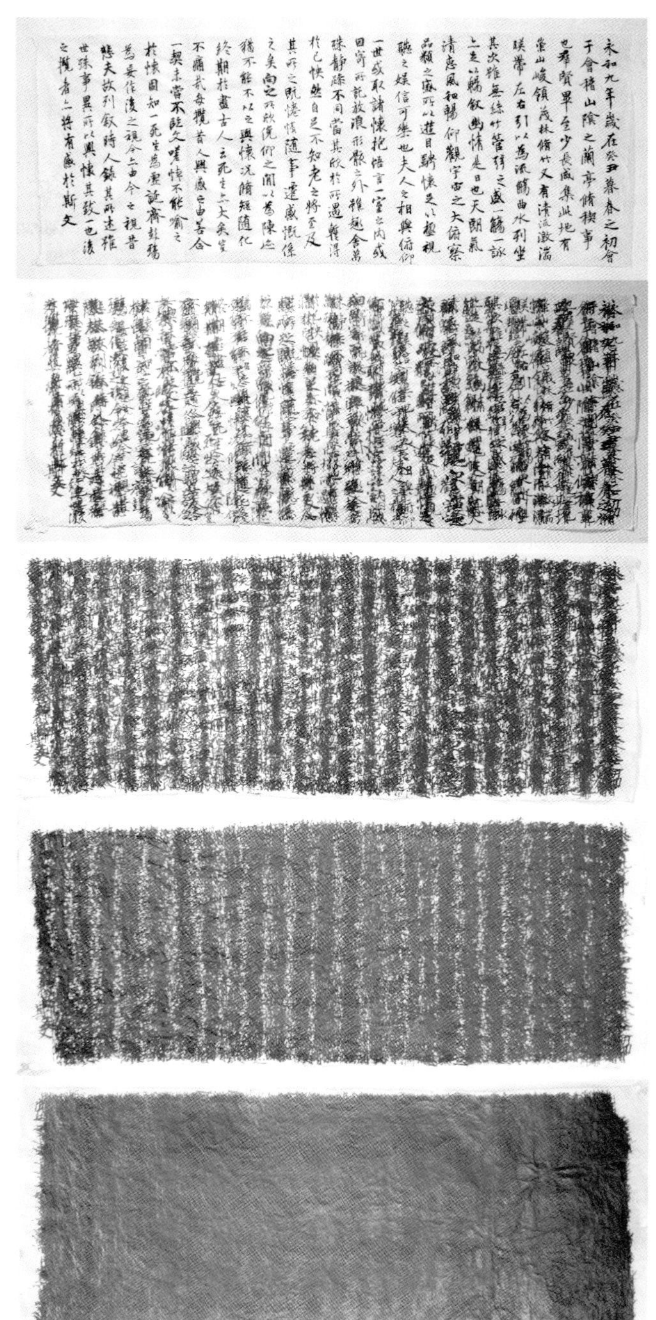

73 Qiu Zhijie, *Copying Orchid Pavilion Preface One Thousand Times*, 1992–95

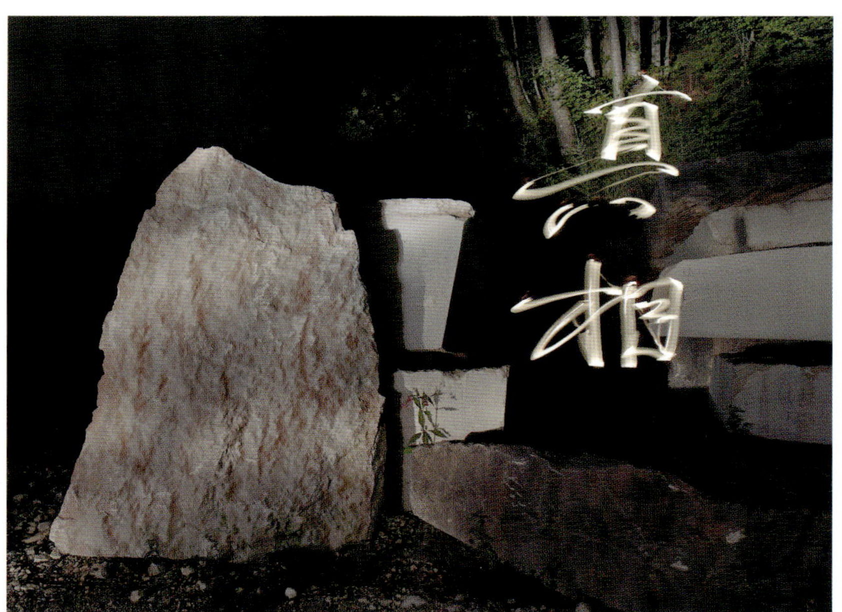

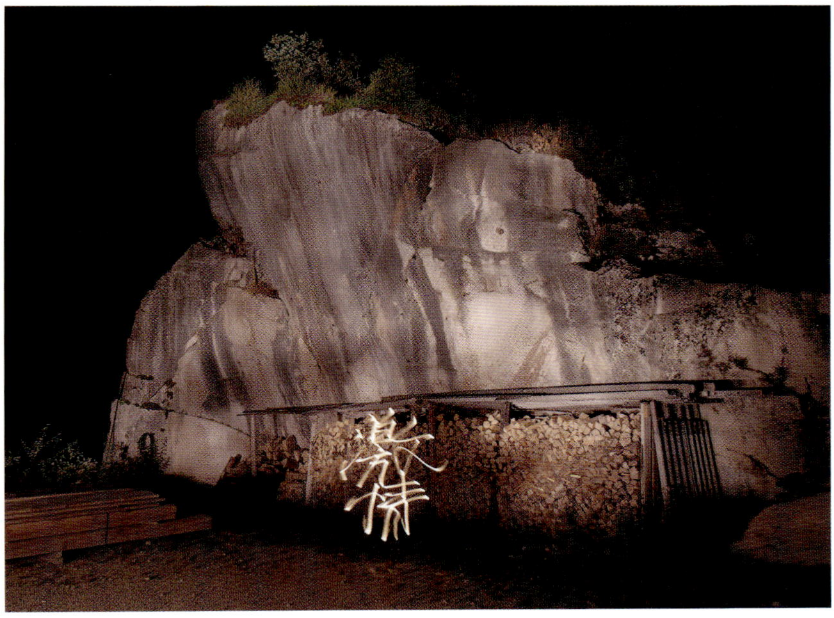

74 TOP Qiu Zhijie, *Light Calligraphy: Truth*, 2006
75 ABOVE Qiu Zhijie, *Light Calligraphy: Passion*, 2006

Calligraphy is also metamorphosed in Qiu Zhijie's *Light Calligraphy* series, in which the artist used a light source – a simple torch, treated like a pen, or indeed a brush – to write Chinese characters in the air against a background of dark night. The calligraphy was written backwards, creating a mirror image, so that it reads correctly to the camera and viewer. The long exposure enables the camera to arrest the otherwise invisible traces of the movement of the torch-brush; at the same time, the artist's performing body escapes the picture frame, as if the words write themselves, reflecting on the present moment, which the image always occupies. Calligraphy in China was often executed at historically or politically charged places. Unlike in the European tradition, in Chinese visual culture a public commemorative monument would have been dominated by calligraphic writing, carved on wooden plates or engraved in stone. Arguably, in his work, Qiu Zhijie has been commenting on places with particular significance, whereby the textual form expressing the artist's perceptions and reflections is fused with the backdrop, like inscriptions in painting scrolls. Of his methodology, the artist states: 'Light and time form the essence of photography, whilst the essence of man is to perceive, to transform, and to write [bodily].'[24] Here, calligraphy makes photography, and vice versa.

With his fellow artists Chen Zaiyan and Sun Qinglin, Zheng Guogu set up the Yangjiang Group in 2002 as an art collective, primarily focusing on experimental practices of calligraphic writing through playful collaboration and participation, with attempts to subvert the sociocultural norms and values of calligraphy. No conventional format of calligraphic practice has been followed; instead, the work is produced through the events of cooking, eating and drinking, and through audience participation, which has been vital to the production process.

In the ongoing series *After Dinner Calligraphy*, usually at a performative installation, the artists use left-over party food to improvise calligraphic assemblages on paper. They tried different tools with various actions to deliver the writings in order to break away from what they had inherited technically and culturally. But still, 'it is almost impossible to calligraph'. As Zheng Guogu has stated: 'As soon as you hold and lift your brush, you see a powerful tradition haunting you, right behind you.'[25] The artists deliberately started to practise calligraphy

while getting drunk on alcohol. For them, this became the only way to 'forget' about well-established cultural and aesthetic values; perhaps it also enabled them to join the inebriated state of the master calligrapher Wang Xizhi.

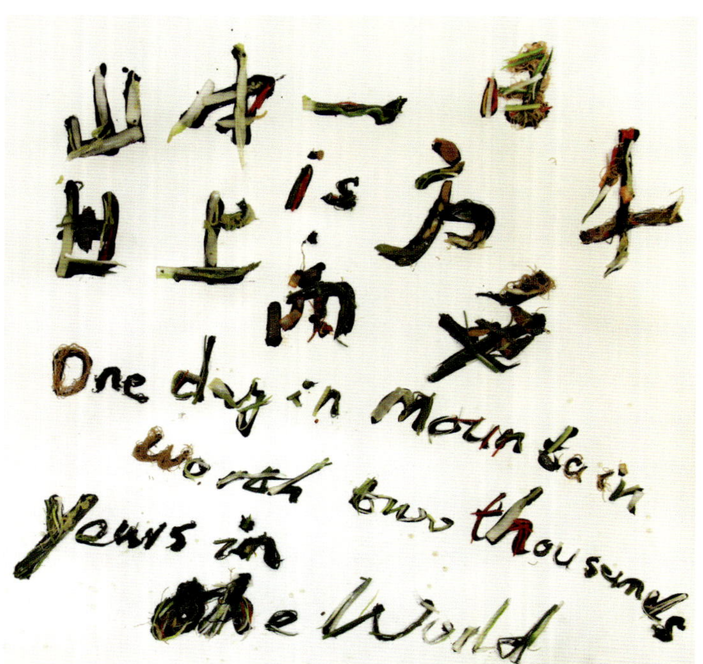

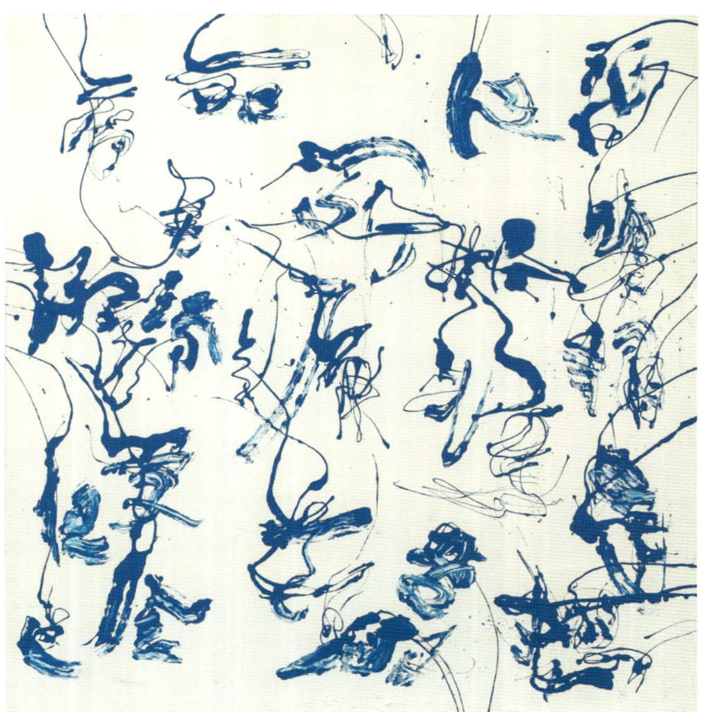

76 ABOVE Yangjiang Group, *After Dinner Calligraphy: One Day in Mountain Worth Two Thousand Years in the World*, 2012
77 LEFT Yangjiang Group, *Drunk Calligraphy: I Drink in Order to Drown the Agony, but the Agony Has Learnt How to Swim*, 2012

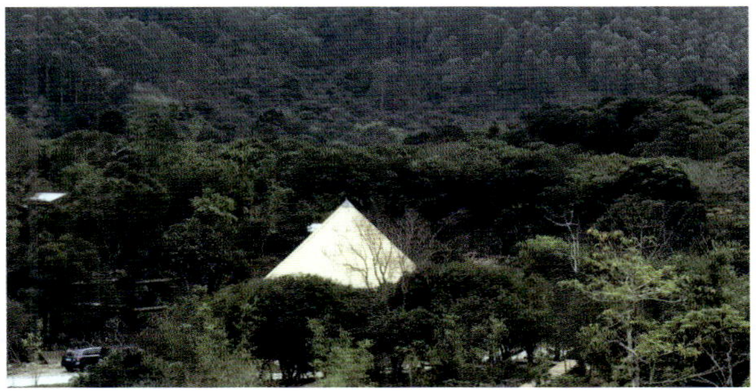

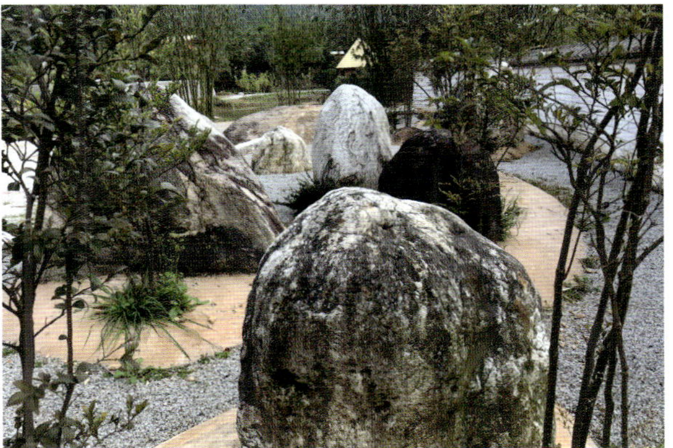

78 ABOVE Zheng Guogu, *Liao Garden*, 2000–present
79 RIGHT Zheng Guogu, *Liao Garden*, 2000–present

Over and above the practice of calligraphy, tradition in general can be extended as a 'legend' in everyday life today. Based in his native Yangjiang, on the southern coast of China, Zheng Guogu seems to have retreated from the contemporary world, like a literati, for a calm observation of the tensions between tradition and modernity in a rapidly globalizing China, amid the impact of Western culture and digital technologies on contemporary Chinese life. In his pursuit of such transcendence in the midst of ordinary society, he started his ongoing project, the *Liao Garden* (in Chinese, 'Liao Yuan'). Basing his work upon the video game *Age of Empires*, Zheng has gradually developed and constructed a 30,000-square-metre (325,000 sq. ft) complex of buildings and gardens on the outskirts of Yangjiang, as a constantly and anarchically evolving utopian domain. Life in Yangjiang is quiet, away from busy cities. While the local labourers and their physical experiences provide an important reference point for the development, the plan of the garden is improvised on a daily basis. It has been growing as a living project, with its own independent ecology, for some twenty years.

The pronunciation of the word *liaoyuan* has a Buddhist allusion – to fulfil a destiny. For Zheng, this can be corroborated through the process of building his garden. 'The whole thing is an artwork,' he says, 'although some visitors cannot find it; it is a visualization of my own experience … in connection with nature; it is a laboratory.'[26] This experimentation is rooted in Chinese tradition – not only the physical practices in relation to calligraphy, tea gathering, medicine making and other everyday experiences in China, but also in evoking the Buddhist belief in the impermanence of the physical realm and other forms of energy, actual or imagined. As the art critic Lu Mingjun suggests:

[For the artist] only in pyramid-shaped buildings such as Liao Garden … can we feel another form of energy. It eliminates and consumes reality's chaos, conflicting magnetic fields … bringing people and space together and balancing them out. Therefore, this seems to go back to an older logic of viewing, but apparently one that is more universal. The purpose for Zheng is not only to activate the magnetic field and open more spatial and temporal dimensions but also to reveal to more people that every body, mind and thing in the universe contains a structure of energy and spiritual mechanism.[27]

The project refuses the modern exhibition system: it cannot be presented in a white-cube space, and the site-specificity does not allow any part of the work to be transported. One can only travel a long way from one's home, and be utterly disconnected from this, in order to encounter the artwork, or indeed a different form of everyday. The work is not just to be viewed; it is to be experienced, with the bodily perceptions of sights, sounds and smells, and with the dialogues between human, natural and unknown energies.

Huang Yong Ping, who was based in Paris, used to claim that every artist has a motherland, but art does not. This seemed to be his tactic to avoid some of his work being considered simply as a collection of Chinese symbols – a challenge faced by other Chinese artists too.[28] For example, the imagery of a snake-like dragon, the dragon being a central figure in Chinese culture, was appropriated in his *Ressort* (the French for 'spring', or 'resilience' and 'energy') to dominate the museum space, spiralling from ceiling to ground; and also in his *Serpent d'océan*, where a 130-metre-long (425 ft) curving skeleton rises from the banks of the Loire estuary near Nantes, and appears and disappears, depending on the level of the tide. Through this Chinese mythological representation in the West, shown

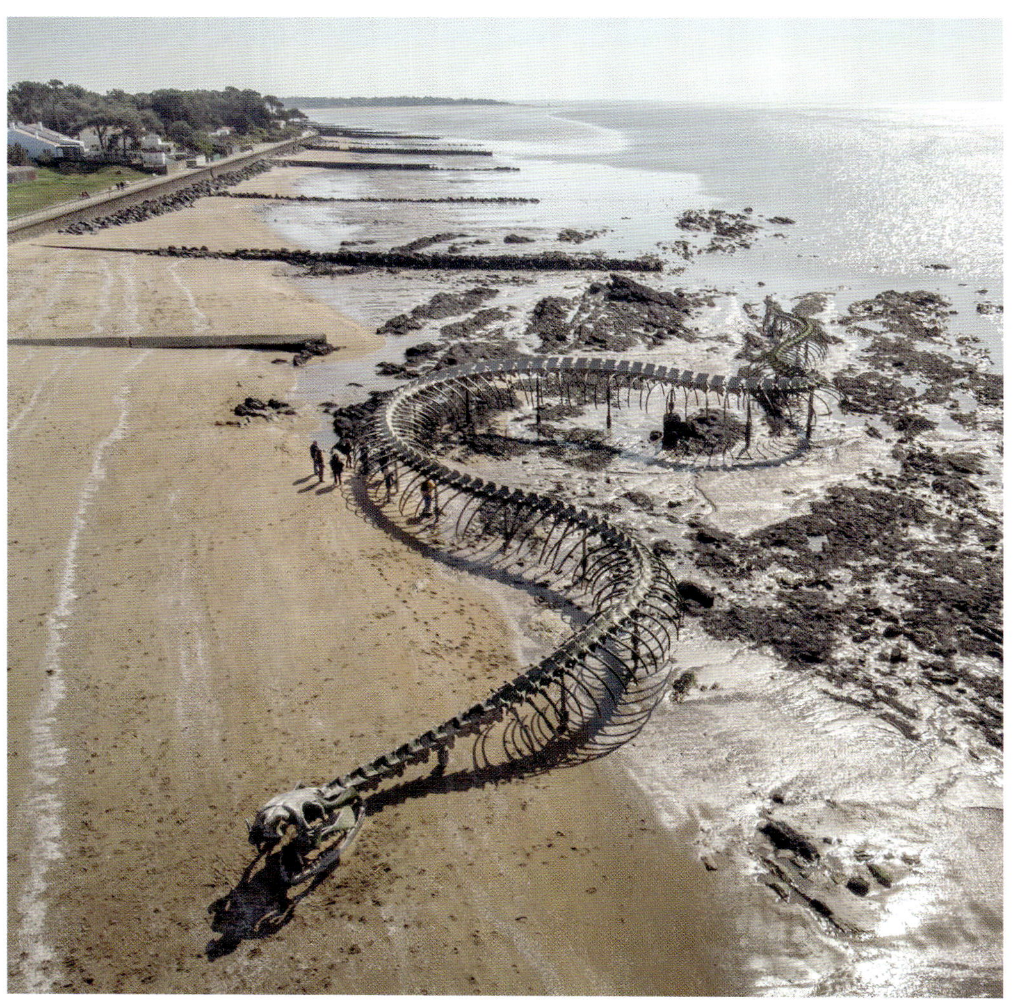

80 Huang Yong Ping, *Serpent d'océan*, 2012

either descending from the sky or rising from the ocean, the artist discusses the notions of identity and cultural hybridity, and draws on the various artistic and philosophical traditions to reflect on new global realities. His work plays on different interpretations of tradition, histories of creation and tenets of wisdom from Chinese mythology, and on temptation and deception from biblical narratives. It comes from places of nothingness, heavens or waters, that are abstract, cosmic and sublime. And, more importantly, it is visualized only as a set of

skeletons, as if factual, but avoids a full fleshing out. No one
has ever seen a dragon, and therefore the skeleton can become
a form of evidence. In this case, it is not evidence of what has
truly existed, like fossils for Darwin's theory of evolution, but
instead it is evidence of our ability to imagine.

Coda

The 'Everyday Legend: Reinventing Traditions in Chinese
Contemporary Art' collaborative research project (2016–18)
involved multiple visits to towns and villages that were well
known for traditional craftsmanship.[29] One of the objectives
of this cross-disciplinary project was to examine the condition
of traditional arts and crafts in China (some still surviving,
some fragmented, some discontinued) and the implications
for the present and future, both in China and across the world.
Naturally, only a limited selection of the vast possible array
of arts and crafts could be surveyed, but these included the
remaining ceramic and porcelain factories, workshops and
museums of Jingdezhen in Jiangxi Province; the *kesi* tapestry/
embroidery work carried out in Suzhou in Jiangsu Province,
specifically for the imperial family of the Qing dynasty; and
the figural/landscape wall paintings, glazed roof tiles, clay
sculptures, woodblock prints, flour figuring, inkstone carvings
and paper-cutting of Shanxi Province.

One paper-cutting shop, in Pingyao in Shanxi, was owned
by the craftswoman Wen Tao. In 2001, like many others in
the town, Wen had been laid off as a consequence of China's
economic transformation. Having been taught paper-cutting
by her grandmother from the age of six, she decided to
open her own shop. As she recalled: 'Through paper-cutting
Grandma told us stories with allegorical meanings: images
of corn for the harvest in the autumn, for example, or fish for
wealth during the year, gourds for peace, and pomegranates
for prolificacy...'[30] Her shop became a popular tourist site, and
Wen's offerings included 'life cutting', with her subject seated
in front of her, as in a traditional portrait sitting. Her paper-
cutting differs now from the styles taught by her grandmother.
In the past, the primary site of display was the window, and
indeed these paper cut-outs were also known as 'window
flowers' (*chuanghua*), traditionally made to celebrate special
events like Chinese New Year or weddings. Their uses became
multiple, both educational and religious: as prayers to gods; as
stories when the cut-outs placed in windows cast shadows on
sunny days; as beliefs to endow hopes in the everyday. Today
these functionalities have been lost. Instead, the paper-cutting
needs to be visibly skilful to legitimize the piece as a work of

art. As Wen said, 'Based on what I learned from Grandma, I can now multiply patterns and make the image more complicated, with much finer cuts.' It needs to be exotic enough for a tourist to want to take it home as a souvenir. It also needs to be overtly practical and representational, more like a street drawing, thus shedding its symbolic and literary nature.

In contrast, inkstones are more expensive to buy and too heavy for a tourist's suitcase. A site visit to the craftsman Hui Dongcun's workshop in Dingxiang, in Shanxi Province, led to a feeling of pessimism for the future of the industry. Traditionally, the inkstone was an essential tool for calligraphic writings. Its decline might be explained by four events. First, as with the invention of photography affecting painting from the early nineteenth century, the advent of ready-made ink meant that calligraphers were now freed from having to spend time grinding ink on an inkstone. Secondly, the arrival of manufactured pens and pencils from the West in the early twentieth century further challenged the practice of brush-writing with ink. Thirdly, in recent decades, alphabetical keyboards have played an increasingly dominant role in Chinese character writing, and have almost overthrown calligraphic forms altogether. This does not represent a mere change of writing instrument, following the development from brush to pen; it also affects the manner of inputting, the mode of understanding, the form of being cultivated and, ultimately, the way of thinking. The inkstone, then, could only survive as a non-functional, aesthetic object with cultural connotations – the functional tool becoming a decorative object, or a living specimen – and primary sales had to rely largely on the inkstone being presented as a creditable and valuable gift between friends and officials within social relationships.[31] However, fourthly, in 2014, in order to prevent government corruption, the giving of so-called 'cultural gifts', including inkstones, was prohibited.

The craftspeople who participated in the research project showed enthusiasm and often pride, but also anxiety and regret. It is impossible to know for how much longer the fading images of Qing dynasty generals will last on the painted walls of Shanxi, or who will succeed the lone warden of Nanchan Temple, one of only two surviving temples from the Tang dynasty. China is a special case of the cultural transition from past to future, and yet all things must pass. Contemporary art itself will not be able to save traditional arts and crafts, but it can provide a critical view to raise awareness of how culture evolves and, more importantly, a creative energy to let them be reborn.

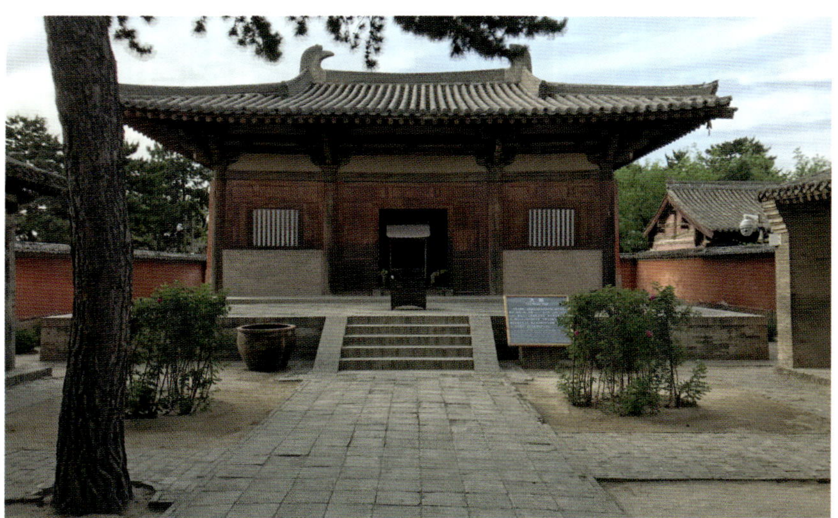

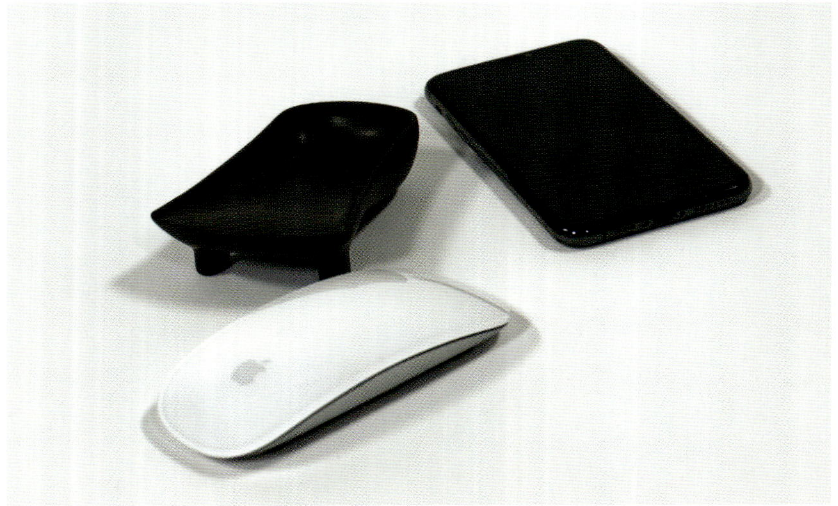

81 TOP Nanchan Temple, 2017
82 ABOVE A reproduction of a Song dynasty hand-held inkstone,
a computer mouse and an iPhone

At his workshop in Dingxiang, Hui Dongcun kindly presented a 'cultural gift' of a mobile inkstone (*chaoshou yan*; literally, hand-hold inkstone). In the early Song dynasty, this type of inkstone was designed to enable the mobility of the calligrapher and to free the writing or other brushwork practice from the literati desk. It is more or less the same size as the mouse of a desktop computer, or a smartphone – both now indispensable items in everyday life. The inkstone was no doubt indispensable, too, to the Song literati, with more or less the same function: communication in elegant style.

Chapter 3
The Art of Urbanization

In the last few decades, China has seen the most extraordinary economic growth, fuelled by rapid urban development, the scale and speed of which are unprecedented in human history for both the increase in construction projects and the increase of the urban population.[1] Buildings, architectural complexes, streets, and even whole cities can be transitory, leaving little trace of what has gone before. Existing scholarship on the topic concerns the tangible and quantifiable aspects of this transformation, such as policy changes, the physical expansion of the cities, the migration of massive populations, the construction boom and the widening social inequality. At the same time, more attention should be given to the intangible processes of the transformation, such as how individual urban residents experience and perceive their changing cities through cultural means, for a more holistic and multifaceted understanding of urban aspiration and its consequences in China and beyond. Many scholars have rightly referred to the recent transformation of China as an 'urban revolution'.[2] From a historical perspective, the spirit behind the urban de/construction in contemporary China can be traced back to the early years of the People's Republic, when urban spaces, residential areas and everyday experiences were rearranged for both practical and ideological purposes.[3] It was reported, for example, that 'China is pushing ahead with a sweeping plan to move 250 million rural residents into newly constructed towns and cities over the next dozen years'.[4] The changes have continued all the way through the 'revolutions' in the last century, and are evident in the acceleration of economic and urban development since the Open Door policy, shaping a moving reality that is almost surreal, beyond normal and perceptible daily existence.

Throughout Chinese history, at every change of dynasty, the emperor would rebuild China into a very different empire. This reconstruction rarely took the form of small repairs and amendments, but rather great upheavals, as the emperor established his own political and cultural regime amid the ruins of the former. One after another, brand new eras began. 'No construction without destruction' (*bupo buli*) – Chairman Mao's conclusive teaching – was extended as an axiom for his Cultural Revolution, but it was also a prophecy for the dramatic urban developments of today. Construction in China does not merely constitute an effort towards improvement; it is a revolutionary action fundamentally to replace the old with an entirely new visual experience.

The Qing dynasty bequeathed us the great Forbidden City, a marvel of a palace complex. However, after 1949, intellectuals and architects such as Liang Sicheng were naturally at a loss as to how to impede the march of New China. By the 1980s, Beijing had already turned from a city of ancient culture and history into the second-biggest centre of heavy industry in the country, after Shenyang. This process of transformative reconstruction remained unstoppable during the era of economic construction and the urbanization process that characterized the period of reform and opening up. Traditional architecture can now be made to exist in two different ways: the first is through fake copies of the original, and the second is through protection of originals as scenic highlights in the visual landscape. The former has become an extraordinary phenomenon, whereby pseudo-Ming and pseudo-Qing styles of architecture are fabricated, adorned with sundry archways, and themed communities replicate whole towns and cities as well as monumental constructions in Europe and the Americas. 'Given China's tradition of embracing a more permissive attitude towards duplication and architectural imitation,' author Bianca Bosker argues, 'there is an element to these simulacrascapes that is deeply conservative and consistent with distinctive, traditional Chinese cultural practices.'[5] The second approach involves restoring the original by detaching it from its urban context and cultural ecology. Be it the Beijing *hutong* (small alley) or the Shanghai *shikumen* (literally, stone gate, a typical style of residential architecture in Shanghai since the 1860s), some of these traditional constructions are saved, renovated and isolated as limited editions, while the surrounding residential areas continue to be transformed into tourist and commercial sites, such as at Xintiandi in Shanghai.[6] What we are witnessing here is not a continuously emerging and steadily advancing cultural context, but rather a fragmentation of reality.

If the mission of an artist is to think, imagine and critique, is it even possible to keep up with a society in such flux? As daily changes are experienced as part of urban existence, what does China really *look* like, and what are the relationships between visual reality and the instability of what has been seen and experienced; between artistic response, imagination and memory? In reaction to the incessant changes, artists have shaped a moving reality, an illusive one, beyond the normal and tangible environment of everyday life. This chapter will discuss artworks that respond to the urban transformation in China through three different but interconnected forms.

Fragmentality

First, 'fragmentality' – the state of being fragmented – has become one of the most representative features of developing urban China. In Qiu Anxiong's 2009 animation work *Temptation of the Land*, the ruins of the Old Summer Palace of Yuanmingyuan, the Great Wall of China and a panoramic landscape open an ambitious visual narrative of the previous 150 years of Chinese history, filled with political and cultural struggles. From portraits of the last emperor Puyi, Sun Yat-sen and Mao, from wars and the Great Leap Forward movement to revolutionary parades, and from devastated rivers and mountains, and Shanghai's port, to the Great Hall of the People and the Monument to the People's Heroes, the fragmented scenes are woven together through the artist's black and white brush strokes. The country is built, destroyed, and then re-built. Fireworks blossom over the Tiananmen Tower, celebrated in turn by the flags, sickles and hammers of communist ideology and the righteous fists of the people. Finally, huge industrial chimneys rise to symbolize another revolution, while urban landscapes are replaced completely, yet again, by super-modernized skylines. At the end of every story, there must be a triumph. However, in Qiu's work, the triumph is not attributed to the prosperity of the urban development, but to an exceptional household who refused to have their home relocated. The house remains, after many months' resistance, its foundations now exposed as it appears to stand alone, heroically, as a last tenacious fort besieged by growing high-rises all around. It is an exemplary fragment of the evolving cityscape, defending the surviving patch of home, or a temporary monument to the excitements and frustrations of urban change.

Following the approval in 2001 of Beijing's application to host the 2008 Summer Olympics, urban development began to accelerate in China's capital, starting from the areas within

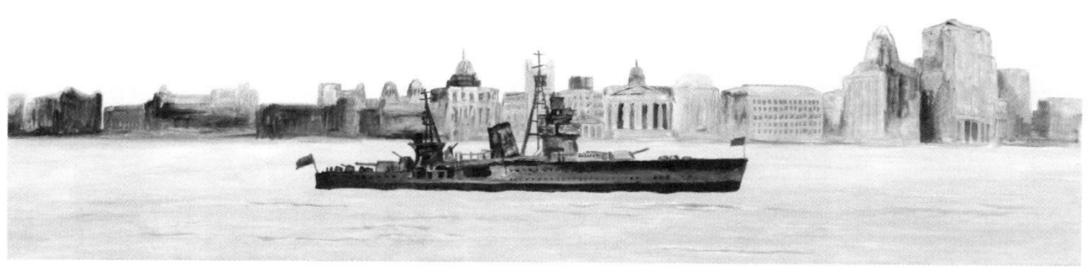

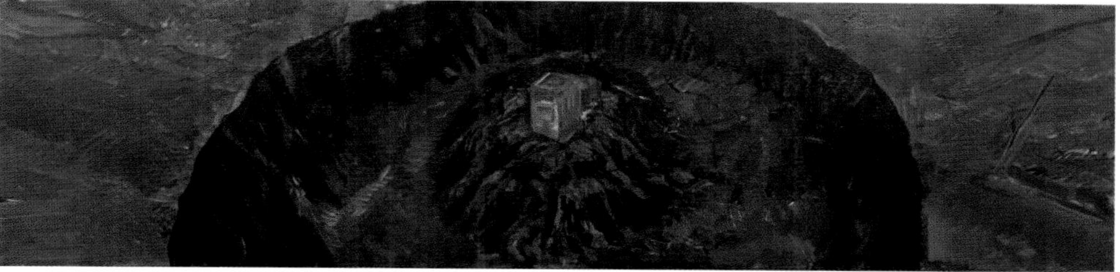

83 TOP Qiu Anxiong, *Temptation of the Land*, 2009 (animation still)
84 ABOVE Qiu Anxiong, *Temptation of the Land*, 2009 (animation still)

85

the third and fourth 'rings'. The citizens of Beijing, the home city of artist Wang Gongxin, became alienated due to the rapid changes. Wang's 2002 video installation, *Red Doors*, is presented in a four-walled compound surrounding a central space, reminiscent of the layout of *siheyuan*, a traditional style of residence in northern China, usually belonging to wealthy families, which is fast disappearing, in line with the swift pace of urbanization. The central space is encompassed by four screens, presenting four doors that look like regular *siheyuan* entrances. When viewers walk into the space, they can randomly open one door after another, or they can open multiple doors simultaneously, to reveal public scenes that are apparently taking place inside 'homes'. The doors act as theatrical curtains to frame and stage everyday happenings in Beijing, including the rush-hour traffic and people's social lives – playing mahjong, singing Beijing opera, performing tai chi and morning exercises in the park – and, in addition, rather disturbingly, the remaking of the city. In fact, more than a theatrical curtain, they are the vital instrument of a magician. Open and close these doors, and, in the blink of an eye, they will offer an entirely different view. The worlds behind the doors are fragments of urban reality, in which bulldozers and cranes dominate the landscape and constantly ruin the peaceful rhythm of regular lives. On the one hand, the slow opening of the doors encourages a desire to understand the

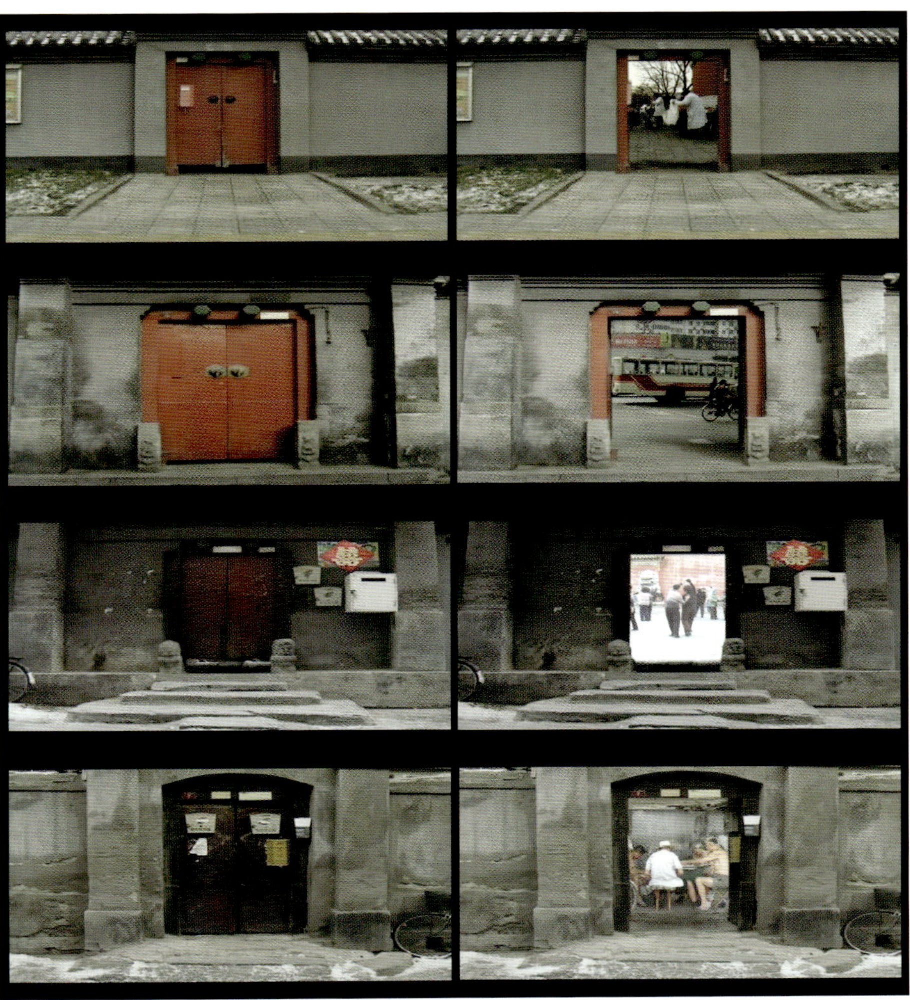

85 Wang Gongxin, *Red Doors*, 2002 (video stills)

past and the present of the city; on the other hand, their sudden and loud closing shatters the narrative and induces a subtle sense of nostalgia. In Wang Gongxin's work, the private courtyards behind the doors are turned into public spaces, and yet the views to the public scenes are constantly and forcibly interrupted by the closure of the private spaces. 'I had a strong feeling of instability at the time,' the artist explains. 'If you have experienced these frenzied urban constructions, you do not even know if you are inside or outside, and if you are watching or being watched.'[7] Wang played dual roles: as the inhabitant who has lived through the changes, and – asserting some independence – as an observer of the transformation. The four-channel video work shows the daily realities captured by the artist in Beijing, but they seem to be sliced realities that perhaps cannot be put back into one entire piece. The doors keep opening and shutting, and practising their magic tricks for the audience, allowing them to see only fragments of urban lives at a time.

In China, demolition and reconstruction never cease, making way for the next determined phases of urban development. When numerous old residential houses are unable to survive, there is the spectacle of ruins. Xu Zhen's large installation consists of debris spread on the ground in a rectangular shape. This alludes to the rubble of a house that has been torn down, or, more metaphorically, the silence that typically falls straight after a disaster. Any perceptions of stillness are broken, however, if one observes the ruins

86

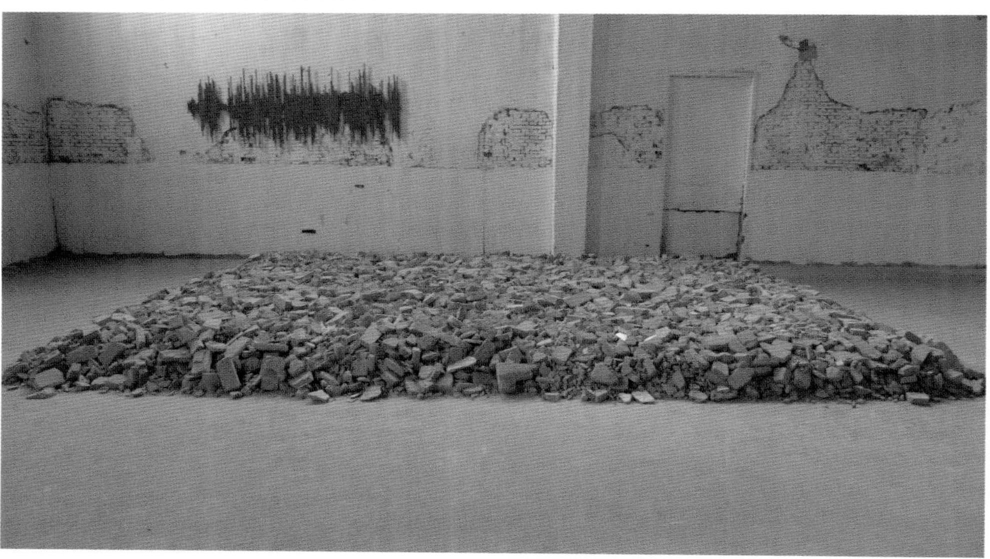

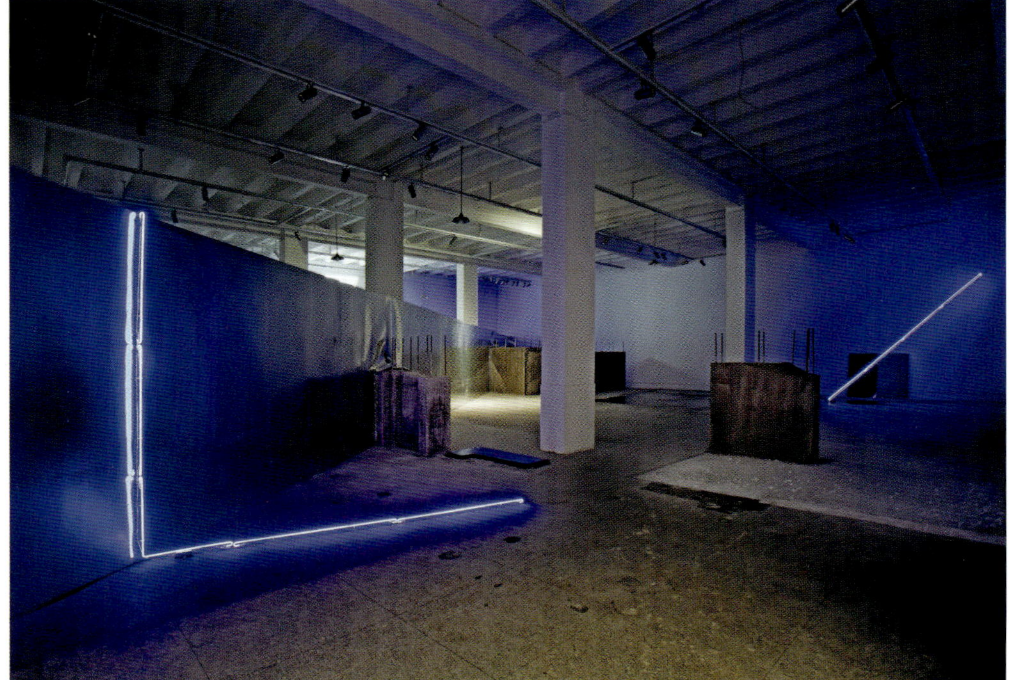

87 He An, *Who Is Alone Now Will Stay Alone Forever*, 2012 (installation view)

closely and sees that the entire carpet of broken bricks is in
fact 'breathing', rising and falling slowly, quietly and almost
imperceptibly. As the title of the work suggests, it exposes a
specific state of 'calm' – a pivotal point between what might
have already happened and what might be to come; in other
words, between the existent and the imagined. But one thing
is certain: the present is fragmented, either by a disastrous
force or by an urban plan. At the same time, the preternatural
undulation embodies a latent energy, one that is somewhat
threatening, and which might lead the present to a new phase
of success or might precede an imminent danger ahead.

87, 88   He An's site-specific installation reimagines the industrial
ruins generated by the social transformations. The title of the
work, *Who Is Alone Now Will Stay Alone Forever*, is an excerpt
from the poem 'Autumn Day' by Rainer Maria Rilke (1875–1926).
In this work by the Austrian poet, the description of the
transition from summer to autumn serves as a metaphor to
express melancholy and, ultimately, the liminal sense of a
lack of belonging. In an abandoned factory site in Shanghai,

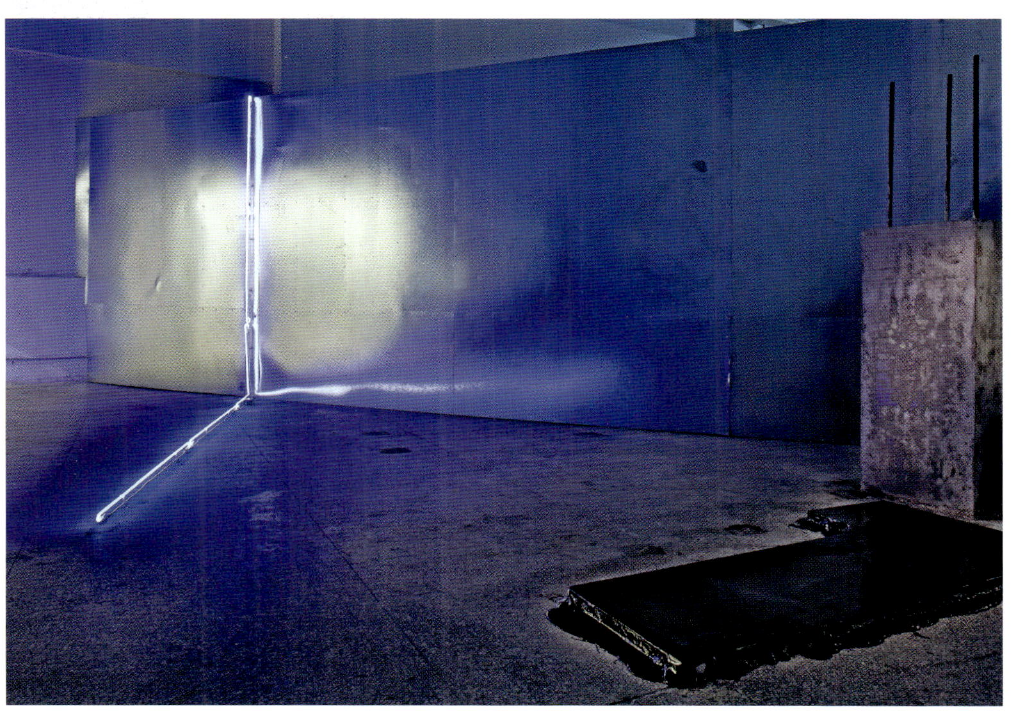

88 He An, *Who Is Alone Now Will Stay Alone Forever*, 2012 (installation view)

there are the remains of building structures: concrete blocks
with their reinforcing steel bars protruding like monstrous
antennae, abstract forms made with black viscous oil, and the
traces left by industrial machines after they have been moved
away. The space has been split in half diagonally by a series of
continuous metal sheets, which are usually used as billboards
to present advertisements. Here, they have mostly blocked
access to the other side of the exhibition, except for a ripped
section that has been 'violated' by some of the concrete blocks.
Through that vertical crevice, one can peep into the world
next door, which seems like a virtual space, but apparently
contains random collections of industrial materials – ruins and
scars – from its previous life, and, more importantly, maintains
memories through materials, shapes and smells. Blue neon
tubes – carefully designed in line with the original traces of
the industrial activities at the site – traverse both sides of the
divide, like bolts of lightning, to ignite the fading energies of
the industrial space. These lights are reflected on the surface
of the panels, helping to create a futuristic past.

89   One of Song Dong's ongoing series involves remnants of old houses, which originally made up the historic residential areas of the *hutong*, and which have now been demolished in favour of new constructions. These materials, such as retrieved door and window frames, have become useful elements of vocabulary throughout the artist's body of sculptural work, while the typical set of colours that carry the collective memory and their worn textures are the accent. These materials are symbols of home. In being completely reshaped and rearranged, sometimes as geometric abstractions and sometimes in the form of traditional screens, they are transformed. In particular, when the transparent glass of the windows is replaced with colour-tinted mirrors, and when each of these is thoughtfully manipulated with another layer consisting of a coloured frame, the past and the current aesthetic values meet. As experienced in China's rapid development, urban memories are fragmented, like Song's windows and doors, connected with each other like neighbourhoods, and reinterpreted as familiar yet alienated structures.

90   In his early work of 1999, *Broken Mirror*, Song Dong swings a hammer to destroy a mirror that reflects a city street scene, shattering the viewer's conception of what has been perceived, and presenting a different scene. At first, it seems to be illusory when the mirror image of the city disappears in a fleeting moment and is succeeded with a different view. This view reveals the new reality, on the one hand, but on the other it reveals the

91 fragile nature of its medium. Similarly, in *Crumpling Shanghai*, a hand is shown crushing pieces of paper, one after another, on which everyday street scenes in the city have been projected. The images vanish into darkness, nothingness, and then are restaged with a set of entirely new landscapes. The subversive act of the artist reiterates the transience of urban existence. Since 2003,

92 Song's installation *Eating the City* has travelled the world. With the help of local volunteers, the artist uses tens of thousands of biscuits to meticulously shape miniatures of buildings and urban landscapes. Starting from the opening day of the exhibition, visitors are invited to consume the city. Although destructive, this is also part of the *constructive* process of the art production. According to Song:

*The purpose of my work is for the city I build to be destroyed...
As cities in Asia grow, old quarters and buildings are knocked down
and new ones built, almost every day. Some cities have even been
built from scratch in twenty years... We eat the city we have built
and tasted through our desires and demolished it at the same time
until it became a ruin.*[8]

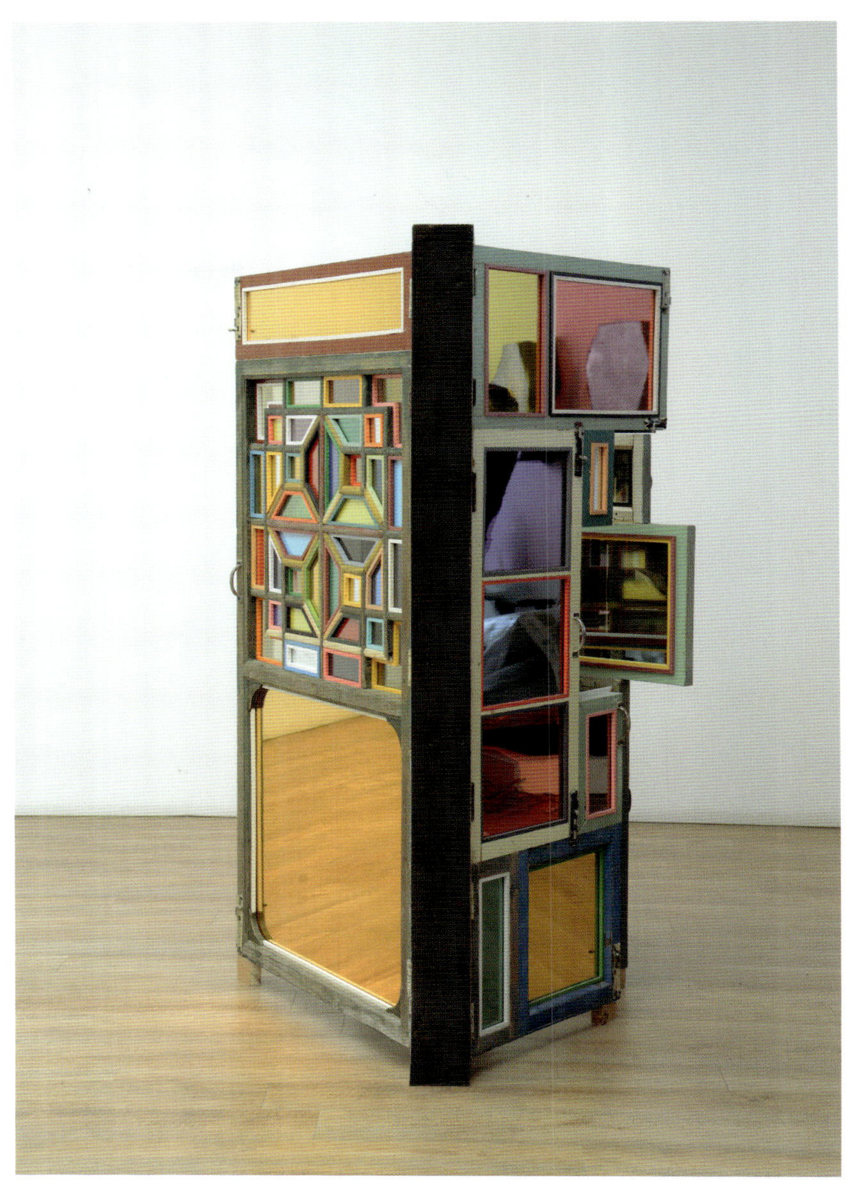

89 Song Dong, *Usefulness of Uselessness: Window Door No. 3*, 2019

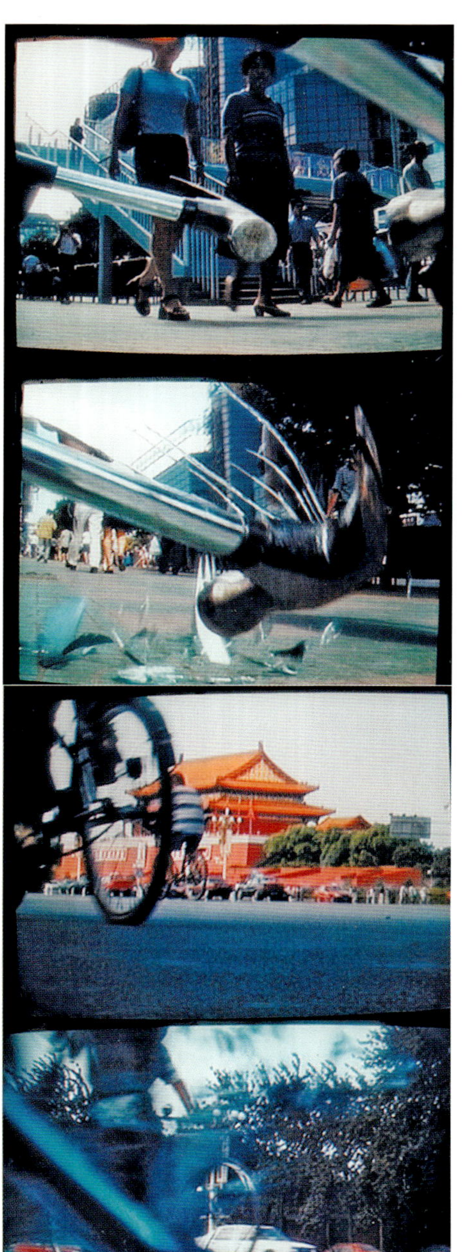

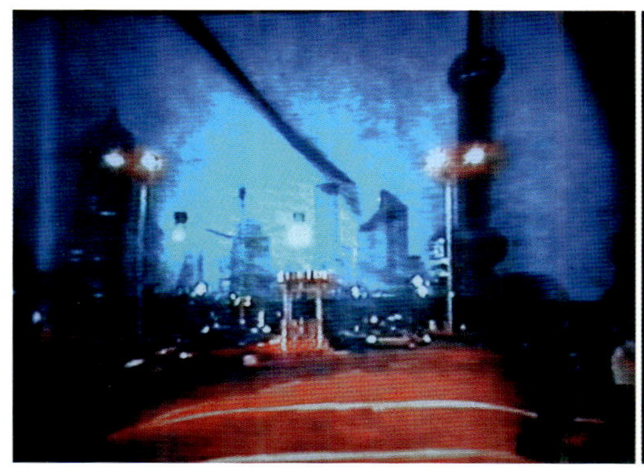
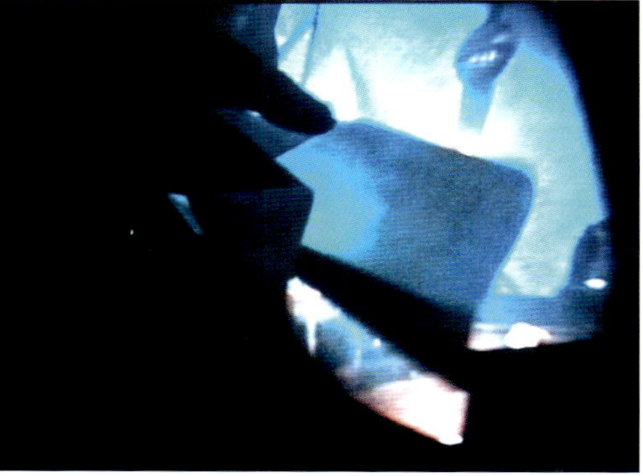

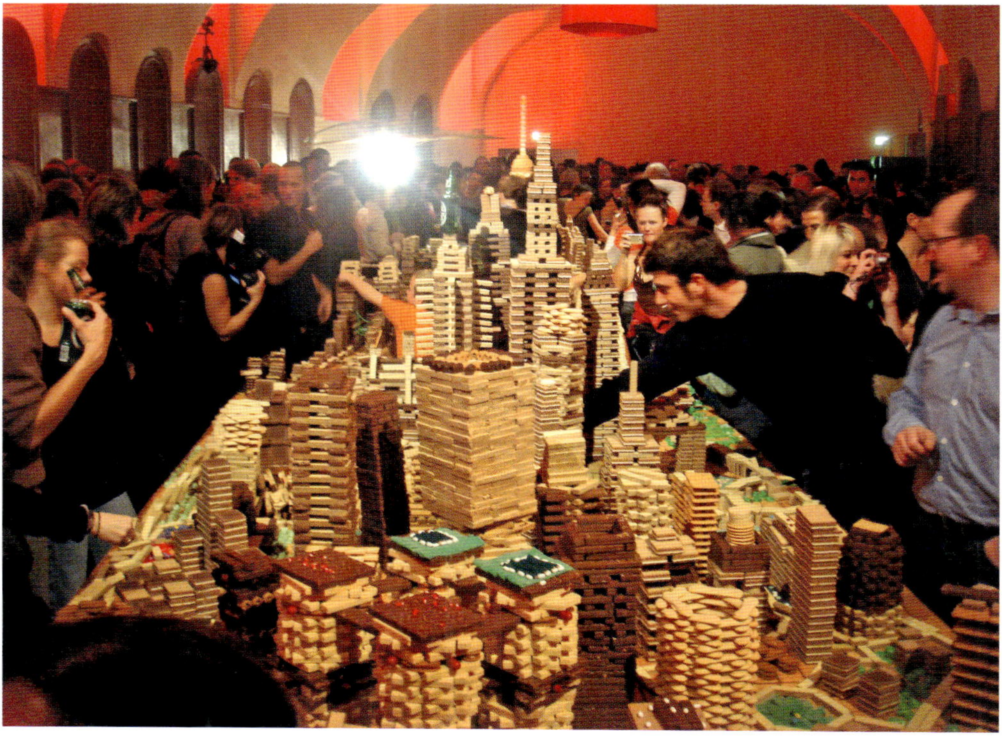

90 OPPOSITE Song Dong, *Broken Mirror*, 1999 (video stills)
91 TOP Song Dong, *Crumpling Shanghai*, 2000 (video stills)
92 ABOVE Song Dong, *Eating the City*, 2003 (installation view)

There is no need for the artist to identify any particular buildings or landmarks in his displays of edible food; his constructions are symbolic presentations of the metropolis in our globalized world. While each installation looks orderly and delicious at the outset, it quickly starts to look catastrophic, as if approaching the end of the Anthropocene era.

Fluidity

In the performance work *Safely Manoeuvring across Linhe Road*, Lin Yilin uses large bricks, like a builder, to construct a wall of approximately 3 by 1.5 metres (10 by 5 ft) on one side of a busy main street in the new centre of Guangzhou, with multiple high-rises under construction. He then takes some bricks down from one end of the wall and moves them to the other end, where he starts to build them up again. Moving brick by brick from top to bottom and row by row for hours, the artist gradually manages to migrate the construction of the entire wall across the street to arrive at the opposite side of the ongoing busy traffic. As if responding to the changes in the city, this unstable wall seems to be attempting either to block off or to give way to the flow of urban life. The temporality of the wall is reinforced by every movement of the artist – the central focus of the work, and a symbolic sample of the fluid construction of high-rises in the background. Similarly, the work *Sand Dune* took place on an anonymous construction site in Guangzhou. The artist started to build a brick wall at one end of a pile of sand, and then moved this wall forward, brick by brick. It was physically challenging to realize the project, as the bricks kept sinking into the sand, and the wall was consequently unable to maintain its full shape. Although fewer and fewer bricks became available to be moved, the wall eventually rose over the sandy hill, leaving the 'casualties' buried behind.

In the urban transformation in China, nothing can be fixed. Through a semi-fictional approach, Chen Shaoxiong's series of three-dimensional photo-collages consists of several layers of images collected from a city, including of pedestrians, vehicles, passengers and traffic signs, forming a normal street view. As indicated in each image by the deliberate inclusion of a pair of hands, the portable cardboard collages were then positioned against new everyday backgrounds of urban landscape. Each reconstructed photo-narrative offers a miniature theatre, in which an ordinary street view is excerpted, reassembled and restaged as a fluid everyday reality; in fact, from the actual background behind itself.

For the span of an exhibition that took place over the course of seventeen days, artist Wang Wei invited ten labourers to act as

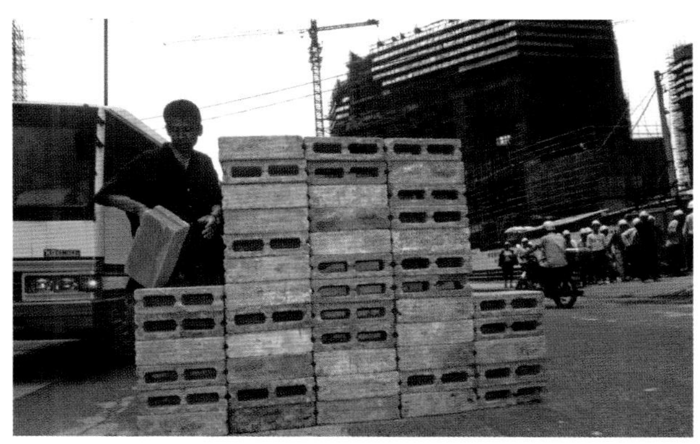

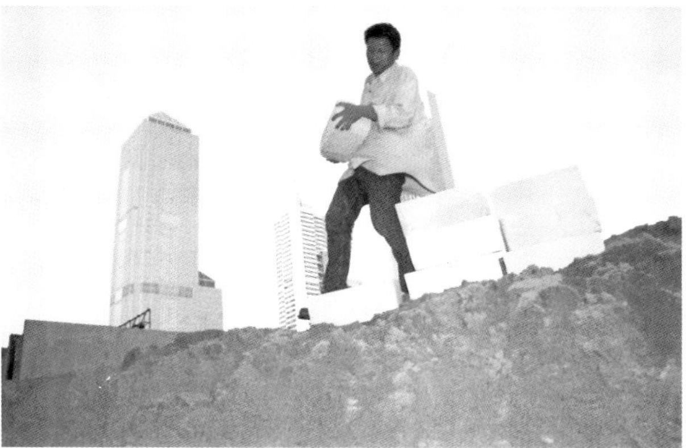

participants. They had been making a living by recycling bricks in Beijing – collecting these from demolition sites and reselling them for new constructions. For *Temporary Space*, they searched around the city for bricks, collected them over a few days, then began to make a structure in the exhibition space. Gradually, 20,000 recycled bricks were assembled and used to build four 4-metre-high (13 ft) walls, which resulted in a 100-square-metre (1,075 sq. ft) room inside the existing gallery space. The walls were constructed without any doors or windows, so the building presented as a large architectural body, inaccessible, extending from floor to ceiling. What it housed remained unknown. Two days later, it was deinstalled; the bricks were removed by the workers to be resold back into everyday construction work. The action constituted an additional stop on the recycling journey of those bricks in the dynamic flux of urban development – their destiny manifesting from old sites, via a gallery space as an artistic pause, to new sites, and no doubt further onwards.

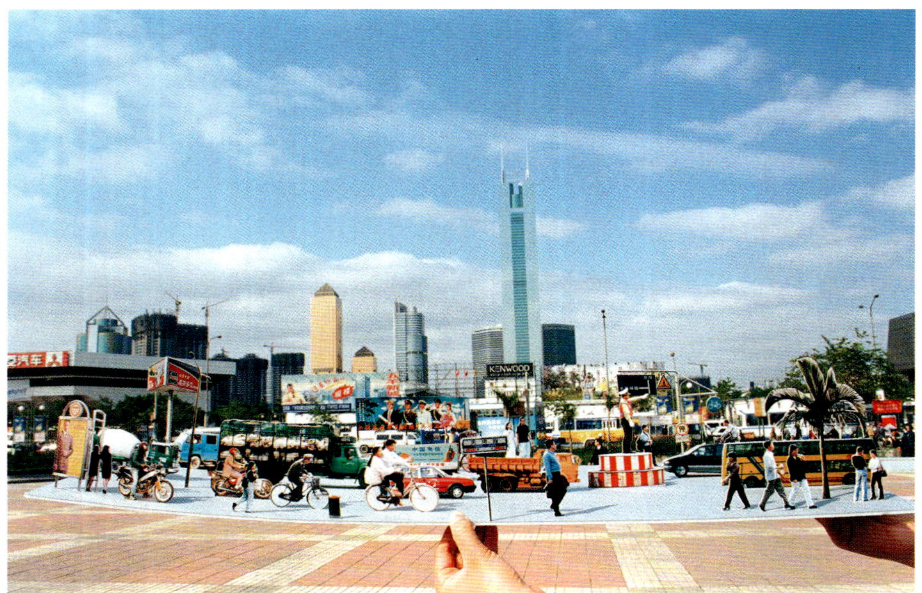

95 ABOVE Chen Shaoxiong, *Street, No. 1*, 1998
96 OPPOSITE ABOVE Wang Wei, *Temporary Space*, 2003 (installation view)
97 OPPOSITE BELOW Wang Wei, *Hypocritical Room*, 2002 (installation view)

97 Wang Wei's *Hypocritical Room* also discusses the 'mobility' of reality. This time, a large cubic structure was made using metal supports and photographic prints that reflected the interior from various points of view. The space appeared to be a temporary site in a transitional state, either to be demolished or to be converted for other uses – the same pillars and beams are shown, covered in the simplest of paints. The interior was migrated to the artist's cube through a calculated process – first being 'flattened' by the camera, and then being 'inflated' again in a kind of three-dimensional form. It becomes an illusion of an 'interior' inside an interior. Illuminated by the lights installed inside the structure, this false space could be moved around on castors in the real space. The two appeared to be developing a dialogue – between the old and the young, between the actual and the metaphysical, and between the permanent and the provisional. In addition, the work was not just a new imitation of the existing space; it also made the existing space itself new, through a shift from placing content within a context to making the context itself the content. In contemporary China, floors and ceilings, walls and windows, constructions and cities, are all on the move.

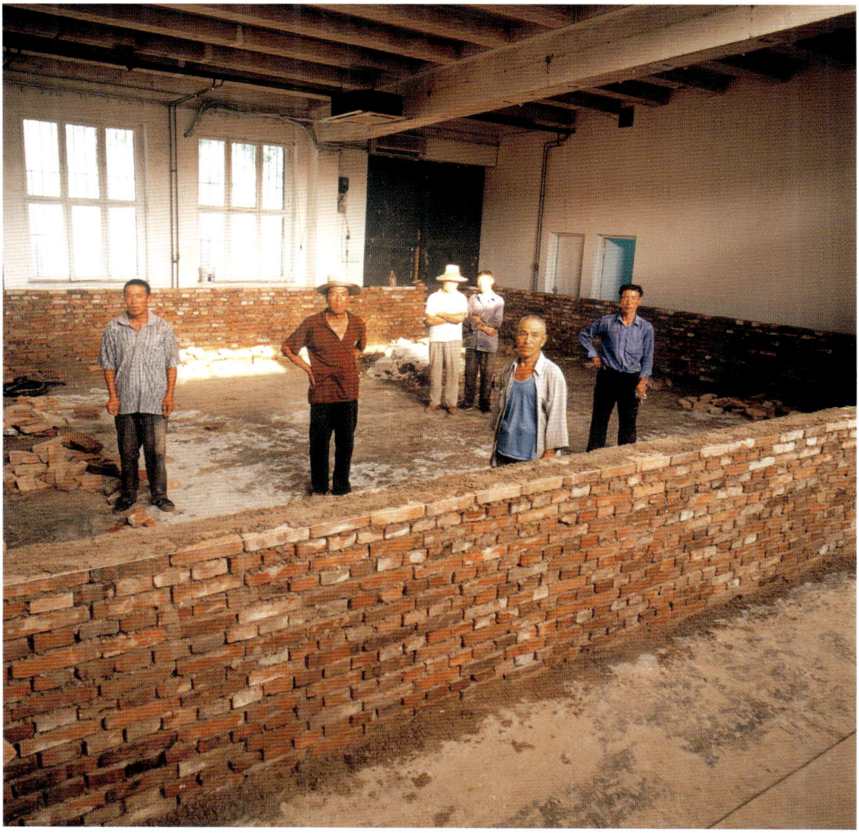

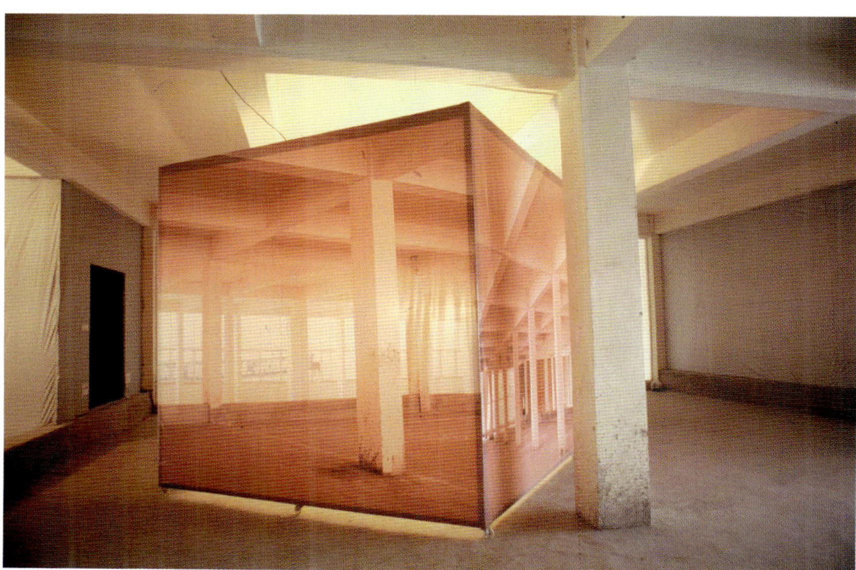

Having moved to Beijing in 1999, artist Nabuqi, like many of her fellow inhabitants, witnesses constant changes in the living environment on the outskirts of the capital. Travelling daily from home to studio, following the same route, she notes that the path sometimes gets narrower and sometimes wider, and the buildings and walls on its sides evolve from time to time. Furthermore, she can experience the anarchic transformation and expansion of urban territory by moving further and further out from the centre. There is neither a suitable long-term rental to stay in, nor any sustainable neighbourhood to move to. The city keeps growing, with ambition and greed. For Nabuqi, the term 'urban-rural fringe' (*chengxiang jiehebu*) remains only a term, or a concept, without specific reference to any identifiable location. Everything in her urban experience seems to be temporary, both constructions and people left in an in-between state. As the artist has stated, they become 'many empty shadows left behind'.[9] In the work *A View Beyond Space*, Nabuqi developed a series of miniature architectural models, or architectural objects. They are all detached from the urban context, deliberately positioned as having an independent existence. Some are representational, such as stairs, ladders or a horizon of construction; others are more abstract, such as lines to form shapes of views or silhouettes of views. With her sculptural language, the three-dimensional work has been developed with a certain quality of flatness, and it often appears predominantly monochromatic, like shadows. If a shadow can be seen as a shaded area that either floats on a plain surface or occupies – or, more accurately, is attached to something that occupies – a three-dimensional volume, then in Nabuqi's work this shadowiness becomes a series of monochromatically hued and somewhat compressed views that consciously minimize their three-dimensional volume. In addition, although they may look refined and solid, parts of them are often wearing away, like wax burning or ice melting, to reinforce the nature of temporality.

Yang Zhenzhong's earlier work, *Light as Fuck*, depicts the ease with which a single finger holds up the feather-light skyline of the representative urban construction of Lujiazui, the new financial centre of Shanghai, and China's most condensed district of skyscrapers developed since the early 1990s, as epitomized by the Oriental Pearl Tower. At the artist's fingertip, the entire cityscape is turned upside down; it wobbles, and never

98 OPPOSITE TOP Nabuqi, *A View Beyond Space No. 13*, 2016
99 OPPOSITE CENTRE Nabuqi, *A View Beyond Space No. 16*, 2017
100 OPPOSITE BELOW Nabuqi, *A View Beyond Space No. 4*, 2015

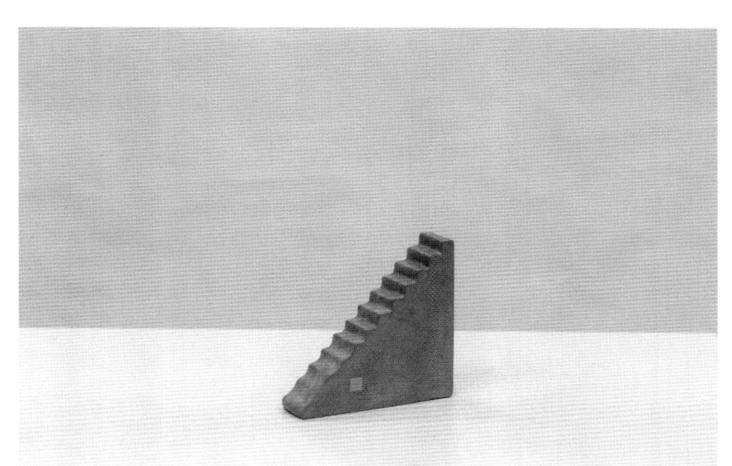

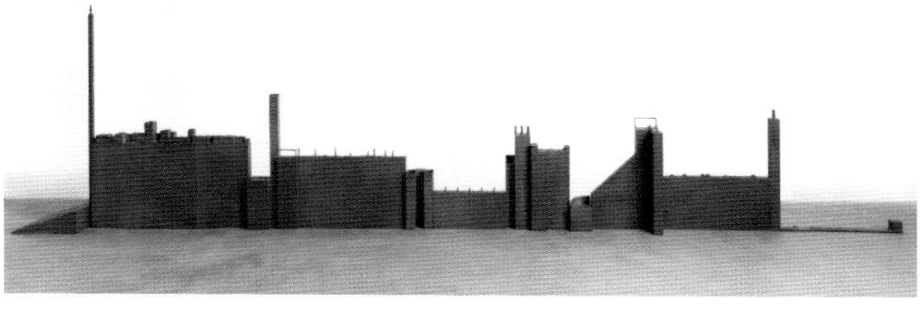

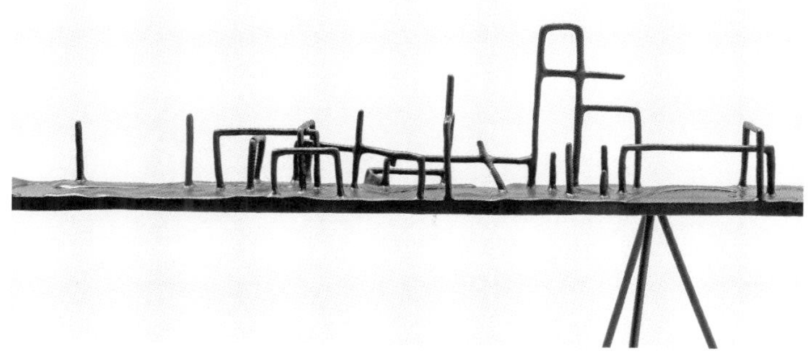

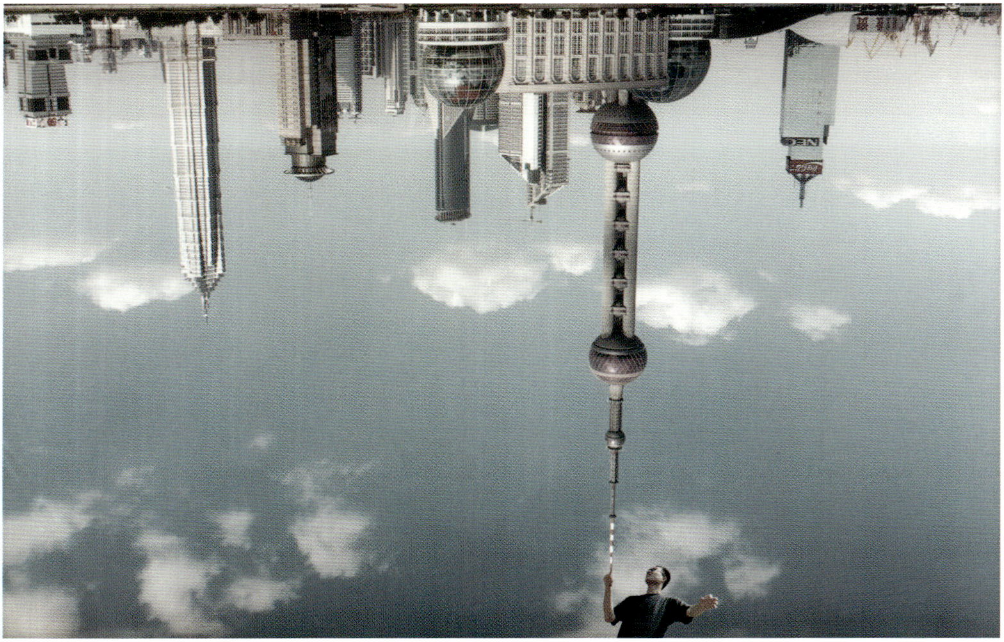

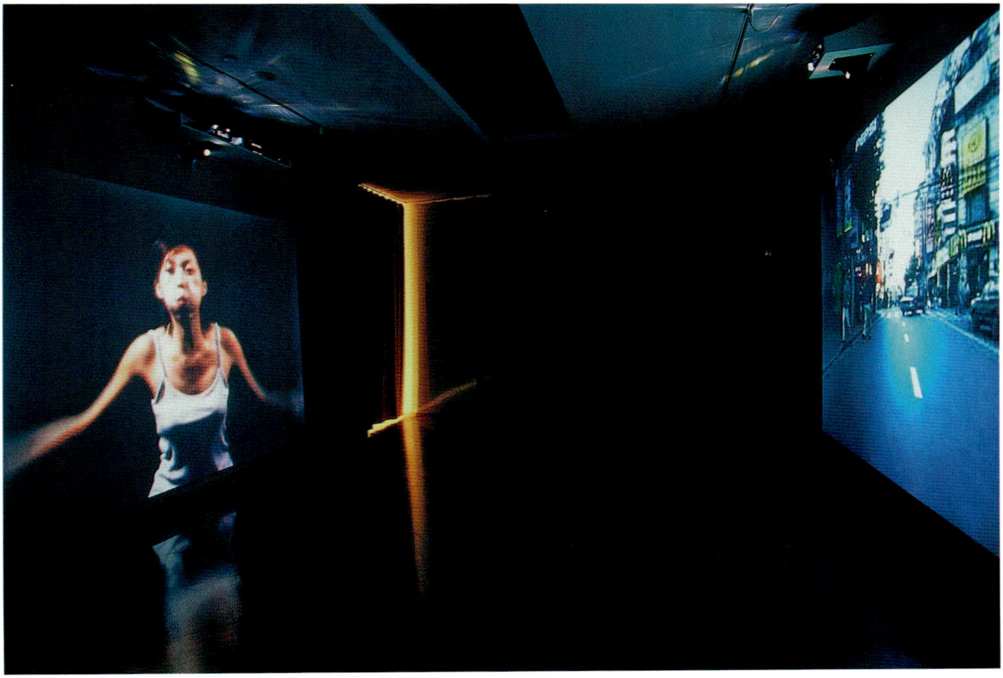

101 TOP Yang Zhenzhong, *Light as Fuck*, 2002 (video still)
102 ABOVE Yang Zhenzhong, *Let's Puff*, 2002 (installation view)

stops moving, in order to balance itself in collaboration with the artist. Also focusing on Shanghai, the work *Let's Puff* is a video installation, involving two projections screened opposite one another. On one side, a young woman, dressed casually, blows air in sharp bursts towards the opposite projection, which features footage of the Nanjing East Road, the city's iconic thoroughfare developed as a retail area connecting the Bund. With every exhalation the street scene is pushed backwards slightly, suggesting an impermanence in this urban environment, as if it is being pushed all the time. Interestingly, the majority of pedestrians and shoppers on the Nanjing East Road look as if they are visitors from other cities, provinces and countries; to many Shanghainese, they are foreigners or outlanders. With too many guests, 'home' can feel alienated. Between the two screens, we too are caught in the illusion, travelling along as 'others'. In Yang's interpretation, economic revival and the ambitions of urban development become part of a circus act in which the performance can never stop so that the charade can continue. By using playful images – the exercises of balancing and puffing – the disturbing unpredictability of the situation, as well as the temporality and uncertainty behind urban prosperity, is divulged through a sense of humour. Yang Zhenzhong neither tells us how the city of Shanghai can possibly be put back down again, nor does he provide any alternative for the moment when the girl one day runs out of breath.

In a 2019 series of video works by Hu Weiyi, everyday vistas – residential building blocks during the day, or illuminated cities at night – form ordinary and yet somehow strange urban scenarios. *The Window Blind* comprises three sets of windows, which are in the style of 1980s or 1990s buildings, collected by the artist from construction sites. Translucent curtains move in front of them, automatically, gliding from one side to the other. Beyond the windows, on one side the viewer looks out onto a more contemporary urban scene, as one would expect from any residential high-rise building; as if – on the other side – the gallery space were a kind of home. The buildings on view include some unusual ones, their windows covered by concrete and integrated into the walls. They are in effect windowless, and only bear the shapes of windows, like scars on the skin; they are lifeless, or like giant tombstones. Gradually, however, these blocked windows start to 'breathe', 'blossom' and come back to life, until the curtain travels back over to the relevant section to veil them. Hidden by the airy sheets of the fabric, the windows can only fade away back into the walls, as if life had been silenced once again, or withered. But those that have been exposed revive again, and the curtains must work

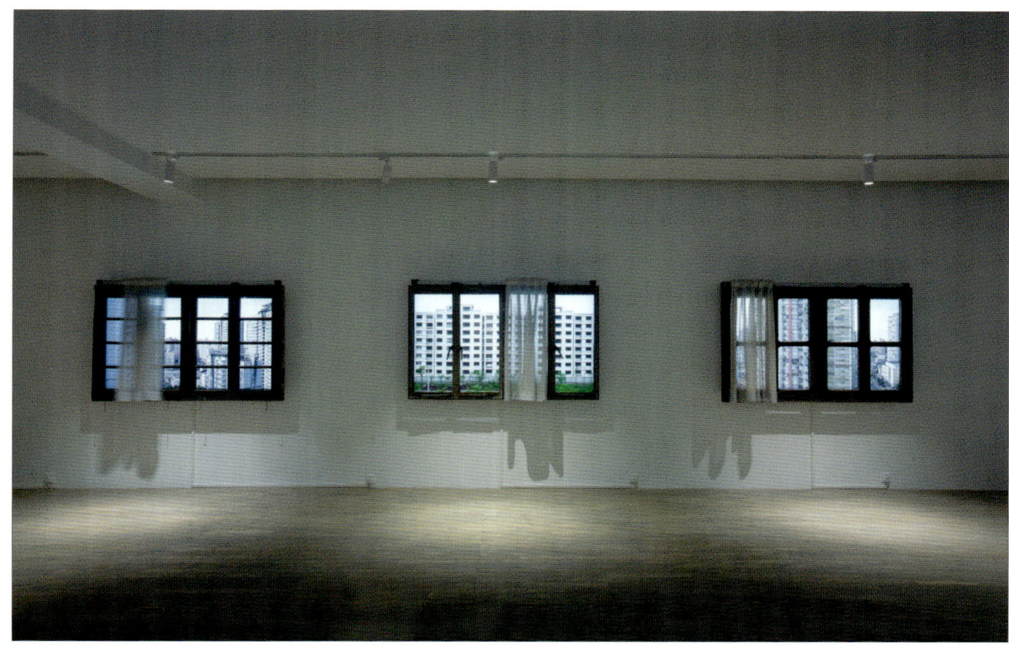

103 Hu Weiyi, *The Window Blind*, 2019 (installation view)

hard to keep up with the pace of 'blossoming'. The central video installation shows a building possibly under construction with windows uninstalled, the gaps appearing as rectangular holes. As with the other high-rise windows in the work, the viewer might notice some staged scenes of buzzing family life – the watering of plants, or the hanging of washing – which the artist has integrated from other sources. And yet, these are erased, emptied or expelled as soon as the curtain arrives with its quiet violence. In what seems like a game of hide and seek, the curtain on the one hand acts as a form of obstruction, albeit a symbolic one considering its translucent nature; in fact, paradoxically, it might actually stimulate curiosity. On the other hand, according to the artist, the curtain becomes an embodiment of censorship, surveilling and forcibly intervening in daily life. Contrarily, the curtain both conceals and reveals.

Having grown up as a new-generation artist in Shanghai, one of the most dynamic cities in China, Hu Weiyi has his own observation:

This sense of powerlessness, concomitant with nothingness, also reflects the existential state of each individual in the city. People

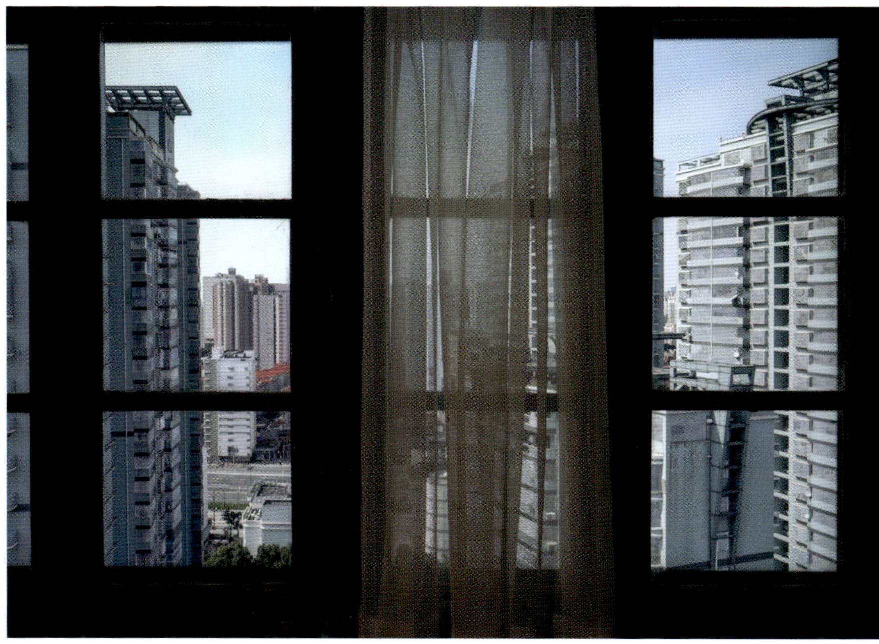

104 Hu Weiyi, *The Window Blind, No. 1*, 2019 (detail)

endure a power that can integrate a rule and a standardized lifestyle, though they are not capable of suppressing their inner desire. The city is a mixture of power and desire... It is an exhausted urban dance in which each living object is involved, and becomes an indispensable interconnection of the hierarchy, systematically exporting itself to the same process.[10]

In a pair of video works by Hu, *The Rule of the Wind* and *The Rule of the Water*, the city is in control. Two different street views are presented, as if on monitor screens, focusing respectively on a junction at an urban-rural fringe zone and on a bridge across a river. They have one thing in common: dual sets of traffic lights, either in the centre or in the distance, but dominating the image. When the red light comes on, the flow of the river ceases immediately, as if 'frozen' into an uneven sheet of glass; on the adjoining screen, the wind stops, too, and the plants are halted in their swaying, as is the flow of traffic. Urban life becomes static. Only when the green light comes back on does the 'glass' river start to run again and the plants resume their response to the wind. The only elements that can break the rules which control normal urban existence are the traffic

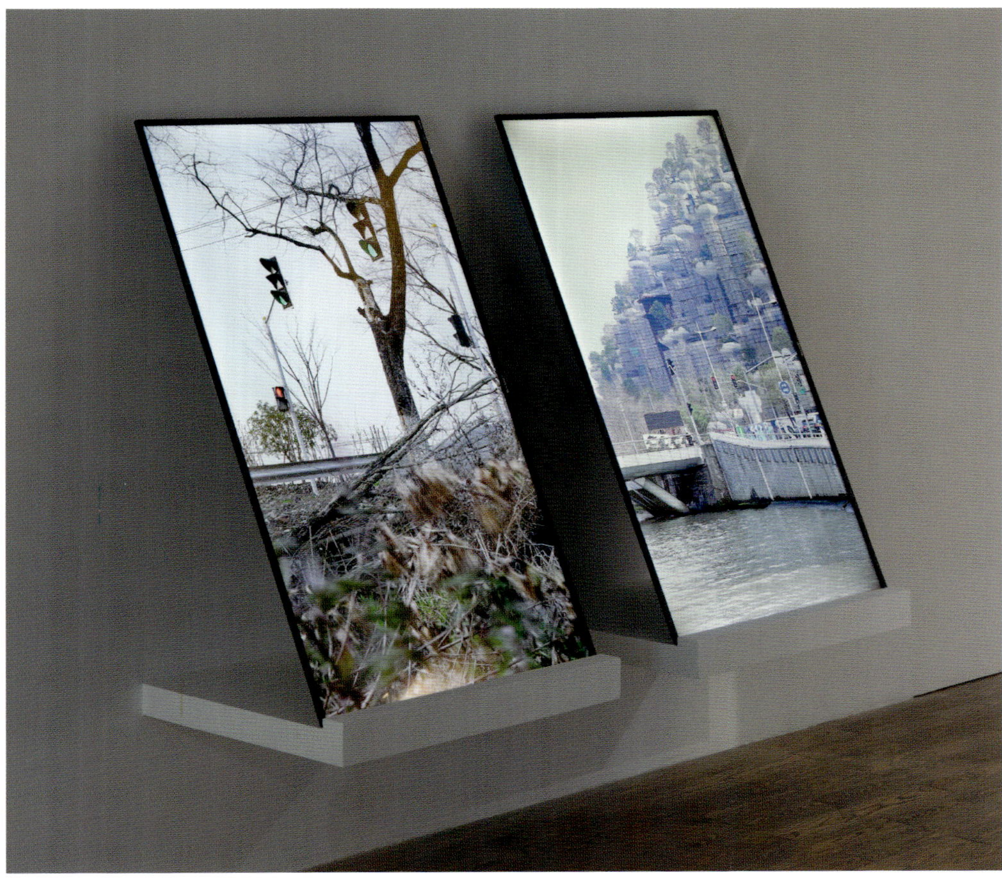

105 Hu Weiyi, *The Rule of the Wind* and *The Rule of the Water*, 2019 (installation view)

lights: in fact, they are both the makers and the executors of the rules, or indeed they are the rules themselves. In Hu Weiyi's videos, as with his curtains, the lights are the ultimate power that authorizes, or invalidates, the fluidity of urban progress.

The Illusive

Since late 2012, across the country, the term 'China Dream' (*Zhongguo meng*) has been popularized, coined to take the place of 'Harmonious Society', which was introduced by former president Hu Jintao in 2005. The new term encompasses 'a dream for peace, development, cooperation, and mutual benefit for all. It is connected to the beautiful dreams of the people in other countries. The Chinese Dream will not only benefit the

Chinese people, but also people of all countries in the world.'[11] It enables people 'to project their own personal dream on the official concept', but it 'is also designed to help the Chinese leadership unite the Chinese people at a time of growing political and economic uncertainty'.[12] The term 'China Dream' is culturally engaged, representing a specific political agenda, and providing an imaginative space for artistic response. As a new model, it does not project an *exact* direction, but instead, a *sense* of direction. It forms a distance – an almost permanent one, which is never reachable, but which is simultaneously romantic, or even artistic. The intention is that the ultimate destination is not to be clearly defined; rather, it can be imagined and interpreted from a variety of perspectives. It is neither far from one's current situation, nor close to it, but the implication is that the destination is only a dream away. To capture and reflect China's extraordinary economic development and accelerated urbanization, and, indeed, an image of the 'China dream', new artistic strategies must be prepared.

106   Jiang Zhi's *Rainbow* series shows an elusive spectacle, though seemingly a natural one. The artist depicts an urban reality dominated by consumer culture and commodity fetishism as an ironic fairy tale in which a splendid rainbow traces an arc across the sky above Tiananmen Square. The image of the rainbow is perfectly symmetrical, aligned with the architectural arrangement of the square, too perfect to be true. Jiang's rainbows actually consist of images of hundreds of neon signs, both Western and Chinese, sourced from across the city, ranging from promotions for fast-food restaurants, household products and news media to signs for theatres, shops, clubs and banks – representations of almost every kind of commodity one would expect to see on a high street. The details contained within the artificial rainbow require a careful reading. Neon lights belong to our cities and are associated with the prosperity of urban life. In Jiang's work, with their strategic, seductive power blinking on top of buildings, these interconnected lures keep forming and nourishing our urban desires. As the artist has stated:

[The rainbow] is constructed as a surrealistic prospect, representing commercial consumptions that take place every day on the way towards the future. When all cultural and spiritual values have disappeared or been lost through urban development, then the pursuit of the material becomes the sole impetus in contemporary life. The previous utopian ideology is transformed into consumeristic ecstasy and greed, which can still be romantic, as ever.[13]

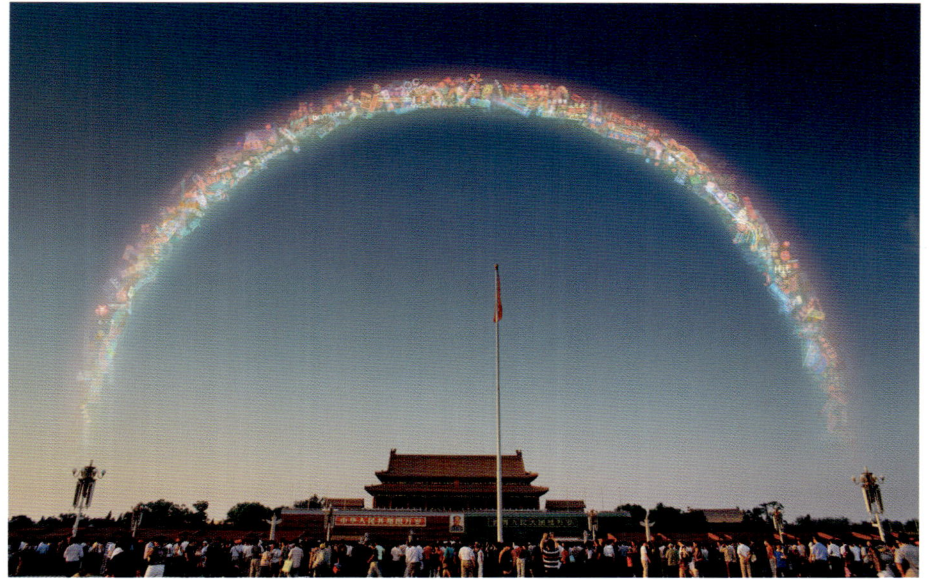

106 ABOVE Jiang Zhi, *Rainbow, No. 3*, 2005
107 OPPOSITE ABOVE Jiang Zhi, *Rainbow*, 2007 (installation view)
108 OPPOSITE BELOW Hu Jieming, *Somewhere: Square*, 2004

107 In the 2007 video installation that was an extension of
this work, a modest interior is seen, featuring old-fashioned
radiators and a single bare lightbulb hanging from the ceiling.
Central to the piece is the window facing out of the damp
wall, with a hopeful view beyond its metal frame: a forest of
skyscrapers illuminated by the rainbow of glinting neon lights.
It seems to be the vision of the owner of the space, or perhaps
generally that of urban inhabitants; a celebratory firework
commemorating economic success, or else a sequence of flares
warning of coming uncertainties.

108 For the 2004 series *Somewhere*, Hu Jieming appropriated
images from postcards around the globe and fabricated new
scenes. The photographs feature some of the world's most
renowned tourist sites; but at the same time, through digital
manipulation, they appear to be of unknown places. For
instance, in the centre of Tiananmen Square, instead of the
Monument to the People's Heroes and Mao's Memorial Hall,
there appears a different set of monuments – the Sphinx
and the pyramids – located on the central axis. The image
of the square must have been taken from the balcony of
Tiananmen; or it is as if it was formed by the dignified gaze

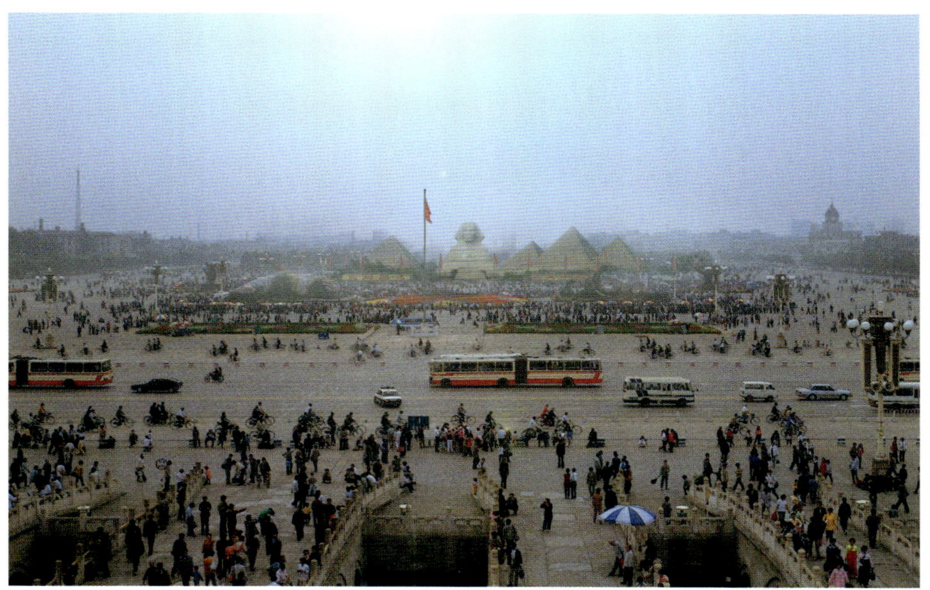

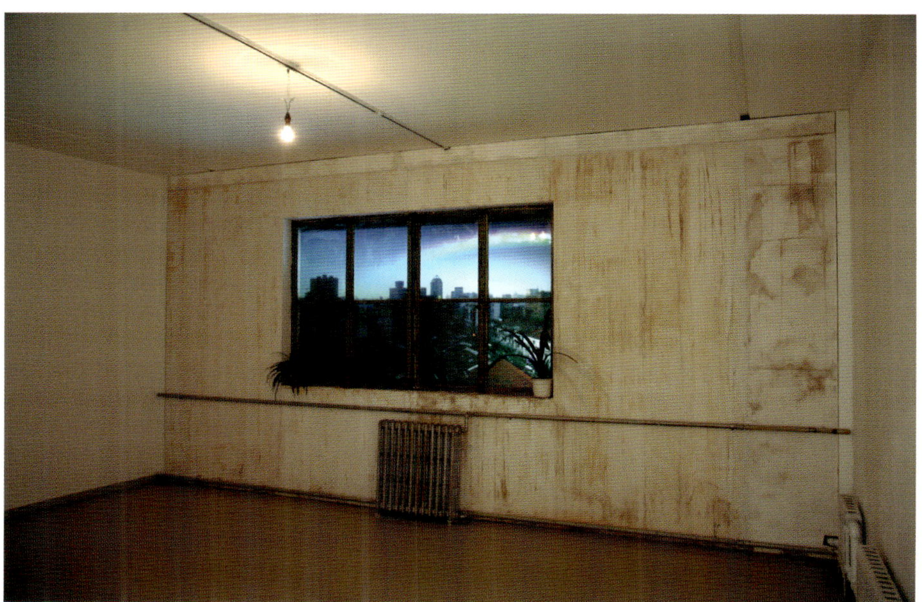

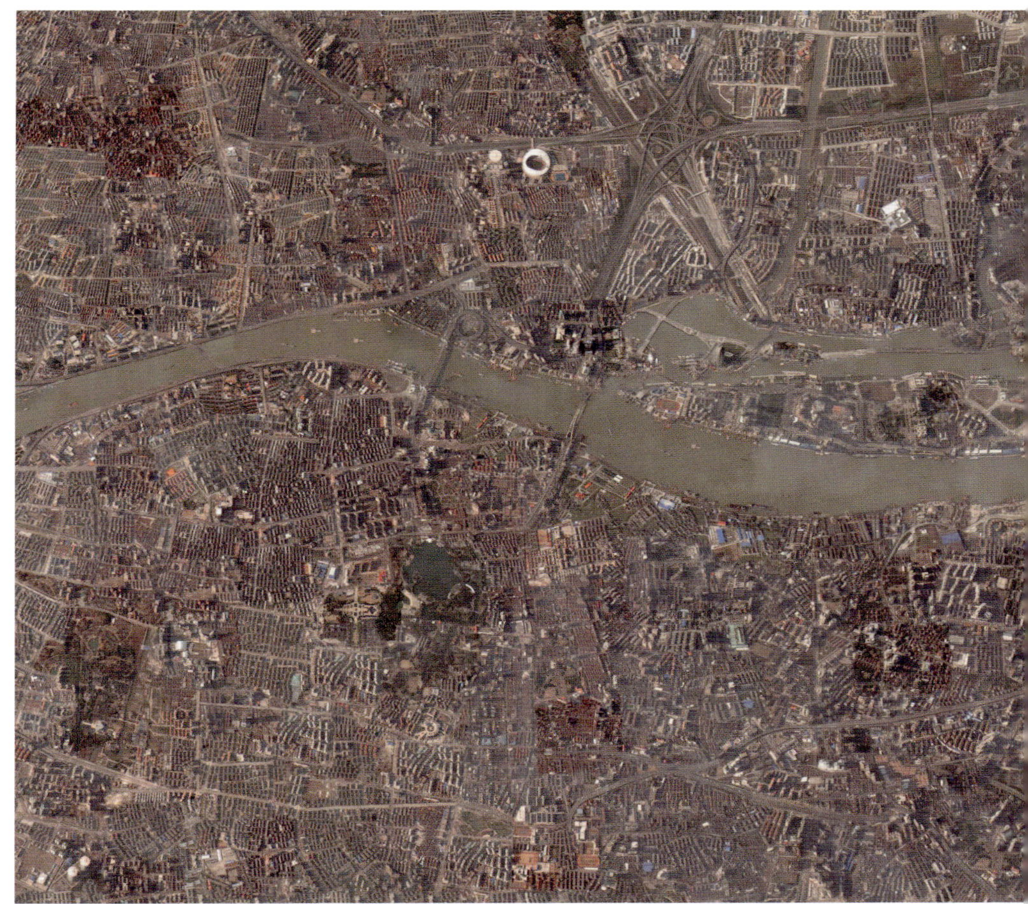

of Chairman Mao looking out from his portrait hanging above
the Tiananmen Gate. The individual components of the image
are all perfectly real, including the Golden River Bridge in front
of the Gate, the pedestrians, traders, tourists and cyclists, and
the late-1980s-style buses passing through Changan Avenue …
until the eye reaches the Egyptian complex that merges into
the background. The gaze of Mao Zedong continues to look out
over the country and his people, and extends its sight into the
world for a global 'harmony', or, in fact, a chaotic coexistence.
In another example, the Nine Zigzag Bridge in Shanghai's Yu
Garden leads visitors beyond the pavilions in the lake towards
the skyscrapers of Chicago only a few miles away. Hu Jieming
composes images of everywhere and nowhere.

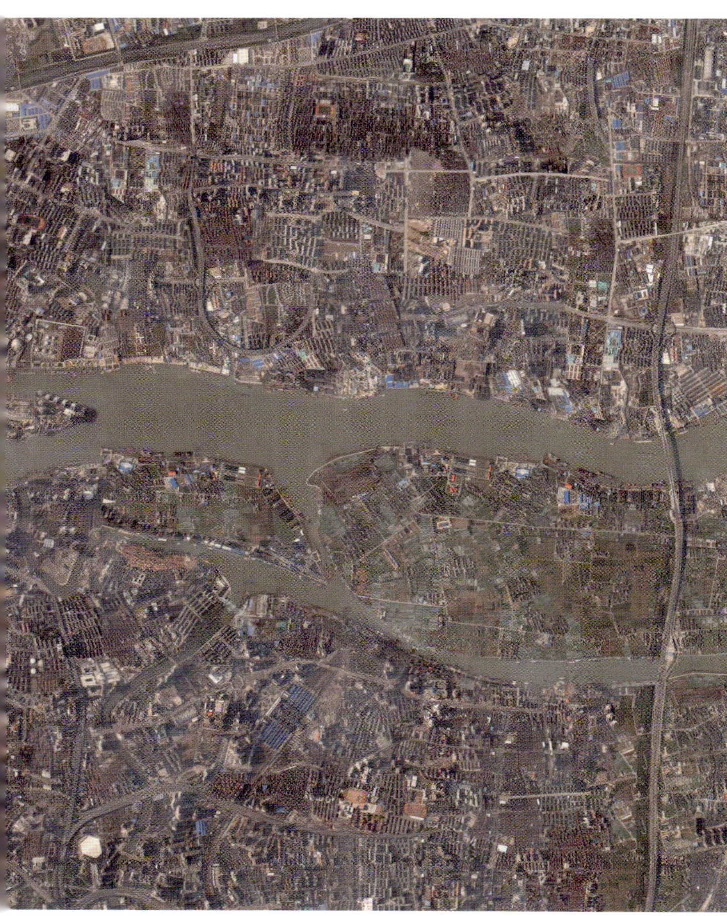

109 Hu Jieming,
Where Is My Home,
2011

109

As a further extension, in the project *Where Is My Home*, Hu imposed his home city of Shanghai on the landform of Guangzhou, 1,600 kilometres (1,000 miles) away in southern China. From the work's satellite viewpoint, the Jiangwan and Haiyin bridges that cross the Pearl River which runs through Guangzhou, for example, have been replaced respectively by Shanghai's Nanpu and Lupu bridges on the Huangpu River. All the local streets, elevated roads and buildings of Shanghai have, where possible, been transplanted into the topography of Guangzhou, including landmark buildings, such as the Oriental Pearl Tower and the Shanghai Stadium. Every element of urban structure in the two cities has been compared and removed/relocated to match as closely as possible, using any

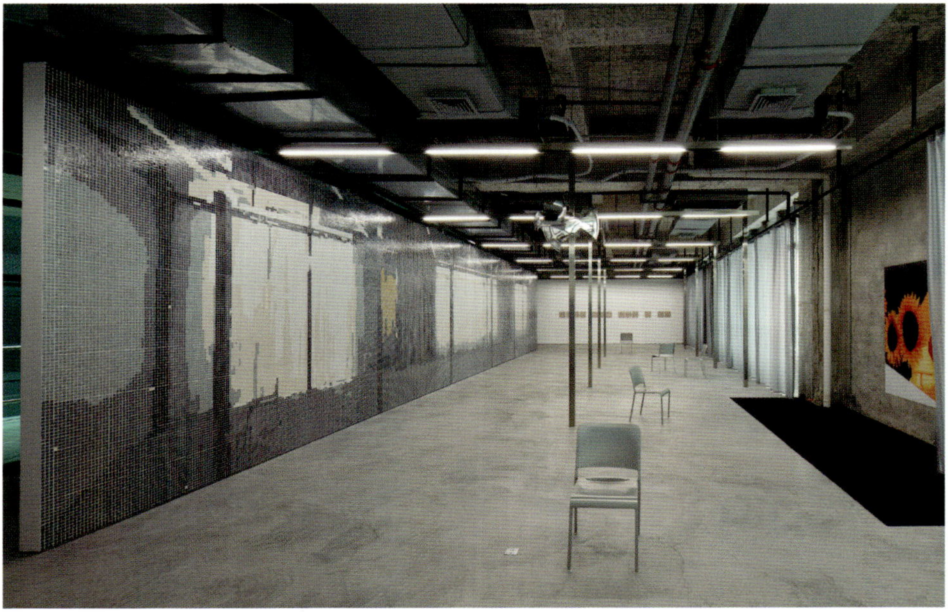

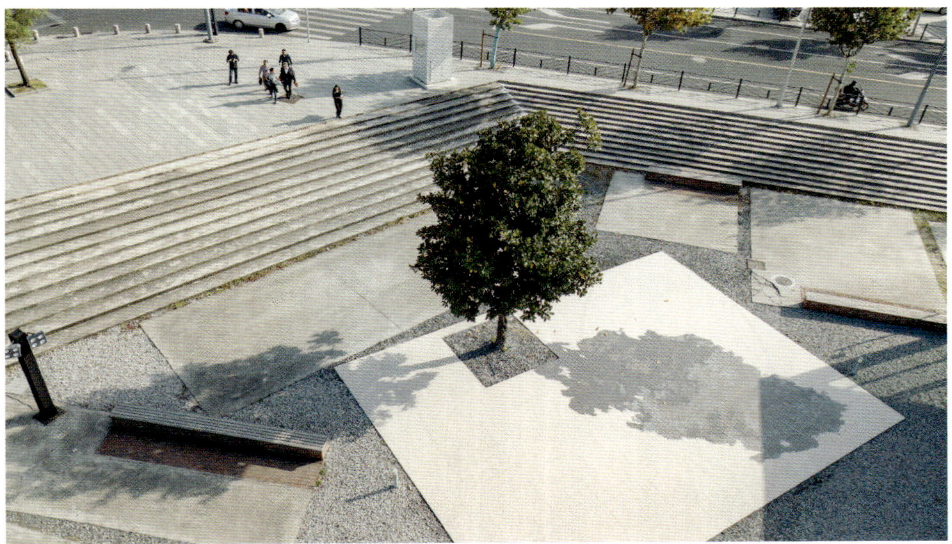

110 TOP Wang Wei, *What You See Is Not What You See*, 2017 (installation view)
111 ABOVE Wang Wei, *Shadow*, 2017 (installation view)

necessary discreet alterations that were supported by the digital technology available at the time. Like undertaking an extremely ambitious jigsaw puzzle, completing the task seems to have involved the complete migrations of two entire cities, segment by segment. In fact, it is more than a puzzle: a new physiognomy has been built, a hybrid appearance of the two cities. In line with the rapid urban changes in China, if this were a moving image, the cityscape would have continued to evolve over the years, even over months and days, as long as lost jigsaw pieces could be found or reproduced.

In order to arrest such an illusive reality, Wang Wei immobilizes it. In the 2017 installation *What You See Is Not What You See*, the artist referenced the existing spatial arrangement of an exhibition space, including the decorative metal pillars in the middle, the chairs found scattered around the room, and the diaphanous curtains hung in front of a row of large windows. A temporary wall was built and covered with mosaic tiles that mirrored the existing environment, the interior as well as the landscape beyond the windows. The wall maximized the size of any graphic piece that could fit in the space; but at the same time, despite being a visible artwork itself, it somehow retreated from the space, to become a passive part – or a fixed shadow – of a fluid exterior reality. In an outdoor site-specific work, again made with mosaic tiles, Wang simply imitates the shadow of a magnolia tree in front of the West Bund Art Centre. Unlike its authentic shadow, this artificial one seems to be frozen onto an existing concrete floor. It is relatively permanent: whenever the sun moves, or natural conditions change, such as cloud or rain, day or night, it stays absolutely still, as if it is in a timeless moment. The real shadow, on the other hand, changes in size, flickers and dances around the tree and against that immobile element, the shadow of a shadow. Wang's works with mosaic tiles are neither abstract nor completely realistic. They are faithful in imitating the real scene but obscure because of the nature of the material; through the lens of the digital era, they are *pixellated*. In some sense, then, perhaps we are seeing a co-existence of the actual and the virtual – a full and comprehensive reality of our time.

Cao Fei's *RMB City* was a fictional city constructed in the online virtual platform Second Life, which allows users to build their own dream world. In the work, Cao took the name 'China Tracy' for her avatar. Writing in 2007, the artist said:

In RMB City, we will be able to cruise the digital ocean, witnessing a Ferris wheel rotating on top of the Monument to the People's Heroes; looking down from the sky on the water of the Three Gorges reservoir gushing out of the Tiananmen rostrum ... walking across a vast, desolate state-owned factory area in Northeast China; and finally hovering over the Grand National Theatre in Beijing. Also in our view will be gigantic planes gliding over terraces in the crevices of the central business district, and aerial super-malls. We will see water flowing into huge toilets on the container piers of the Pearl River Delta area before traveling through the sewage system into an ocean with floating statues of Mao Zedong. The rusted steel structure of the Olympic Stadium aka 'Bird's Nest' will be washed in splashes of ocean spray, while an aerial band on a floating sheet of the national flag filled with five-pointed stars makes a deafening noise that shakes Rem Koolhaas' CCTV building, causing it to collapse...[14]

Author and academic Chris Berry discusses Cao's work through the prism of Foucault's effort to make a clear distinction between utopia as a space which is 'fundamentally unreal' and heterotopia which *does* exist but is somehow apart from the real world. *RMB City* becomes a mirror heterotopia of rapidly urbanized and highly industrialized China, when the artist 'opens up an *alternative* rather than *oppositional* space for thinking, feeling, and doing that is parallel to the world of Chinese culture and society beyond the artwork itself'.[15]

Back in reality, the idea of urban power can be further expanded. In February 1950, almost immediately after the founding of the People's Republic, Zhao Zhao's grandfather was sent to Shihezi in the province of Xinjiang, which in Chinese means literally, 'new frontier'. In June that same year, Xinjiang Production and Construction Corps was established to garrison the border region. The Uyghur Autonomous Region was declared on 1 October 1955, replacing the former province of Xinjiang, when the Uyghur ethnic category was officially recognized. As part of the Corps, the Zhao family was stationed in the region to open up the wasteland in northwest China, which had previously had little connection to the outside world. Zhao Zhao was born in 1982 and grew up in the Corps.

Having been based in Beijing for many years, in 2015 Zhao Zhao decided to make an ambitious project in connection with Xinjiang, which he considered to be both a homeland and a borderland. The Taklamakan Desert lies between the Kunlun and Tianshan Mountains in Xinjiang, forming the greater part of the Tarim Basin. With its epic proportions and intimidating size, almost the same as Germany, 'Taklamakan' means – in the local Uyghur language – 'place of no return'; it is also widely known as 'the sea of death'. However, like Everest or the moon, it has become a focal point of challenge, and this applied to Zhao Zhao too. For him, the project aimed 'not to explore a future in

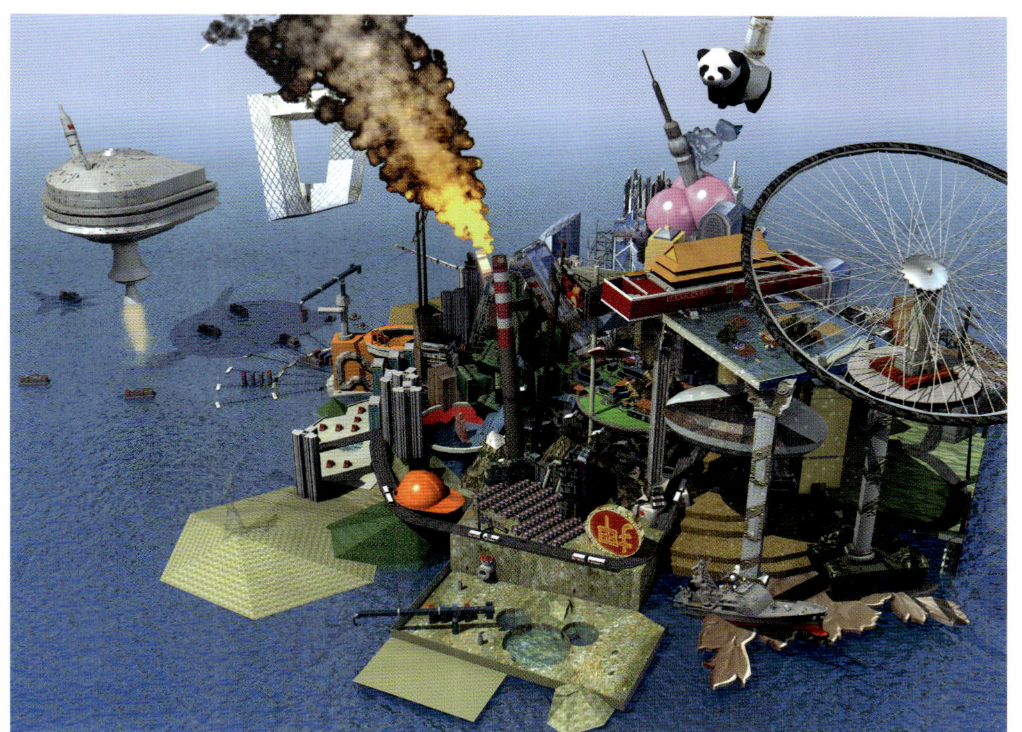

112 Cao Fei (SL avatar: China Tracy), *RMB City: A Second Life City Planning*, 2007 (video still)

any scientifically significant terms, but to discuss a future of our daily existence'.[16] Together with a team of 27 people, Zhao Zhao drove from Beijing to the desert, carrying a 100-kilometre-long (60 mile) 4-core cable and a double-door refrigerator. After arrival at the northern part of the Taklamakan, the process of transporting these materials into the desert was not a straightforward one, as a request relating to an art project could easily be apathetically declined. The artist had to play dual roles of contractor and advertising director in order to pass the strict inspection system and to get his team and equipment through. The cable was finally connected to the power from a household in the Uyghur community in Lunnan, then trailed out towards the centre of the desert. It took 23 days to install the project, which also ended up involving ten transformers to minimize any losses in power transmission. At the end of their journey – a destination in the middle of this vast and uninhabited land – the artist and his team heroically erected the refrigerator, full of Sinkian Beer (the local beer in Xinjiang), to operate for the following 24 hours. When night fell, the refrigerator was illuminated, shining like a beacon as soon as the doors were opened, navigating and embracing all desires.

The urban expansion in China seems to be encouraging, in the sense of prosperity and progress being made, but at the same time, it is aggressive. It follows a political agenda. In the Taklamakan Project, Zhao Zhao could easily have chosen to use one or more powerful industrial spotlights, whose full beam would have appeared more abstract and utopian, but a refrigerator was the choice. This is a symbol of the 'daily bread' manufactured by our commercial society. The refrigerator was transformed from being a simple home appliance, a storage unit functioned by electricity, to being a piece of weaponry, commanded by power; indeed, it became an ensign of the expansive force of urban life with its cultural and political agenda.

Wang Yuyang also uses everyday urban materials to extend his re-imagination of the natural world. In 2007, he made an *Artificial Moon*, which consisted of 10,000 energy-saving light bulbs arrayed in a 4-metre-diameter (13 ft) sphere. It became, as curator and academic Zhang Ga has described, 'an artefact of formidable brilliance, reacting and penetrating, that entertains no meditative serenity, no nostalgia of lost innocence, confers no apologies of nature foregone, and elicits no allegorical signification'.[17] Rather than reflecting light, it is made as the

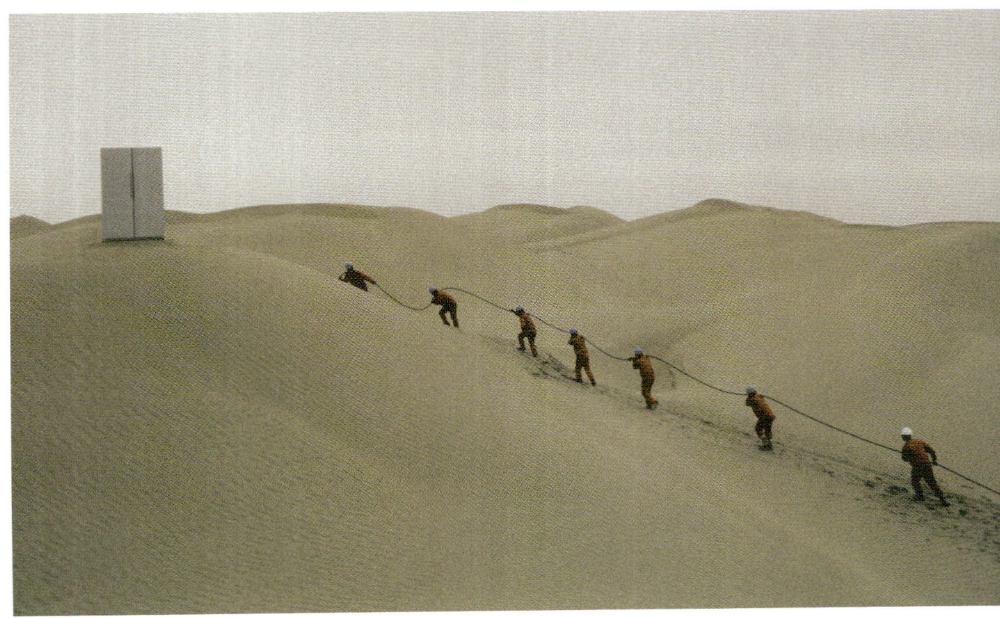

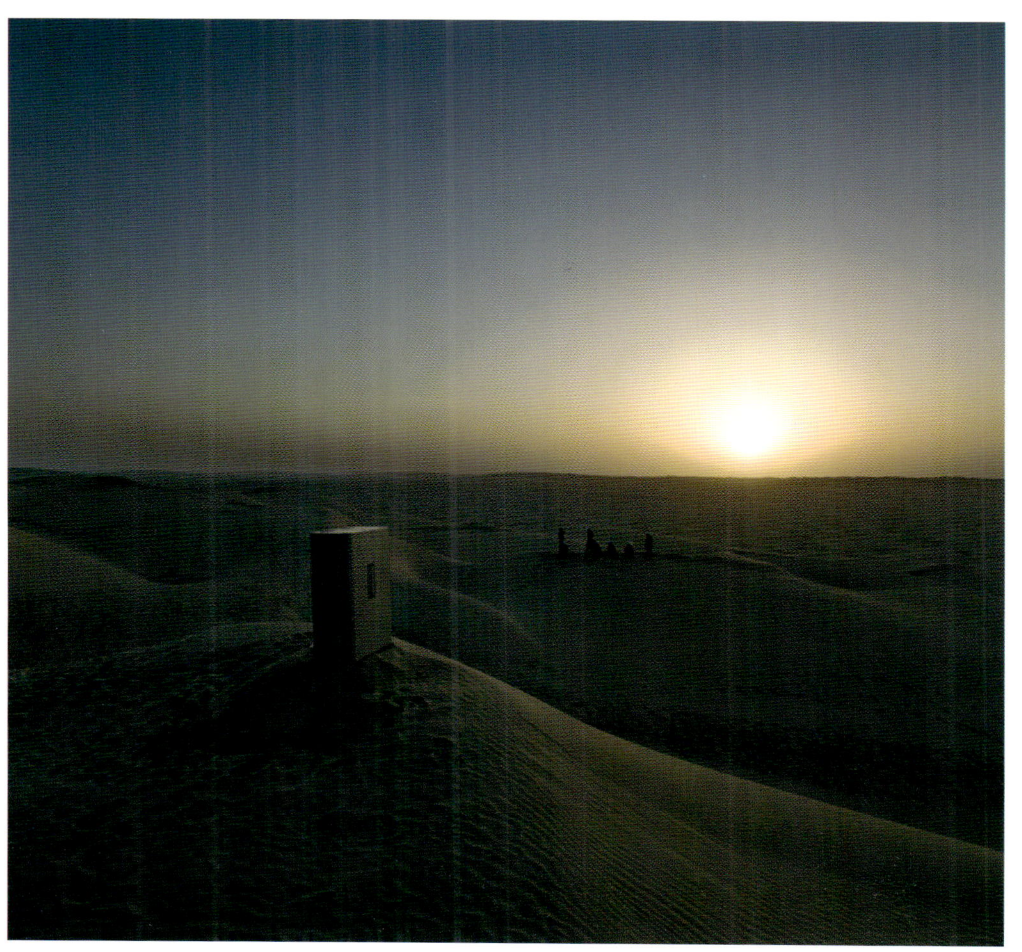

113 OPPOSITE Zhao Zhao, *Project Taklamakan*, 2016 (detail of performance)
114 ABOVE Zhao Zhao, *Project Taklamakan*, 2016 (detail of performance)
115 OVERLEAF Zhao Zhao, *Project Taklamakan*, 2016 (detail of performance)

The Art of Urbanization

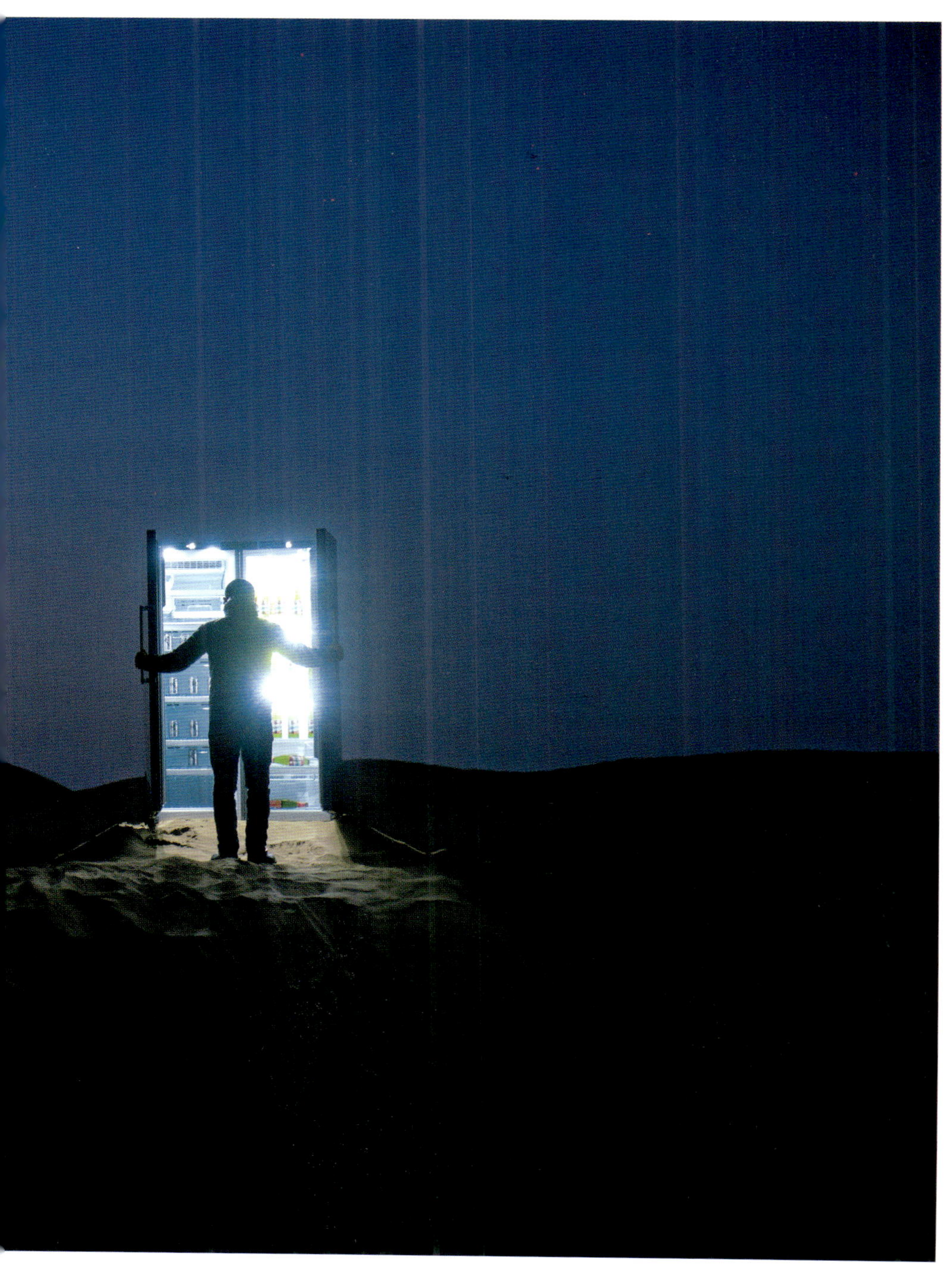

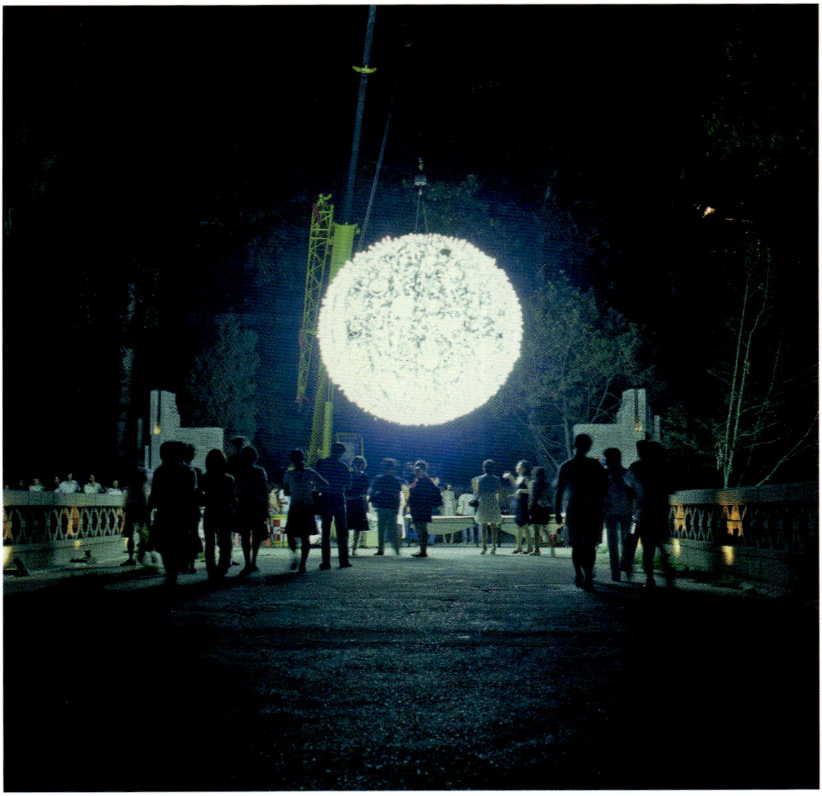

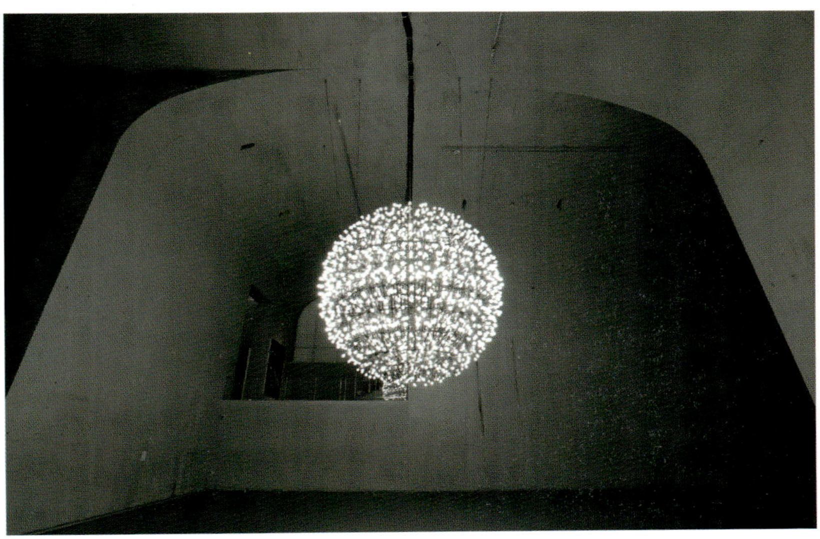

116 TOP Wang Yuyang, *Artificial Moon*, 2007
117 ABOVE Wang Yuyang, *Singularity*, 2015

light source itself; it imitates the natural by utilizing the man-made. It is no longer the peaceful and/or sentimental moon appreciated in Chinese classic literature from the era of the dynasties; instead, it dazzles with electric power to celebrate a poetic narrative of our own time. As a further development, Wang's 2015 installation *Singularity* is also a large bright globe, but this one is animated, revolving in its own time. It consists of dozens of rings placed in a row vertically, from the biggest in the middle narrowing down in size to the top and bottom edges of the sphere. The structure of the circles is formed by metal tubes, each ending in an LED light bulb of varying luminance. The bulbs radiate outwards from the central point and rotate, clockwise or anticlockwise, in a disorderly order, according to a computer-generated programme. If the static *Artificial Moon* can be seen as a reflection on a fictional reality shaped by cities, or a gigantic warning light for the environmental crisis today, then *Singularity* offers a futuristic and illusive vision of urban China.

Coda

Over the past couple of decades, the city of Changsha, in Hunan Province, has been transformed beyond all recognition: the streets, the traffic, the buildings. Right in the city centre sits a four- or five-storey construction, looking like a large market or a microcosm of a multi-layered town of the 1970s or 1980s, with a banner at the entrance that reads, 'Wenheyou Unlimited Company'. This entrance leads to a seemingly endless world of little alleys, residences, retail stores, takeaways, barbershops, games rooms, cinemas, massage parlours and public bathrooms. They are all named after original Changsha shops of the past: for example, the hundred-year-old Sanji Zhai for a traditional bakery, or Dongting Chun for a tea vendor. However, the whole complex is primarily one entity, named the Wenheyou Old Changsha Restaurant, developed to form this mega-mall, one of the so-called *wanghong* ('Internet-famous') restaurants. Various dining units have been discreetly designed between homes and shops, between private areas and public. Some are open-plan, accommodating multiple tables and benches, and some are more exclusive, housed in the reinvented homes of, say, 'Aunty Peng' or 'Uncle Xu', as labelled on their door frames. The room of 'Teacher Zhou' is located on the third floor. It is nothing like a commercial restaurant; instead, it offers a home-dining experience. The 'host' may be absent, but the spice of the food is authentic.

The project was set up by a group of young men, led by the two founders Wen Bin and Weng Donghua. Over several years, while numerous building demolitions and home relocations were taking place as part of the process of urban development, they collected hundreds of thousands of discarded architectural components, items of furniture and everyday objects, which they planned to use to create a complete 'home town'. Every detail – the doors, the windows, the particular green of the walls, the chairs, cabinets, televisions, even the broken cables – was either commissioned or faithfully reproduced using what had disappeared. Street slogans, posters of movie stars and popular songs surround the visitor, reinforcing the immersive experience, while artisans shout out their offerings of local street foods and souvenirs.

Wen Bin and Weng Donghua were both born in the late 1980s and grew up in Changsha – more precisely, in the very area where the current mall stands. They have noted:

Although the housing conditions were poor and the streets were muddy, it was our home, the place where happiness began... This work completely restores everything to when we were children – homes, shops and the community; it invites disappearing craftsmen of the community to produce traditional things and local food, and to restart their businesses for living in an organic and sustainable way... During the last thirty years, China has undergone tremendous changes due to the explosive urban movement, resulting in the same appearance of cities, the same designs, and the same rich people. To find our own way of survival and to return to the origin of our happiness are the sources of our inspiration.[18]

118 Wenheyou Old Changsha Restaurant, 2019

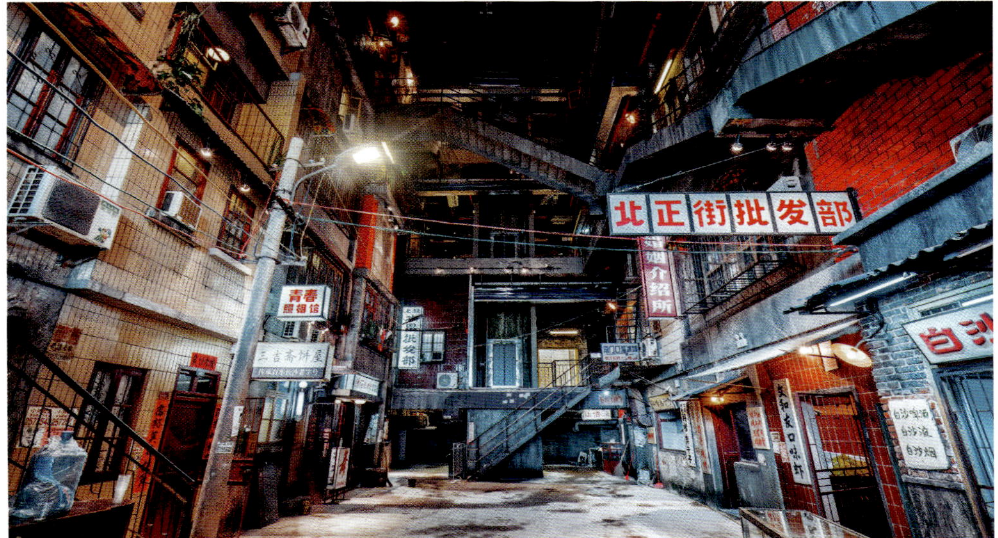

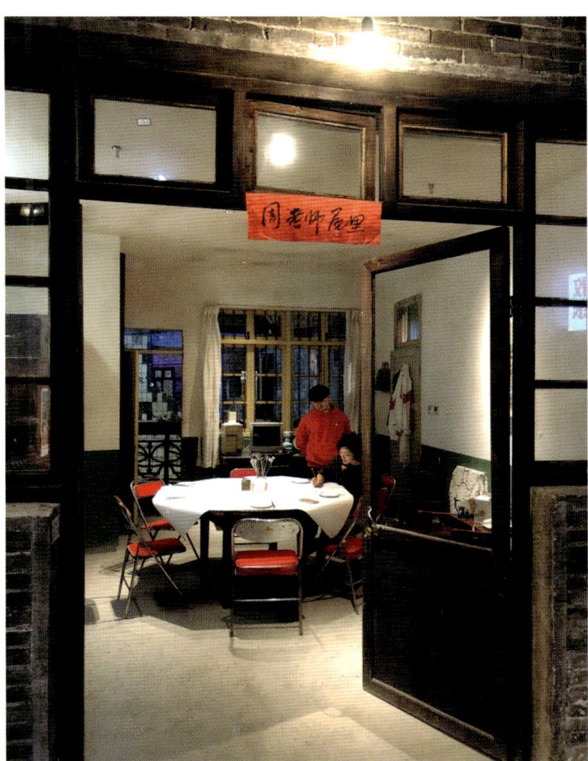

119 'Teacher Zhou' room, Wenheyou Old Changsha Restaurant, 2019

Rejecting the idea of creating yet another restaurant in an identikit shopping mall, in the familiar globalized style of urban development today, the team developed the strategy of achieving an alternative. Rather than building something glossy and luxurious, with modern glass curtain walls, fancy lighting and delicate tableware, they decided to create something that looked unpretentious and worn. They were not pursuing the new, but rather the old.

Today, memory as a subject has become increasingly important in urban studies worldwide. As the art historian Mark Crinson has commented: 'The past is everywhere and it is nowhere. We seem at times overwhelmed by the oceanic feeling of a limitless archive, of which the city is the most physical example and the "memory" of our computers is the most ethereal yet the most trusted, and at others afflicted by a fear that the material traces of the past might be swept away, taking memory with them.'[19] Given the rapidity of the urban changes, the physical experience of being in today's

China is singular, filled with both excitement and anxiety. We are unsure if there is a place to store our memories in these contemporary cities, in which histories have been destroyed, and both traditions and futures are being reinvented. A project like Wenheyou could only be successful in China, where the past can disappear so quickly – within a few decades, or even just a few years – but when people who have experienced that past are still alive. The project revives a specific and immediate past, rather than a distant, ancestral past. A tourist village built in the Qing or Ming dynasty style, with its tell-tale artificial arches, as in the 'Chinatowns' of the West, can only conjure up curiosity and imagination of the unexperienced. Instead, this project was built for those who had grown up locally, who can now pay a visit to their own past; returning home, like lost children. In a sense, however, Wenheyou is not a past, but rather an interrupted present – as if a tape player had simply been paused, then re-started for the song to continue. While everything else has carried on without cease, here there seems to have been a lag. And yet, it requires no imagination; instead, it has its own intrinsic power and capacity to re-accommodate the original community, its culture and social relations, even amid the evolving urban life of today. Each detail – the visuals, the sounds, the smells – is designed not to recall any memories but to reiterate that this is *now*. The project is anti-memory.

It may be possible to glimpse – through an unintentionally opened fire exit door – the brand-new world of the next-door plaza, full of up-to-date fashions and dazzling objects. While customers in the plaza keep shopping for a tomorrow, as usual, on the other side of the partition wall many are dining, communicating and travelling in today's yesterday of some thirty years ago, as usual. That fire exit door will have failed to keep the 'past' and the 'future' separate. It should be kept closed at all times.

Chapter 4
Art At Large

Contemporary art has perpetually been defined and redefined through both artistic and curatorial practices, and through the ways in which it is produced, disseminated and perceived. In the West, artists and curators show art that is inside, outside and completely away from the gallery setting, while formats may vary from conventional white-cube shows to screenings, programmed discussions and publications, and to performance events and activist projects; sometimes, they put into question the label of 'exhibition' altogether.[1] In China, the situation has an even more disparate sense of momentum. The term 'at large' used here is derived particularly from its political, cultural and linguistic contexts; it is employed to have these multiple connotations in order to facilitate the discussions that follow. The Chinese phrase *xiaoyao fawai* is perhaps the closest translation of 'at large'; it literally means 'being unfettered leisurely outside restriction or sanction of the law'. The first indication of the term 'at large' is a state of being unrestrained and unruly, and it leads us to revisit the rebellious mood of contemporary art practice after Maoist China and works that challenge the authorities. Secondly, it identifies the position of being *outside* of rules and regulations, and being *off-site* in regard to legitimized, hierarchical and conventional institutions. Thirdly, it suggests the turn from an 'exhibition' to an 'event' or 'incident' (*shijian*), which may again take place beyond museum walls, and spark wider debates in society. Through these three approaches, art thrives 'at large'.

The rebels of China were trained through the Cultural Revolution, which has been seen as a watershed – the defining period of the half-century of communist rule in China. Studies on the Cultural Revolution offer more than passing historical insight; they are essential for a deep understanding of China today.[2] The Cultural Revolution was pioneered by the radical actions of the Red Guards, perhaps one of the most infamous organizations in history. The term 'Red Guard' (*Hong weibing*) first appeared as the signature to big-character protest posters made by students at Tsinghua University Middle School in Beijing on 2 June 1966. Other middle-school students in Beijing followed and began to establish their own autonomous groups, which organized to achieve collective strength in preparation for stepping onto the political stage. On 24 June that year, the Qinghua University Middle School Red Guards declared their belief through a big-character poster entitled 'Long Live the Rebellious Spirit of the Proletarian Revolution'. The text read:

Revolution is rebellion, and rebellion is the soul of Mao Zedong's thought. We must pay special attention to 'applying ourselves', that is to say, we must pay special attention to 'rebelling' (zaofan). To dare to think, to dare to speak, to dare to act, to dare to break through, and to dare to revolt, is, in a word, to dare to zaofan. This is the most precious quality of a proletarian revolutionary, and the fundamental principle of proletarian Party spirit![3]

The theories of *zaofan* were followed up and emphasized by another two big-character posters, which appeared in July and were warmly supported by Mao in his return letter to the Red Guards. With such an endorsement – or, indeed, 'according to the highest directive' – the disorder spread nationwide. At the same time, the spirit of rebellion was propagated through numerous textual and visual works produced to exalt the new idea, such as the renowned woodcut print *Revolution Is No Crime, Rebellion Is Justified*. *Zaofan* encouraged citizens to become the guards of red power, and led them 'to criticize the whole old world, its old ideas, old culture, old customs and old habits … to destroy the old world and to establish a new world'.[4] In August 1966, the Red Guards in Beijing went onto the streets and put their rebellion into action. They distributed their fliers, slogans and big-character posters, delivered speeches, and began to devastate the 'Four Olds' (*sijiu*; old ideas, culture, customs and habits) across the historic city. Streets, squares, workplaces and homes became the sites of struggles.

This rebellious spirit was of course exemplified also in the generation of artists who were born in the 1940s, 1950s and even early 1960s, and who participated in the movement as Red Guards themselves or, for the younger ones, as Little Red Guards (*Hong xiaobing*). The movement was inspirational for contemporary art practice in China, and has proved to be fundamental for its acclaimed appearance on the international stage since the early 1990s.

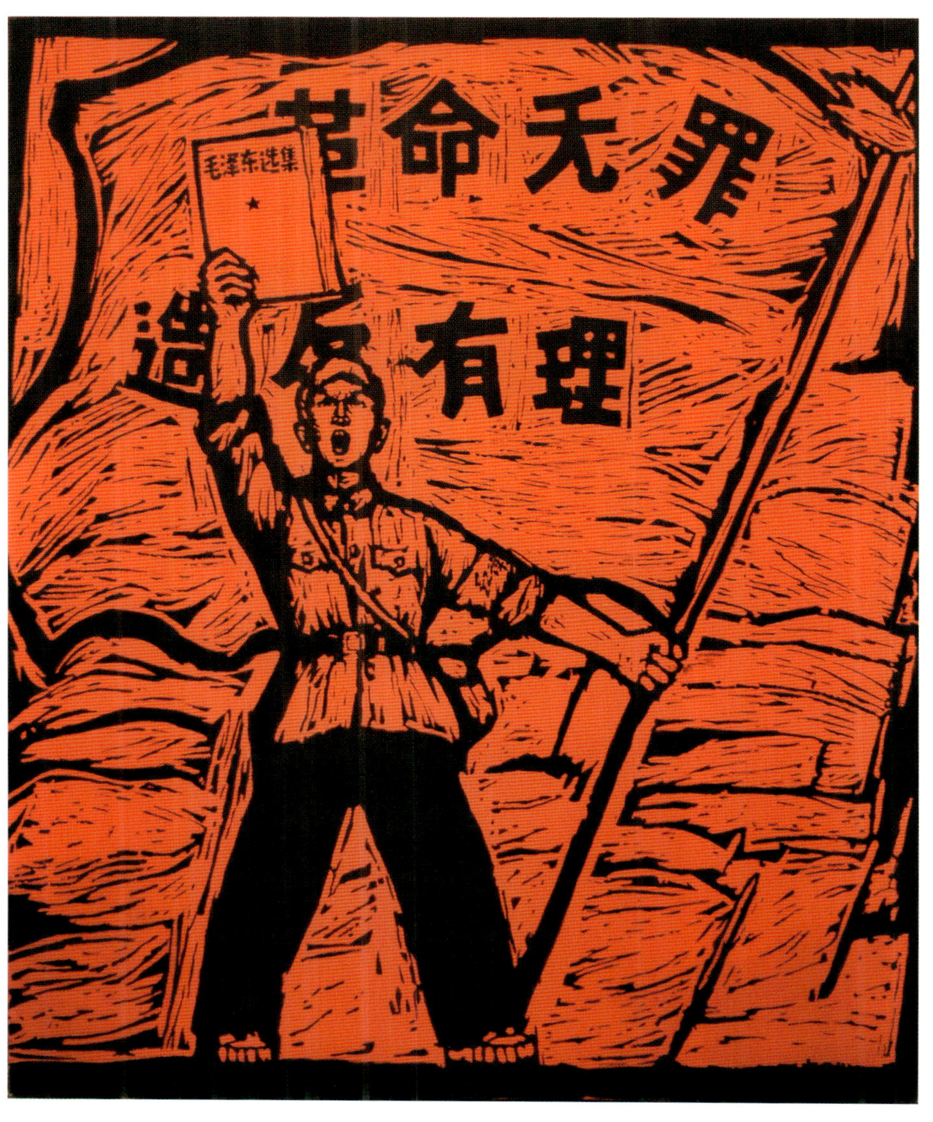

120 Li Bin, *Revolution Is No Crime, Rebellion Is Justified*, 1966

The Rebel

The artistic approaches of the rebels were developed against political authority, cultural power and religious institutions. Nothing could be more obviously rebellious than making irreverent art using the image of Mao, which had been an absolute taboo for many years in China following the Cultural Revolution. Mao's personal cult was fostered after he took charge of the Chinese Communist Party in the 1930s and reached its climax during the Cultural Revolution, in which Mao was praised as the 'Four Greats' (*sige weida*) – namely, the Great Teacher, the Great Leader, the Great Commander and the Great Helmsman – and, above all, metaphorically, as the Red Sun. The man was fabricated as a 'god' for the entire nation. It is estimated that during the Cultural Revolution 2.2 billion of the so-called 'standard portraits' (*biaozhun xiang*)[5] of the Chairman were produced and more than 2.8 billion Mao badges, or four for every man, woman and child in the nation.[6] The image of Mao permeated across the country through all possible forms of visual production and means of dissemination, from a miniature personal belonging to a gigantic public wall. These visual representations appeared as Mao's substitute in both private and public spaces, ubiquitous in everyday life, and providing people with instant and direct access to the Chairman and their belief in the revolution. These images were sacred.[7]

We have discussed in Chapter 1 a number of artworks, including Wang Guangyi's 1988 painting, in which artists manipulated Mao's image. However, if these were produced more than a decade after the end of the Cultural Revolution in order to revisit and examine the cultural and political understandings of the era, then a critical work on Mao produced immediately after his political regime must have been an extreme act of rebellion for the artist. The wood sculpture *Idol*, created by the self-taught artist Wang Keping in 1978, was seen as an extremely daring work 'violating' the divine image of Mao and challenging the autocracy of the state. The work was a hybrid. The subject of the sculpted head remained unclear, but it was evidently intended to be worshipped, as indicated by the title. Some viewers might have said it depicted a Buddha, while others would have immediately identified the pentagram carved above its forehead, evoking a particular significance in Maoist China as reminiscent of the 'red star'. The hybridity presented by such a Maoist Buddha or Buddhist Mao suggests a marriage between so-called 'feudal superstition', which was condemned in the communist ideological context, and, ironically, communism itself; at the

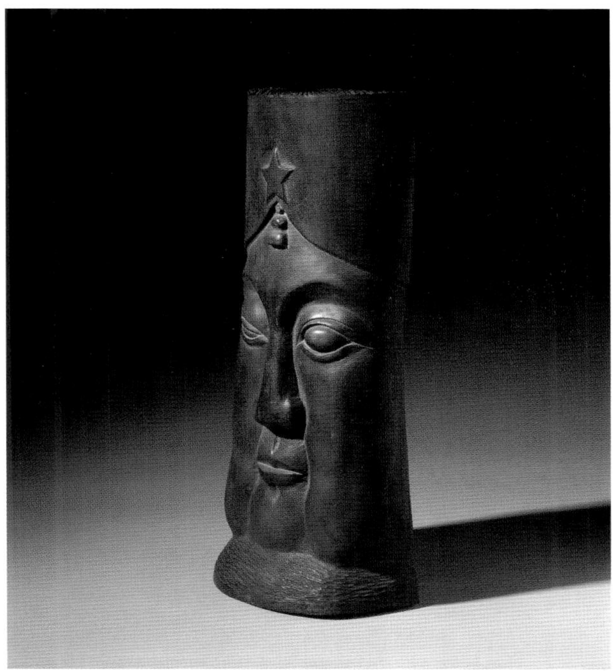

121 Wang Keping,
Idol, 1978

same time, such an absurdity reveals a commonality of their religious nature. As Wang Keping reflected: 'I do sculpture in wood for no other reason than to express my pent-up feelings. I was a Red Guard at the beginning of the Cultural Revolution. All those countless "acts of rebellion" were manipulated by a bunch of conspirators who turned a vast amount of human energy to their own advantage.'[8] It is again important to note that the sculpture was made in late 1970s China, only two years after Mao's death, and to recognize the level of the radicalness of the work and the courage required to make it, in relation to what such a rebellious statement might entail.

122 Political power can also be perceived in a literary format. Jin Feng's *Chinese Plates* present a number of direct citations from the Constitution of the People's Republic of China – 31 articles in total, relating to the rights of 'the people': for example, 'the citizens of the People's Republic of China enjoy freedom of speech, of the press, of assembly, of association, of procession and of demonstration' (article 35), and 'freedom of religious belief' (article 36). Jin's 'plates' are made in the form of slim vertical signboards, normally used for government offices, courts, presses and schools. Each Chinese character has

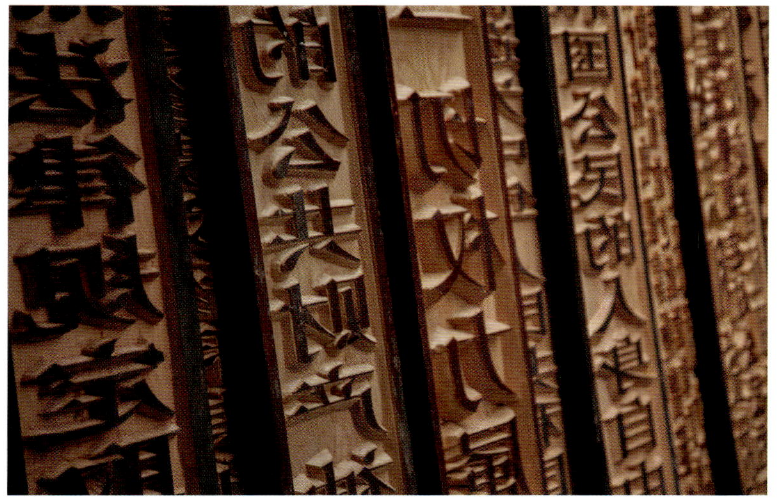

been meticulously hand-carved in the identifiable font for official signboards, demonstrating the power of authority. Here, however, all the characters have been inverted, turning the objects into traditional woodcut plates ready for printing. The wooden panels used in the work are original altar table-tops, collected from individual traditional households. Rather than displaying offerings to gods and ancestors, in the tradition of folk religions, they have been re-crafted to exhibit laws, or beliefs in social justice. And yet, because of their reversal, the words are not immediately legible; indeed, they can be read as 'counter-laws'. The plates now appear merely as attractive objects, with a particular visual quality developed by the craftsmanship. Without being printed to become actual meaningful text, the engraved literature remains ornamental and symbolic, or, in other words, suspended – not to be conducted in practice. In another work, Jin Feng employed police batons – in his view, a symbol of state power, particularly, when used in debatable incidents around the country, such as the eviction of the so-called 'low-end population' from Beijing in 2017. The term, which aroused immediate controversy, refers to workers from rural areas who have migrated to the mega-cities to earn a living. In Jin's series *Aesthetics of Violence No. 1*, family members of migrant workers who remain in the countryside were invited to assist in the production of the work, which involved the deconstruction of 800 police batons. Wives, mothers and daughters of this group of the 'low-end population' worked on the project by peeling

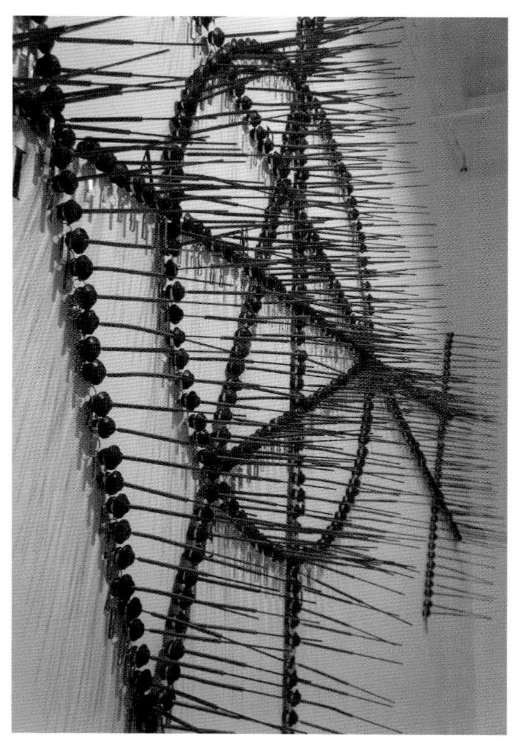

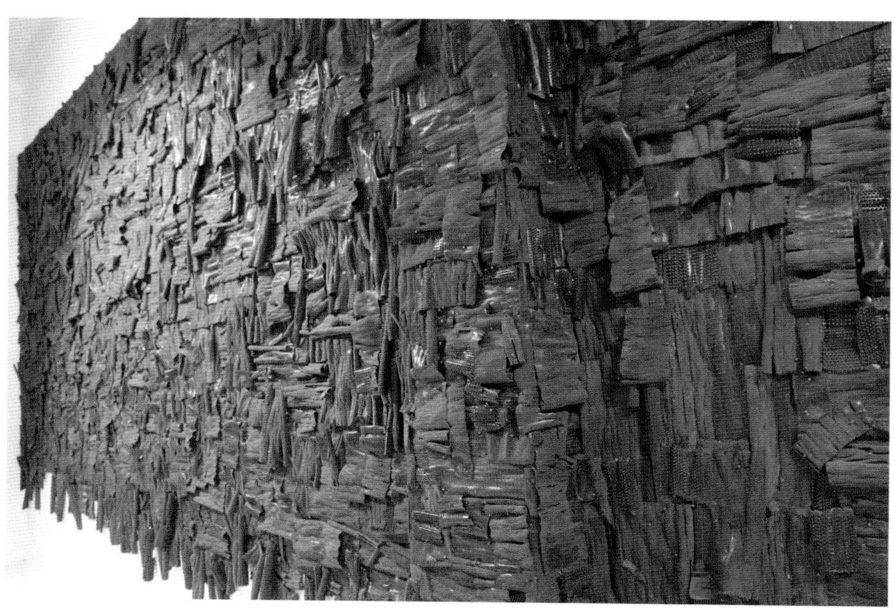

the outer rubber, layer by layer, away from every single spring steel in the core. When the black rubber sheets and steel rods were separated out to form geometric shapes – or, in the artist's words, 'aestheticized, and ritualized'[9] – the original function of the police batons was invalidated.

Ai Weiwei's *Study of Perspective* has been produced as an ongoing photographic series for many years. Throughout the series, viewers see the artist's left hand, with the middle finger raised at cultural landmarks and monuments, such as the Eiffel Tower in Paris, as well as the world's most powerful political centres, including the White House in Washington, DC, the Reichstag in Berlin, the Red Square in Moscow and the Tiananmen Tower in Beijing. As Ai Weiwei discusses:

I grew up in a society where self-criticism was highly valued. Chairman Mao taught us that we should simultaneously conduct criticism and self-criticism, and therefore, I hold my critical view to look upon things around me at all times. Perhaps it is a very simple attitude, but it is my attitude as always, towards for example a cultural organization or a government; an individual or a power system. It could be absurd, insignificant, but it is presented as my personal standpoint.[10]

Neither the consistent middle finger of the artist, nor the changing background of the significant subjects from around the world, should be seen as the focal point of the image. Instead, it is the relationship between them; the tension created by the offensive gesture of an individual, a rebellious act, against political and cultural institutions.

In the late 1960s, China's public properties and cultural relics were attacked by the rebels, with numerous treasures destroyed. Records indicate that, by the end of the Cultural Revolution in Beijing alone, 4,922 of the 6,843 officially designated 'places of cultural or historical interest' had been demolished, by far the greatest number of them in August and September 1966.[11] During the high tide of iconoclasm, hardly any religious buildings – or their statues, frescoes and books – survived these disastrous months. Crying 'smash, burn, fry and scorch', Red Guards pillaged and destroyed countless Buddhist temples with their hundreds of years of history.

This spirit of criticism and rebellion can be revived to challenge cultural orthodoxy in any direction. In one of his most famous pieces, *Dropping a Han Dynasty Urn*, Ai Weiwei drops a 2,000-year-old ceremonial urn, letting it smash into pieces on the floor. The Han dynasty (206 BCE–220 CE) is widely acknowledged as being a defining period in the

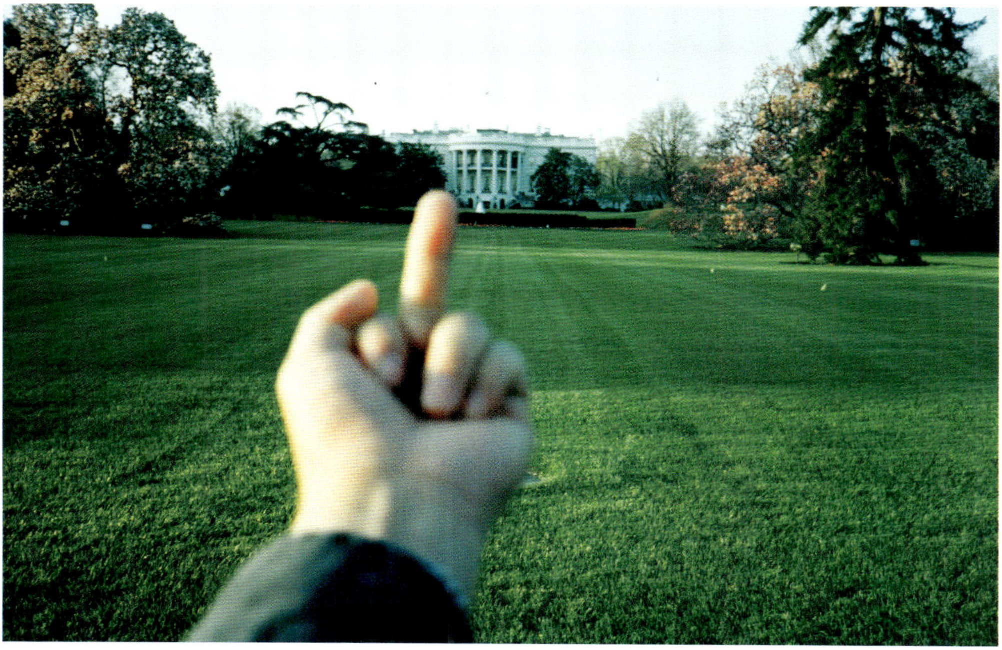

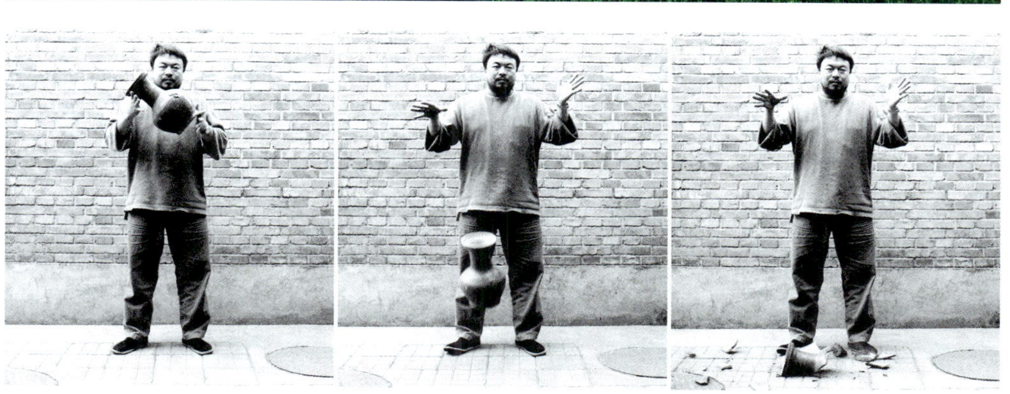

125 TOP Ai Weiwei, *Study of Perspective: The White House*, 1995
126 ABOVE Ai Weiwei, *Dropping a Han Dynasty Urn*, 1995

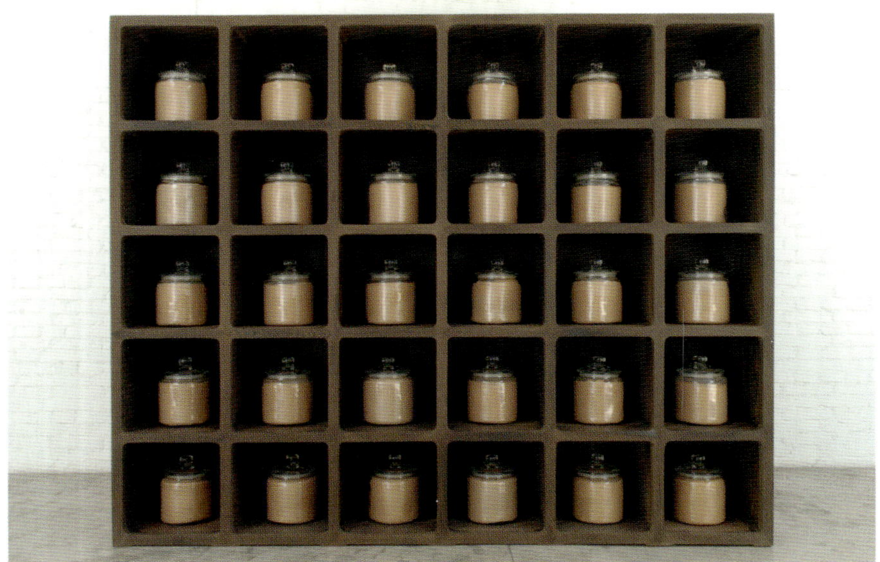

127 Ai Weiwei, *Dust to Dust*, 2008

history of Chinese civilization, and the urn – of considerable value – symbolically represents traditional Chinese culture. To deliberately break such an iconic object – or what Ai Weiwei called a 'cultural readymade' – demonstrates the artist's attitude towards authority; he is clearly performing an act of desecration. The artist's destructive performance, as scholar and writer Birgit Hopfener argues, can be understood 'as not destroying tradition per se, but as destroying a static and essentialist notion of tradition – and related concepts of "Chinese art", Chineseness, respectively – in favour of a temporalized and spatialized concept of tradition as continuous cultural transmission'.[12] *Dust to Dust* is another example of Ai Weiwei's ongoing investigation into the symbolism of cultural despoliation. In this work, thirty glass jars are filled with the powdery fragments of Neolithic pots, which had previously survived for some five thousand years. Hundreds of ancient artefacts as pre-historical relics were destroyed, or transformed through their ruined bodies. In fact, they have been returned to their fundamental materiality – the state from which they were first made purposefully for humankind. The functionality of the original utensils has been demolished, and their shapes are now irretrievably unknown. And yet, they have been reborn, and remain in a different form, beyond their archaeological value.

Natural forces can also be appropriated as a symbol of power. In 2017, when Li Binyuan returned to his home town in Hunan Province, there was a flood across the region. In the video work *Board 100×40*, the artist situates his body standing braced against a powerful and unrelenting cascade of water from a burst roadside dam. He holds a wooden board above his head as a shield against the torrent of water from above. The artist has related that the work is a reference to a childhood recollection of nearly drowning during a similar flood; as such, it is an exploration of bodily memory and a reliving of previous mental trauma and fear.[13] However, when Li confronts the surge of water, being knocked over again and again and being submerged in its flow, it not only reflects the fragility of the human body in the face of a natural force; it also exposes an understanding of the body as a political entity capable of tenacious if futile efforts to heroically exert control over an invincible power. The wooden board – found by chance on a country road – protects the artist from the direct impact of the water, yet, at the same time, it increases resistance to make the performance even more difficult. Although it is a randomly found object, the 1-metre-wide (over 3 ft) board plays a vital role in the performance. It acts as a form of armour or a weapon, a mediator or a provocateur, in the conflict between human body and nature. In another video work, Li Binyuan rebels against the universal laws of gravity when he positions his body completely horizontally, and endeavours to keep his head straight in parallel with the ground. The presentation uses a simple passport photograph format,

128 Li Binyuan, *Board 100×40*, 2017 (video still)

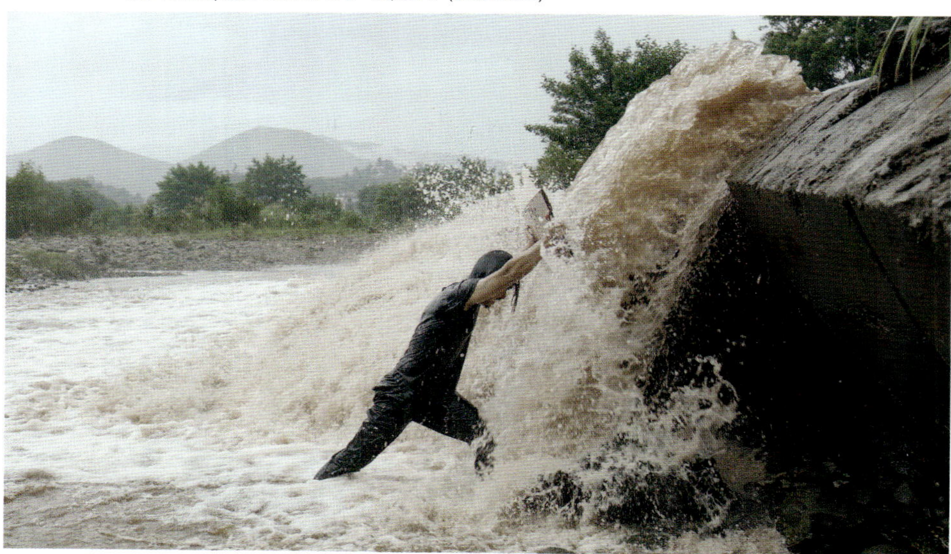

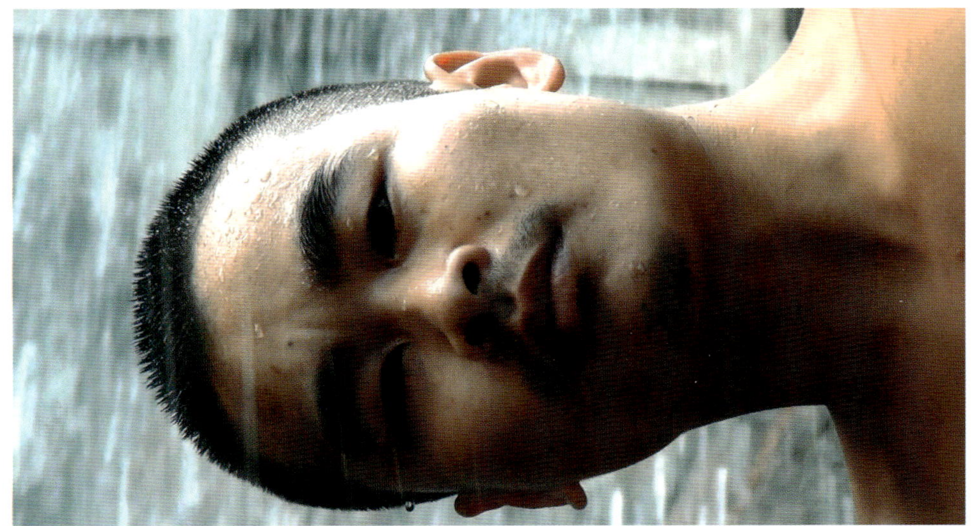

129 Li Binyuan, *Gravity*, 2013 (video still)

but rotated 90 degrees counter-clockwise, the image seeming to be almost completely still, until one detects the slightest tension moving across the artist's face, or realizes that there is a waterfall cascading down from above.

130 The monumental installation work *Freedom* by Sun Yuan and Peng Yu was first exhibited in Beijing in 2009. This gigantic mechanical structure features a rubber hose attached to a water pump and suspended from the ceiling inside a hermetic steel box; the spectator can look through round windows inlaid in metal plates to explore the interior. According to the intermittently timed programme, as soon as the hose shoots hydraulic blasts, it is triggered by the extreme water pressure to thrash around in the space. Bashing against the floor and the walls, or dancing in a frenzied state, it presents a cruelly excruciating – and yet also hysterically funny – spectacle. Curator and artist Josef Ng has observed:

This transferable movement of power, from the generative pump to the 10-meter hose which in turn emits pressure onto the tight stream of water and then finally morphs into unidentifiable shapes, serenaded by a roaring sound... Rust is formed daily on the metal walls by the water vapours ... [and] the random marks and renewed actions etched onto the internal metallic walls and cement floor, analogous to painting on canvas, consequently reveal an emotive density and liberated violence.[14]

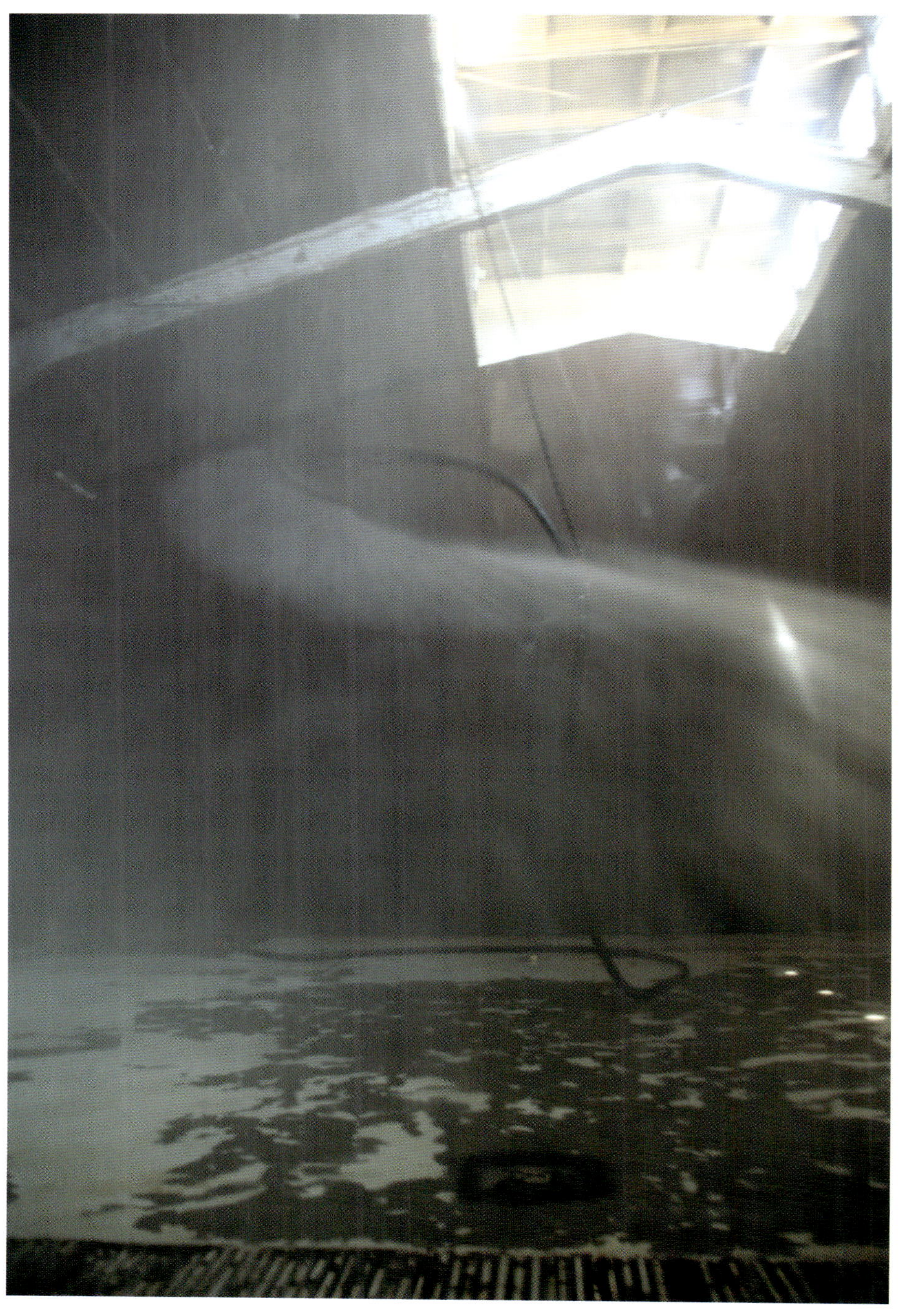

130 Sun Yuan and Peng Yu, *Freedom*, 2009 (installation view)

To the artists, *Freedom* does not necessarily refer to anything specific. 'It's very independent,' notes Sun Yuan, 'unconnected to any reality and unreflective of any cultural phenomena. Yet within the reality in China it is indeed rooted… With a title like that on a work, the audience would feel that this is about China's contemporary reality.'[15] It is, however, still a 'managed' freedom – as long as the neck of the hose is held tightly in the air, and as long as the steel box holds firm. As Sun Yuan further reflects, in China, 'the system is especially strong and the freedom you can imagine is made systematic and formulaic, to be erased under the greatest restrictions'.[16] The work points to a paradox of freedom: the desire for liberation can be expressed and unleashed powerfully, but it only takes shape in a prescribed manner. In other words, it is only within an arena of complete restriction that the rebellious spirit can be fully visualized.

To further extend the discussion on the rebellious spirit in artistic production and execution in China, the following two sections are vital to understanding how art has been developed and positioned beyond institutional confines.

Off-site

The idea of 'off-site' is here developed in relation to the conventional notion of 'exhibition' and its institutional setting. The latter originated in the West, usually as an organized presentation and display of a selection of items in a museum, gallery or other institution that is open to the public. One of the earliest examples was the first Paris Salon, held in the Palais Royal in 1667; by 1699, the exhibition's expansion had prompted a move to the Grande Galerie of the Louvre. This style of 'salon' thus became the public space for art in the modern sense, inviting aesthetic judgments. Soon after, in the eighteenth century, art exhibitions proliferated throughout Europe, perhaps most notably the annual summer show at London's Royal Academy, which was first staged in 1769. From the second half of the nineteenth century, European cities and states began to sponsor large international art exhibitions to build up and secure their identities as cultural centres, including, famously and enduringly, the Venice Biennale, founded in 1895.[17] Since the second half of the twentieth century, and particularly in the last three decades, we have seen biennials and triennials established as instruments of economic and cultural development worldwide, though art has continued to be exhibited mostly in art-museum and gallery spaces.[18]

In China, 'off-site' can be understood as both a cultural and political proposition. First, from a cultural point of view, in the

Chinese tradition of literati art, for instance, artworks were made, shared and appreciated within the format of a scholarly 'elegant gathering' (*yaji*), as mentioned in Chapter 2 (see p. 101). In such a context, artworks were presented to a selective and invited group, not to the general public. The site of *yaji* was not just for displaying and viewing art; more importantly, it was for critique, exchange, connoisseurship, and the actual making of literature, calligraphy and painting. As recorded in many classic paintings, artworks that consisted of visual and textual or calligraphic components were usually examined within a small group of peers, in a way that made viewing a 'social act'; it has even been noted, for example, that, 'as the figure of individual and solitary subjectivity', the horizontal hand scroll is far less commonly seen in these classic paintings, as it represents 'the opposite to the social, collective viewing implied by the [vertical] hanging scroll format'.[19] The *yaji*-style gathering was a site for dissemination and perception in a far more intimate way than at a public exhibition, and, at the same time, it was a site for a kind of modestly competitive art production. These venues were detached from any institutional spaces, and thus were usually private and autonomous, secluded and 'off site'.

Secondly, from a political perspective, 'off-site' immediately relates to the 'unofficial' status of contemporary Chinese art during its early development, regularly labelled as it was with the preceding modifiers 'avant-garde', 'underground' and 'experimental' – something peripheral to the 'mainstream', i.e. officially accepted, art forms. As noted earlier (see p. 8), the *Star Art Exhibitions* have widely been considered to be the starting point of Chinese contemporary art. Significantly, these were born 'off-site'. After being refused permission to exhibit their work inside the main state-run institution, on 27 September 1979 the artists decided to stage the first *Star Art Exhibition* on the iron fence surrounding China's National Art Museum in Beijing, juxtaposed in a timely way with the *National Art Exhibition Celebrating the Thirtieth Anniversary of the Founding of the People's Republic of China*, an official exhibition inside the building. The National Art Museum was built at the end of the 1950s, featuring the architectural styles of traditional Chinese attics, and was opened to the public in 1963. By hanging some 150 paintings, sculptures, drawings and prints outside the museum, the 23 young artists of the Star Group proclaimed their self-identity as 'outsiders' in relation to the official art housed in the China-sanctioned space. Both the artists and the audience could easily see the museum on the other side of the fence. On the one hand, the event demonstrated the institution's refusal to 'legitimize'

131

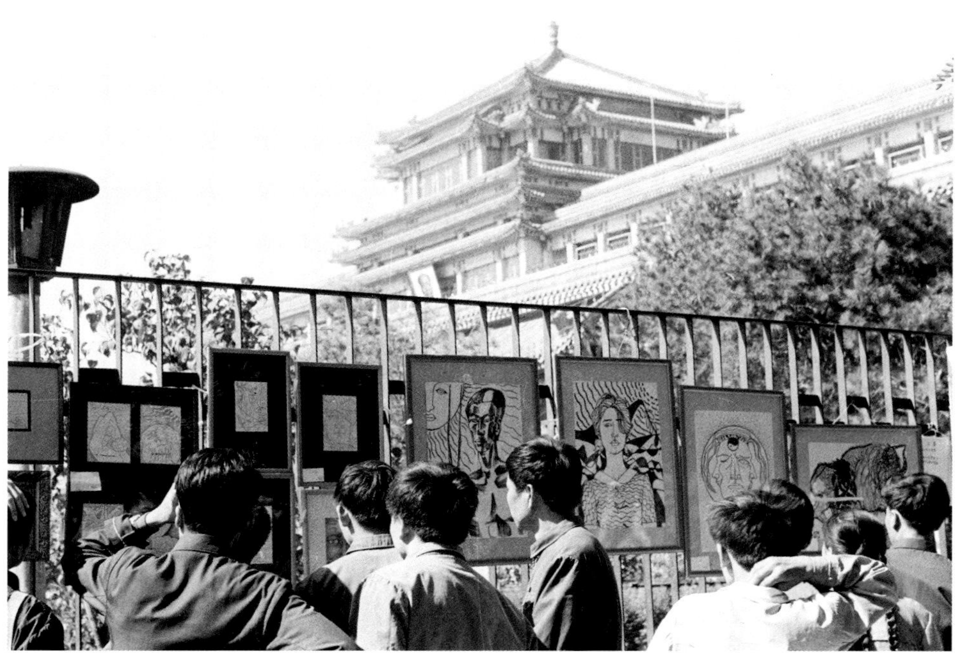

131 *Star Art Exhibition*, Beijing, China, 1979

the Star Group's work; and on the other hand, it brought about the artists' transformation of the exterior into an alternative 'space' for their exhibition. Here, the distance between the main body of the building and the fence was vital to separate and define the 'in' and the 'out', the 'official' and the 'unofficial', and the art space and the everyday; it is apparent and visible. Even so, the police removed the exhibition two days after its opening.[20]

A number of underground exhibitions were staged at 'alternative' spaces or substituted exhibition spaces, such as private residences or public areas. The Garage Show in 1991, for example, was particularly significant in pioneering the showing of new artistic experiments, including Zhang Peili's *Document on Hygiene No. 3* – the first public display of video art in China.[21] Another more provocative example is the exhibition *Fuck Off*, organized by Ai Weiwei and Feng Boyi in a warehouse space, away from the primary site of the 2000 Shanghai Biennale, as a satellite show. The exhibition title in Chinese, *Buhezuo fangshi*, literally translates as 'ways of non-cooperation', thus making the exhibitors' independent position clear. The printed preface reads:

*In today's art, the 'alternative' is playing the role of revising
and criticizing the power discourse and mass convention. In an
uncooperative and uncompromising way, it self-consciously resists
the threat of assimilation and vulgarization. A cultural attitude
that takes a stand against power and makes no compromises
with vulgarization is – together with independent, individual
experiences, feelings, and creations – what extends the pursuit
and desire of art for spiritual freedom, an everlasting theme.*[22]

If the *Star Art Exhibition*, as the first representative, was forced
to appear as an 'outsider', then *Fuck Off* took a more determined
position against institutional authority. 'The "historical
significance" of *Fuck Off*', in Wu Hung's view, 'mainly lies in its
assertion of an alternative position, thus keeping this position
vital in contemporary Chinese art'. He continues:

*But it was far from clear, either in this particular exhibition or
in the general practice of … Chinese art [in the 2000s], what the
'alternative' meant beyond self-positioning, attitude, and verbal
expressions; and this is perhaps why no real confrontation between
the biennale and other shows was found in art.*[23]

According to the analysis of Pauline J. Yao, curator, writer
and co-founder of Beijing's Arrow Factory (see p. 173), 'spaces'
for exhibiting contemporary art in China can be categorized as
'conceptual', 'non-institutional' and 'independent/alternative'.
The first two invite discussions on the contrast between
immaterial and physical spaces, while the third designation
'embodies the immaterial and idealistic tendencies of
"conceptual space" and shares the anti-establishment ethos
or stance of "non-institutional" space'.[24] In the context of
Yao's discussion:

*The adjective 'alternative' does not so much define the
unconventional architectural aspects of a space than describe
its attitude and positioning outside the dominant institutions
of art, particularly the commercial art market. Increasingly the
term does not indicate alternative thinking so much as alternative
practices, the latter being frequently lumped together with self-
organization, institutional critique, collectivity, grassroots
initiatives and other ephemeral exhibitionary tactics.*[25]

Rather than taking a position directly against institutional
power, other possibilities and alternatives can be created. For
example, Gao Minglu uses the term 'Apartment Art' (*gongyu
yishu*) to summarize an important phenomenon in Chinese

contemporary art during the last few decades of the twentieth century. Initiated from the amateur avant-garde activities of the 1970s, through some self-organized groups in the second half of the 1980s, to its peak in the 1990s, a number of Chinese artists developed their own private workspace within public residential complexes. As Gao discusses:

[A]partment art, as a mode of existence of underground, experimental, and avant-garde art, shows the distinct social space of contemporary art in China... [It] is one of the most important ways in which avant-garde artists have committed themselves to the creation of critical and radical contemporary artworks... Rather than as an ordinary alternative space for exhibitions, 'apartment' must be thought of as a way of surviving for avant-garde art... The space of Chinese apartment art was both personal and social ... [and] functioned as studio, salon, and exhibition space.[26]

Taking a more proactive approach, in 1997, Song Dong, with support from Guo Shirui, organized an exhibition entitled *Wildlife: An Experimental Art Project Held Outside the Conventional Exhibition Spaces and Devoid of Conventional Exhibition Forms, Commencing Jingzhe Day, 1997, One of the Twenty-Four Divisions in China's Traditional Calendar, Which Marks the Moment in a Year When Animals Wake up from Hibernation and When All Creatures Revive.* The project involved 27 artists, spread across seven locations (Beijing, Shanghai, Guangzhou, Chengdu, Luoyang, Yangjiang and Haikou), and spanned, unusually, over a long period of an entire year, from 5 March 1997, Jingzhe Day, to 5 March 1998. The project was not developed to oppose art-space shows; instead, it sought to find an alternative approach to presenting artistic practices at a time when exhibition opportunities were still fairly limited in China.[27] On the back of the title page in the exhibition catalogue, the organizers stated:

During this period, the artists formed regional groups, within which they engaged in extensive discussion and communication. These sessions helped them formulate individual art projects ... based on each region's unique cultural and natural environment as well as each artist's different background and experience. Each individual project was carried out over an extended period.
The basic characteristics of this activity included: the use of 'non-exhibition spaces' and 'non-exhibition forms'; public presentations of artistic practices; and decentralized art projects across the country. This activity thus represented a new departure in our artistic experimentation.[28]

Clearly, the main purpose of this project was not to reject the idea of exhibitions *per se*, but to extend it, through experimental work produced and displayed outside conventional exhibition spaces. In the words of the artists, when 'art today has become increasingly dependent on art galleries and museums, and exhibitions of various sorts', the *Wildlife* project was developed to break the seemingly established system, and to urge an 'unpremeditated encounter between art and its audience'.[29] In this way, the year-long project resulted in a number of important works in various locations, such as Zhang Huan's *Fishpond*, and works discussed earlier in this book, including Zhuang Hui's *Group Portraits: Luoyang Cadre Police Academy Students and Staff, Henan Province, May 13, 1997*, Lin Yilin's *Sand Dune* and Chen Shaoxiong's *Street* scenes.

From the position of being 'off' not only institutional but also authoritative sites – being 'at large' – art outside the art space has developed its own agenda. Since the 1980s, contemporary art in China has been produced site-specifically in public areas, working locations and residential communities. This is the everyday of a real world, more dynamic and challenging than any white cube. New artistic strategies must be developed to respond to the different sites and their cultural and political connotations, to further push the boundaries of what we understand as art.

Arrow Factory was a special art space at the time when China was seeing a boom in newly established art museums, and when biennials and triennials were becoming one of the most significant phenomena in the globalized art world. Co-founded by Rania Ho, Wang Wei, Pauline J. Yao and Weng Wei, it was a modestly sized space (15 square metres; 160 sq. ft), a former vegetable stand, located in a small *hutong* named Jianchang (literally, Arrow Factory) in the centre of Beijing. With its mission 'to provide an alternative; a different context in which artists can experiment with pushing the relationships that radiate outwards from the levels of the individual, the neighbourhood, the urban, the region, to finally, the global',[30] Arrow Factory realized more than sixty projects following its launch in 2008.[31] Envisaging the constraint of the size of the space in comparison with large art museums, and its location within the local community, artists had to develop different artistic strategies.

Wang Gongxin's 2009 work, *It's Not about the Neighbourhood*, site-specifically developed for Arrow Factory, was easily missed by the audience. The artist created a 1:1 scale replica of the next-door bakery, and made the façades of the two spaces completely identical, positioned directly adjacent to one another. During the day, the work appeared sculptural, or not even 'artistic' at all: the same aluminium door and windows, with a glass storefront, were commonly found in Beijing's *hutong* communities. And yet, at dusk, when the actual bakers retired and the shop closed, the windows in the artwork were illuminated, showing the people next door at work, as if behind the opaque windows, making and selling their bread and noodles, as they usually did during the day. It was, in fact, a back-projected video piece, filmed by the artist. Depending on the hour of the day, the projection turned on and off to change its relationship with the genuine bakery – sometimes as a physical imitation, sometimes as a virtual simulation, and occasionally as both at once.[32] By imitating the appearance of the adjacent shop and replaying the day-time business during night-time hours, the work juxtaposes the genuine and the imitation, the real and the imagined, and alternates states of absence and presence as everyday life in the neighbourhood community goes on by day and by night.

In He An's *Wind Light As a Thief*, a streetlamp grows out from the interior of Arrow Factory, with the large light half-sticking out of the glass door of the space. It is situated neither inside nor outside. For this work, viewers were invited to use a switch placed on the door to turn the light on and off. What they did not know was that the switch operated not only this streetlamp in situ; it also controlled two other lights – another streetlamp in a close-by neighbourhood, and a primary light in a privately owned shop within the community a few hundred metres away. Each of the three lights, in their respective sites, was linked and outfitted with its own switch. The work physically connected three different spaces – the art space, the public and the private: 'using transgressive methods to intertwine these disparate locations, the artist solicits viewers to traverse the divide between public and private spaces and become willing accomplices in a secret game known only to its participants'. This multi-location installation 'plays with states of lightness, darkness and apparitions of the unknown through the seemingly innocuous action of flicking a light switch'.[33]

We have discussed other relevant subjects in previous chapters: for instance, the importance of site-specificity, such as the traffic on the street to Lin Yilin's *Safely Manoeuvring across Linhe Road*, the magnolia tree to Wang Wei's mosaic shadow, the Taklamakan Desert to Zhao Zhao's refrigerator installation, and, of course, Zheng Guogu's Liao Garden to his life-long

132 OPPOSITE TOP Wang Gongxin, *It's Not about the Neighbourhood*, 2009 (installation views)
133 OPPOSITE BELOW He An, *Wind Light As a Thief*, 2011 (installation view)

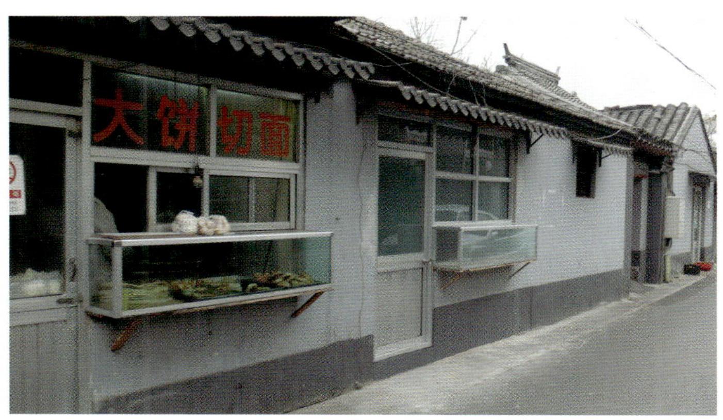

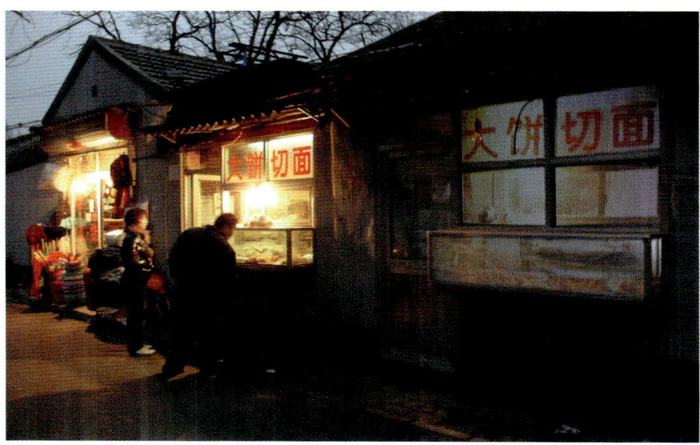

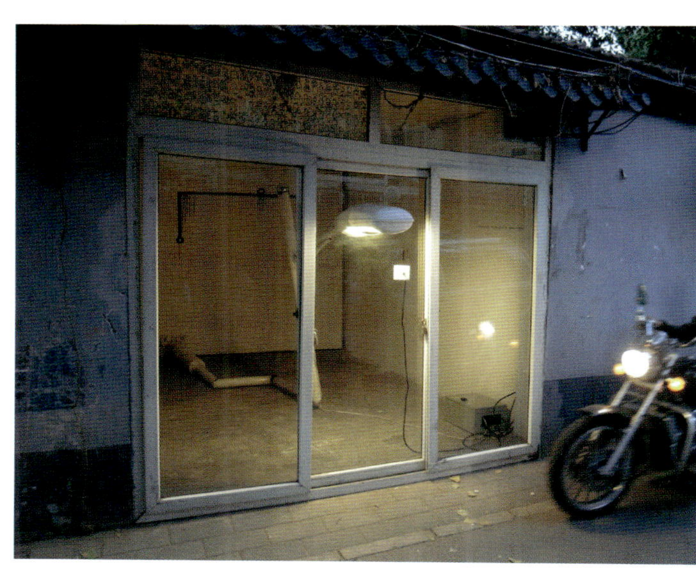

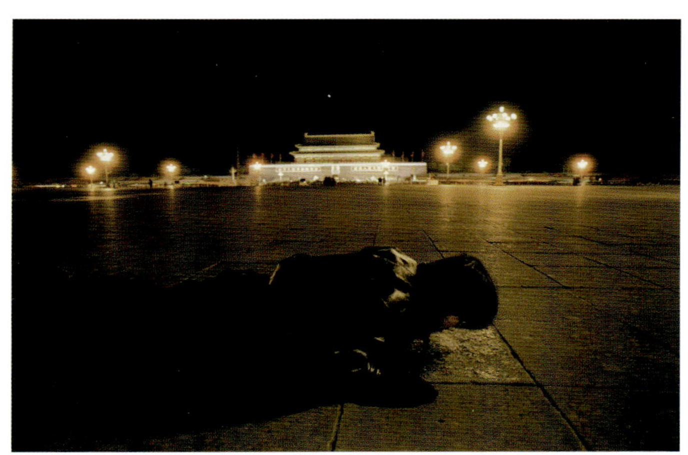

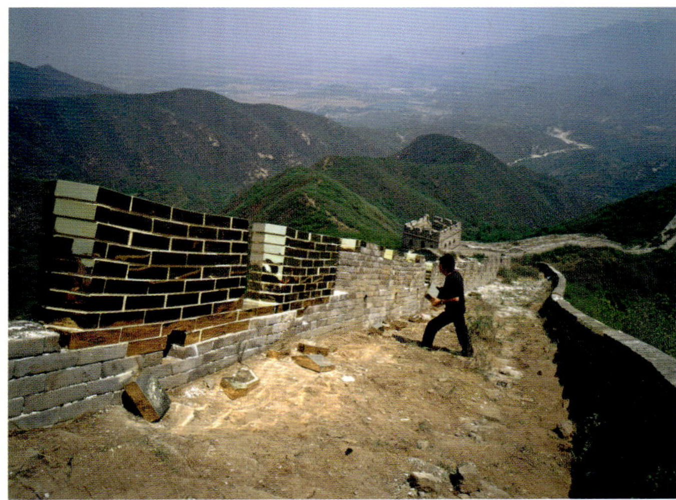

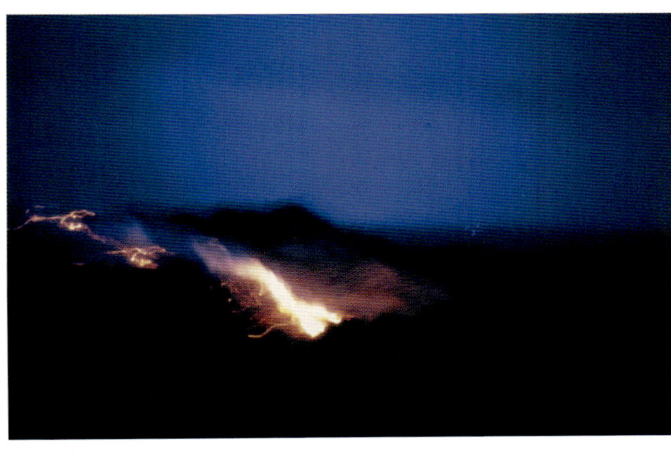

project. Most obviously, some political and cultural landmarks
have become the location of choice for developing 'off-site'
work: for example, Tiananmen, not only as a popular icon
in paintings (for instance, in the works of Wang Jinsong and
Yue Minjun), photographs (Ai Weiwei, Shao Yinong and Jiang
Zhi) and installations (Shen Shaomin and Yang Zhenzhong),
but also as a symbolic site for performance. One night in
January 1996, Song Dong laid his body down prone in the middle
of Tiananmen Square, in severely cold conditions – minus
7 degrees Celsius (19°F). For forty minutes, he kept breathing
onto the freezing concrete ground in order to gradually form
a layer of ice. In comparison with the vast area of the square,
the artist's tremendous effort made minimal impact, either
spatially or temporally. It would disappear soon, leaving no
physical trace. As Wu Hung has noted, the artist's desperate
effort to inject life into that political space was intended to
commemorate the Tiananmen incident in 1989 and the failed
pro-democratic movement. Since then, the artist has continued
to conduct performances in the square and to record these
site-specific works in photographs and videos.[34] The Great Wall
of China, too, lends its unique cultural significance to artistic
discussions. In 2001, Zhan Wang executed his work *Fixing the
Golden Tooth for the Great Wall* in Badaling, one of the most
visited sections of the wall, located to the northwest of Beijing.
Over the centuries, parts of the wall have become weathered,
and some have fallen into ruin. In Zhan's work, the artist fixes
the missing parapets in a section with hundreds of 'golden
bricks'. These are hand-welded, with wafer-thin stainless-steel
sheets replicating the exact dimensions of the original bricks.
The work would lose much of its impact without the cultural
and political significance of the Great Wall. In fact, this is not
a 'restoration', but an 'innovation', in which the brick meets the
gold, the old meets the new, the authentic meets the imitative,
and the cultural meets the pecuniary. Cai Guo-Qiang's 1993
work, *Project to Extend the Great Wall of China by 10,000 Meters:
Project for Extraterrestrials No. 10*, was realized across the barren
ridges of the Gobi Desert, starting at the westernmost end
of the Ming dynasty wall at Jiayuguan in Gansu Province. In
this ambitious pyrotechnic display, the Great Wall, as one of
China's most enduring cultural icons, is central to the piece,

134 OPPOSITE TOP Song Dong, *Breathing*, 1996 (detail of performance)
135 OPPOSITE CENTRE Zhan Wang, *Fixing the Golden Tooth for the Great Wall*, 2001
(detail of performance)
136 OPPOSITE BELOW Cai Guo-Qiang, *Project to Extend the Great Wall of China by
10,000 Meters: Project for Extraterrestrials No. 10*, 1993

revitalized and expanded by the mysterious burning energy. The spectacular nature of the work, as well as the extraordinary feat of its organization through political negotiation and logistical coordination, leads us on to consideration of how the 'off-site' production can turn into the 'event'.

Incidents

Some artworks are only 'true' during the course of the actual happenings. Photographic and video works that have commonly been developed as substituted forms to be exhibited later are essentially 'fake' presentations. The term 'happening' was coined in the 1950s in the West to describe a performance or a situation, often multi-disciplinary, that was to be considered art. In the context of contemporary art in China, the happenings taking place in the public sphere have often become known as 'events', or 'incidents', which, in some cases, owe their existence to the political restraints in China. These incidents happen with or without spectators. Sometimes they can attract a huge crowd of people; and sometimes they are not made to be viewed at all – in fact, they are ultimately 'unseen' – in order to stimulate our curiosity and to allow our imagination and reflection to go beyond any visual documentation.

Arguably, 'incidents' have been seen as milestones marking the early development of Chinese contemporary art. This is most noticeable in the case of the *Star Art Exhibitions* (see p. 8) and, in particular, the public demonstration jointly organized by the Star artists and various literary groups and organizations, including the journals *Today* (*Jintian*) and *Beijing Spring* (*Beijing zhi chun*). In response to the removal of their first *Star Art Exhibition*, the artists held a public demonstration on 1 October 1979, the thirtieth anniversary of the founding of the People's Republic of China. After speeches by the Star artist representatives Ma Desheng and Huang Rui, hundreds of demonstrators marched from Xidan Democracy Wall to the city hall of Beijing Municipal Party Committee, displaying and shouting six slogans led by 'Demand political democracy, demand artistic freedom!'. This was not simply a progression from an art exhibition to an incident; at such a critical turning point for Chinese art, the demonstration can be seen as a fully integrated part of the first *Star Art Exhibition*.

It is generally considered that Xiamen Dada was the most radical and subversive artist group of the '85 Art Movement, with Huang Yong Ping being the key member who led the initiatives of the group. The artists were first brought together by their initial exhibition, *Xiamen Five Men Modern Art Exhibition*, which took place in May 1983, but for 'showing

137

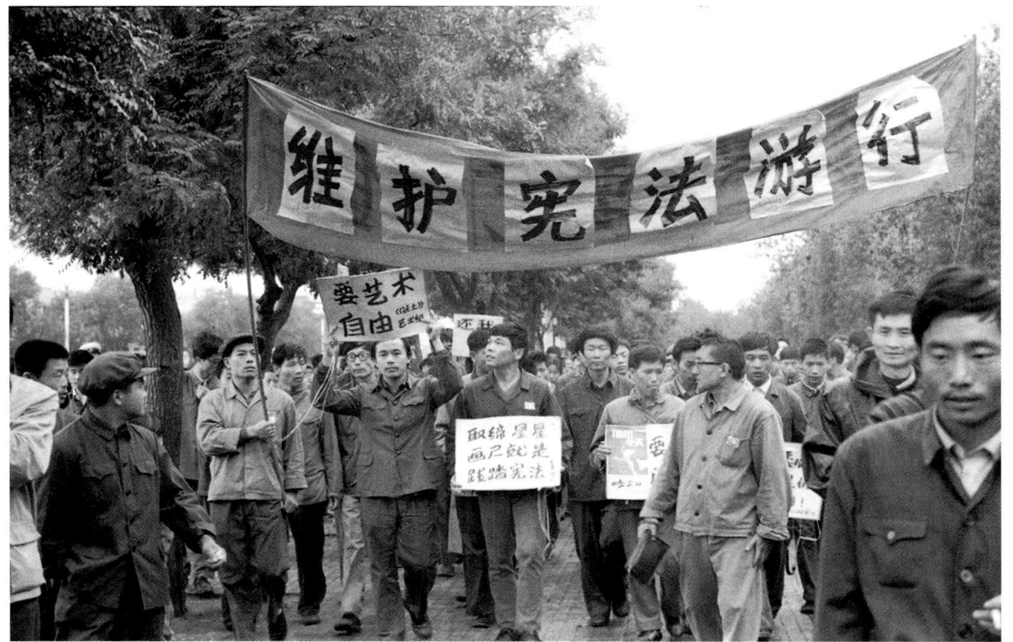

137 Star artists demonstration on 1 October 1979; Wang Keping holds
a raised placard proclaiming 'Demand Artistic Freedom'

internally' (*neibu guanmo*) only. On 28 September 1986, another
exhibition of the group, with an increased number of artists
(fourteen in total), *Xiamen Dada Modern Art Exhibition*, opened
to the public at the Xiamen New Art Gallery. On 20 November
that year, the artists made an extreme decision – to destroy
all the work in the exhibition. A few days later, eight artists
set their work alight on a bonfire in front of the gallery. At the
same time, Huang Yong Ping wrote the following words in
white chalk on the ground, as the statement of the group:

Artworks for the artist are what opium is for men.
Until art is exterminated, life can never be settled in peace.
Dada has died; beware of the fire.

Also in 1986, the group submitted an 'acceptable' proposal to
the Fujian Provincial Art Museum to present an exhibition, but
they did not provide details about the real project they had in
mind. On the day of the exhibition, the artists abandoned the
fake submitted proposal and instead mounted an exhibition
of found materials. They moved items of debris and discarded

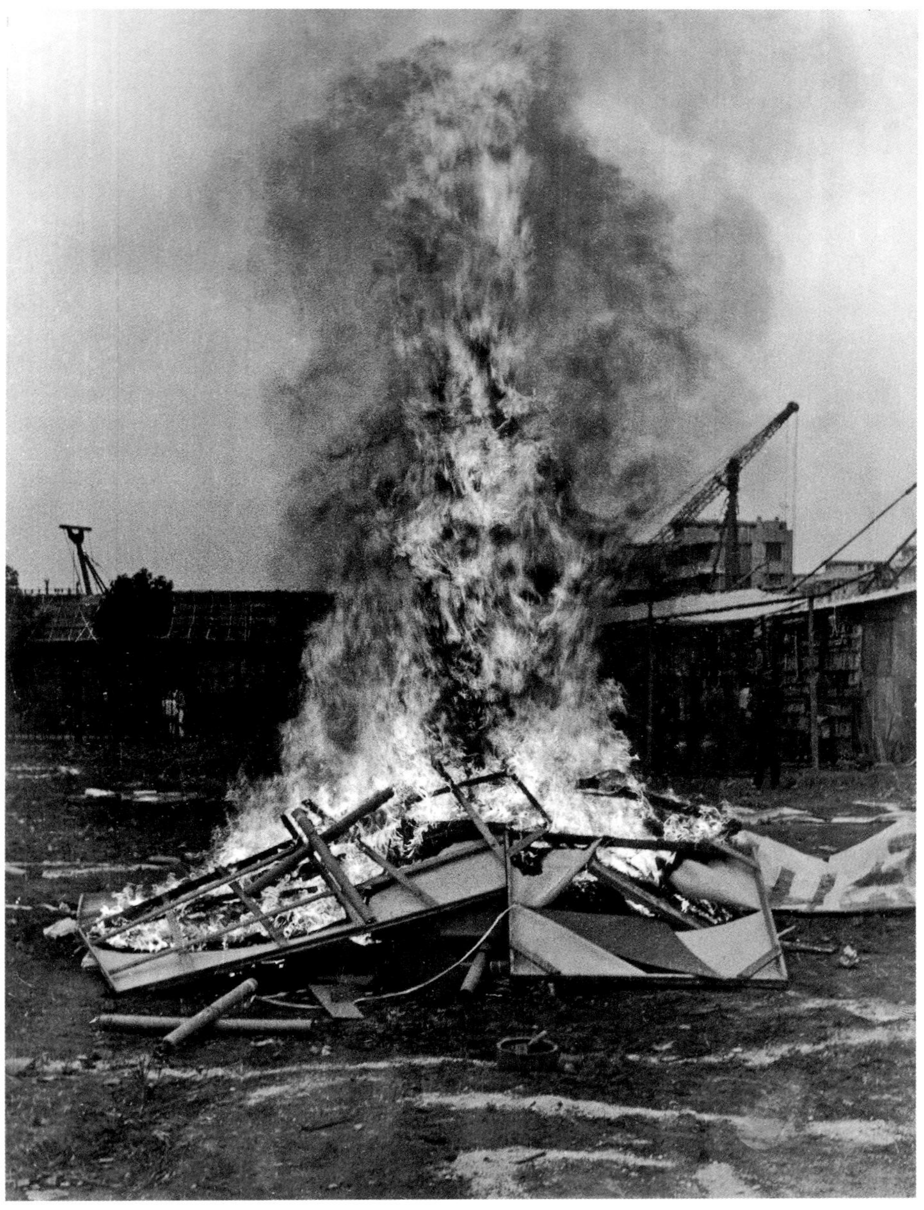

138 ABOVE Burning artworks in front of the Xiamen New Art Gallery, 24 November 1986
139 OPPOSITE Huang Yong Ping, writings on the ground, 24 November 1986

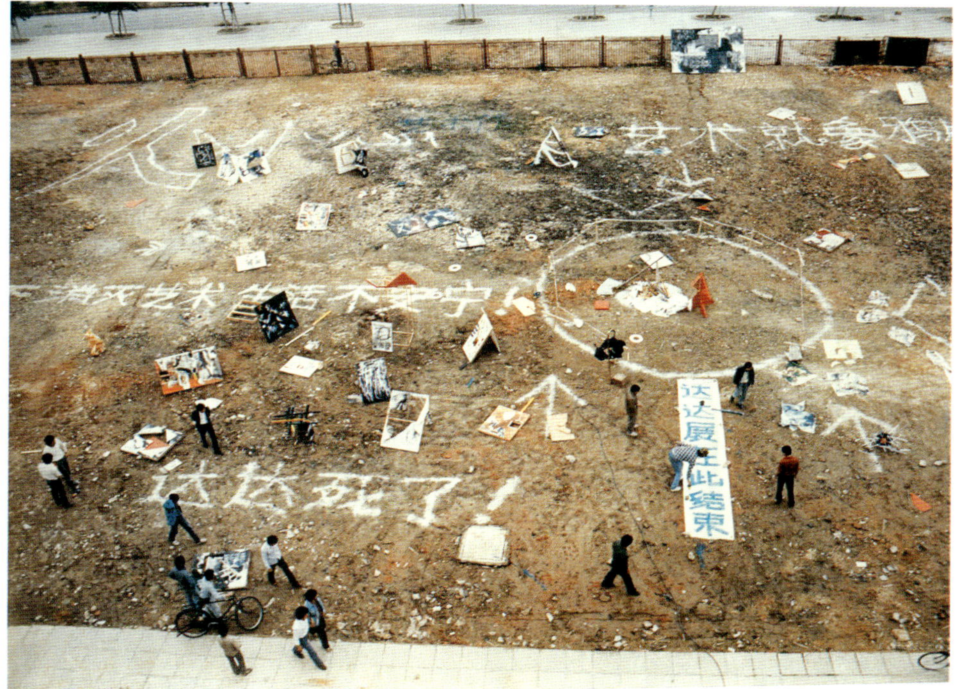

scraps from the museum's surroundings, mostly random items of construction, into the gallery space and presented these as 'art'. The display was up for about two hours before the museum officials realized this was not the original plan and shut down the exhibition.[35] In their printed introduction to the exhibition, the artists asserted:

What is shown here consists of no painting or sculpture; it is an exhibition of an art event characterized by self-definition, offensiveness, and continuity. All works on display must come from the various materials stocked in the open air around the museum. These materials are not used as 'art mediums' to be decorated or constructed from, but are simply displaced to the exhibition hall. Lying on the floor or standing vertically, leaning against walls, or piled up, they are just as they were in the outdoor space. The difference is that these materials are now treated in the same way as works of art found in previous exhibitions – furnished with labels, visited by an audience, supported by art theories, and completed by artists. Moreover, since the entire project takes place in a museum, it can be called an 'art event'. That these materials

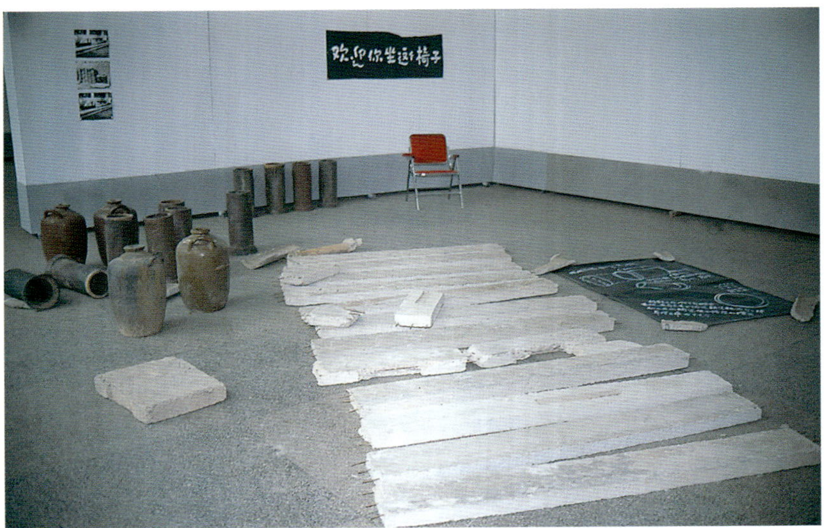

140 Xiamen Dada, an 'exhibition' at the Fujian Provincial Art Museum, 1986

suddenly were rushed into the exhibition hall generates a sense of assault. This assault, however, is not aimed at the visitors, but at their views of 'art'. Similarly, the target of attack is the exhibition hall as a model of the art system, not the exhibition hall itself.[36]

The act of presenting everyday objects in a museum was not new: the Xiamen Dadaists understood the transformative power of the institutional space and the influence of artists such as Marcel Duchamp. However, in the context of China, the way in which the artists broke through the institutional constraints turned an exhibition into something performative, into an 'incident'. There is no individual artwork in the exhibition hall, but the process of installing and de-installing the found materials is the artistic production in itself; and, clearly, the removal of the show by the museum authorities became an indispensable part of the event.

Another famous example in the history of Chinese contemporary art is the gunshot incident by Xiao Lu in 1989. It became one of the most representative works of the *China/Avant-Garde* exhibition at China Art Museum Beijing, curated by Gao Minglu, as a conclusion of the '85 Art New Wave. In the work, titled *Dialogue*, two fabricated telephone booths were installed parallel to one another, with a black-and-white image inside each, representing female and male figures making phone calls. On 5 February 1989, about two hours after the official opening of the exhibition, Xiao Lu fired two shots from a pistol at the reflection of herself in a large mirror placed between the two booths. The exhibition was closed down by the Beijing police for several days, and the artist and her partner, Tang Song, were detained by the authorities. According to various reports, it appears that Xiao Lu did not discuss this performance in advance with the curatorial team. It was completely unexpected, not only for the audience, but also for the critics, theorists and curators of the exhibition. In fact, according to the artist herself, it was not 'meticulously planned', but just happened, as an 'incident'. As she recalls:

I did not necessarily intend to do the gun firing the way I did. I really cannot explain clearly why I did it; it is as if the whole thing was predestined. So many things could have prevented it from happening, but in the end it happened. If I had talked about my plans to anyone on the organizing committee, it probably would never have happened... There were so many coincidences on that day ... so that is how the gun firing came to take place...[37]

The radical essence of a work, then, as well as the specific political context of China, and, in addition, happenstance, are all vital to establishing historical significance in Chinese contemporary art. 'This controversy touched on three issues that would recur in the development of contemporary Chinese art,' according to Wu Hung; namely, 'the nature and purpose

141 Xiao Lu, *Dialogue*, 1989 (installation view)

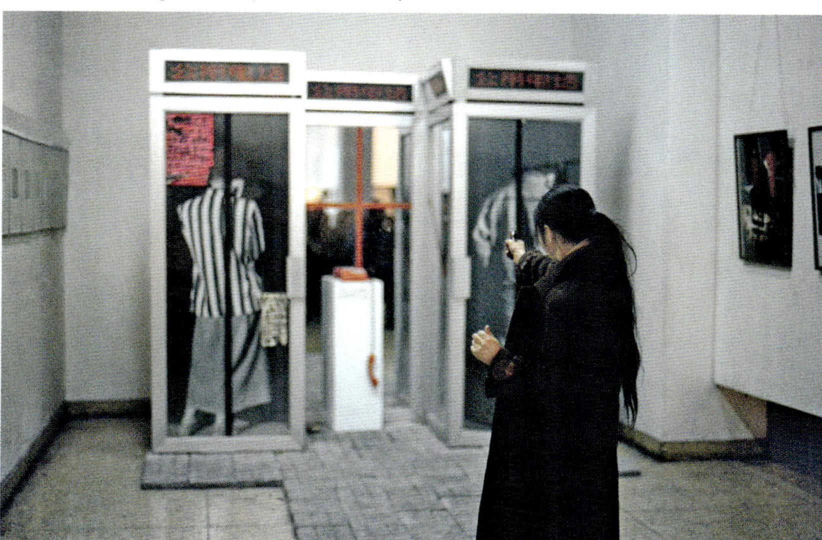

of avant-garde art, the politics of contemporary art exhibitions, and the relationship between artists and art critics'.[38]

In 1996, the Zhengzhou City government commissioned Wang Jin to make a sculptural work to accompany the opening ceremony for the city's major shopping mall. On the public plaza in front of the mall, the artist and his associates built a large ice wall, 32 metres long (105 ft), 2.5 metres high (over 8 ft), and 1 metre thick (over 3 ft). It contained more than 300 objects, including jewelry, cosmetics, toys and mobile phones. Some 100,000 people attended the opening, at which time these attractive consumables became visible inside the blocks of ice. Immediately after the official formalities of the ceremony, the public began to dig the objects out by any means possible, and finally pulled down the entire wall. According to Wang, the significance of the work does not lie in the size of the ice wall, nor in the manpower, resources and scale utilized in its implementation. Instead, 'it is merely an attempt to initiate a new artistic concept through a mode of direct communication with the audience. This prompts the audience's critical participation while also revealing their evaluations of pre-existing experiences and the rules governing their living spaces.'[39] If the above incidents happened, planned or not, and aroused huge public attention and engagement, then some other works seem to be much less viewed in situ, but are still of great political and cultural significance.

Keeping in mind his long-time perception of the restrictive nature of society as a whole, no matter the time or the political system, in relation to individual existence, He Yunchang made a performance piece, *One Metre Democracy*, which also reflects directly the current social environment in China. The artist does not have a big, strong body, but he has nonetheless made incidents with it. In *One Metre Democracy*, without being anaesthetized, he asked a medical surgeon to cut a wound from his clavicle through his chest all the way down to his knee – an incision of 1 metre long (over 3 ft) and 1–1½ centimetres deep (⅜–½ in.). A film documents the violent and painful procedure, during which the artist, lying on a white bed, is surrounded by a group of people as witnesses. He is naked, isolated and vulnerable. The scalpel is ruthless. While it travels across his body, slowly, to ensure the depth of the opening, He Yunchang cannot help but moan in physical agony. Resting on the bloodied bedsheet, when it is done, he pulls out his mouthguard and throws it, determinedly, in the air. As he has commented, 'Surely, you cannot do what you want to do, because of the existing social norms, moral restraints, and laws… However, my body belongs to me, so I can reduce

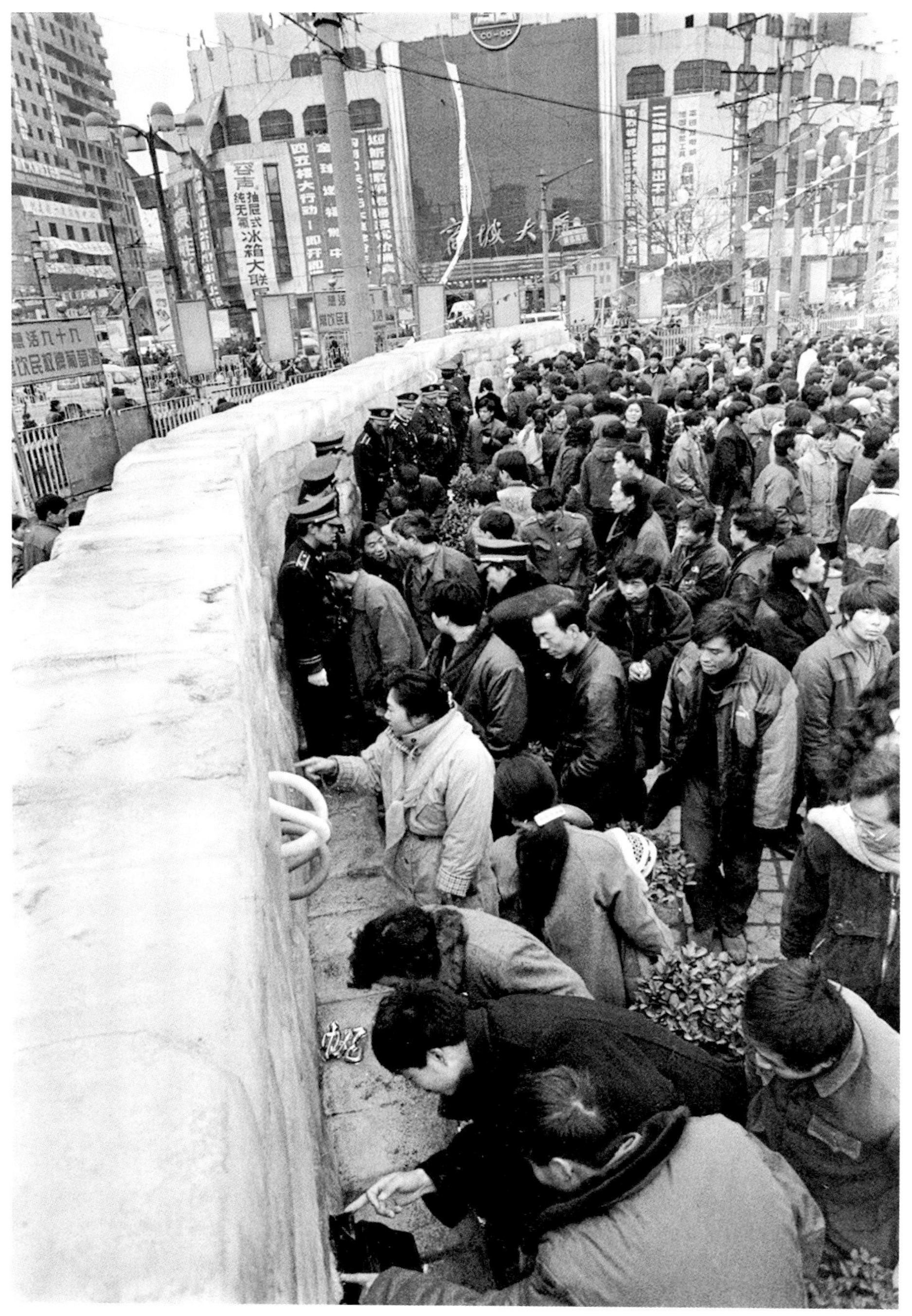

142 Wang Jin, *Ice: '96 Central Plains*, 1996 (installation view)

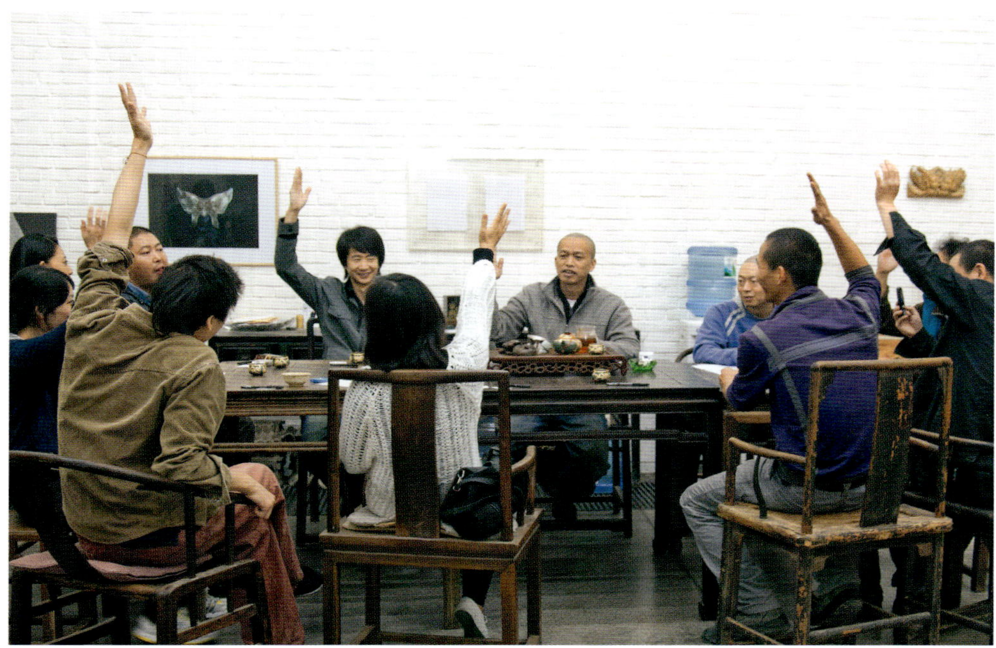

143 He Yunchang inviting 25 people to vote anonymously, artist studio, Beijing, 10 October 2010

its functionality in my way. Therefore, from such a perspective, it means that I can do whatever I like with my own body.[40]

The proposal for the performance was introduced as a 'democratic' decision to be made by twenty-five people, mainly the artist's friends and colleagues, who visited his studio for a meeting prior to the making of the work. The result was that twelve voted in favour, ten against, and three abstained. The performance therefore went ahead as planned; and yet, the 'democracy' of the voting procedure was questionable. In actual fact, He Yunchang had already decided to realize the work by any means. If the idea had not been passed, another vote would have been organized to induce and pressurize the participants in order to obtain a positive result.[41] All the voters were invited to witness the surgery. A photograph documented these participants, who surrounded the artist immediately after the procedure and posed for the camera, but were clearly trying to recover from the psychological impact of the performance. The huge scar left on the artist's body ironically manifests the realization of the 'democracy', but at the same time He Yunchang believes that the work is a realistic one, reflecting both the suffering (on the part of the artist) and the lack of

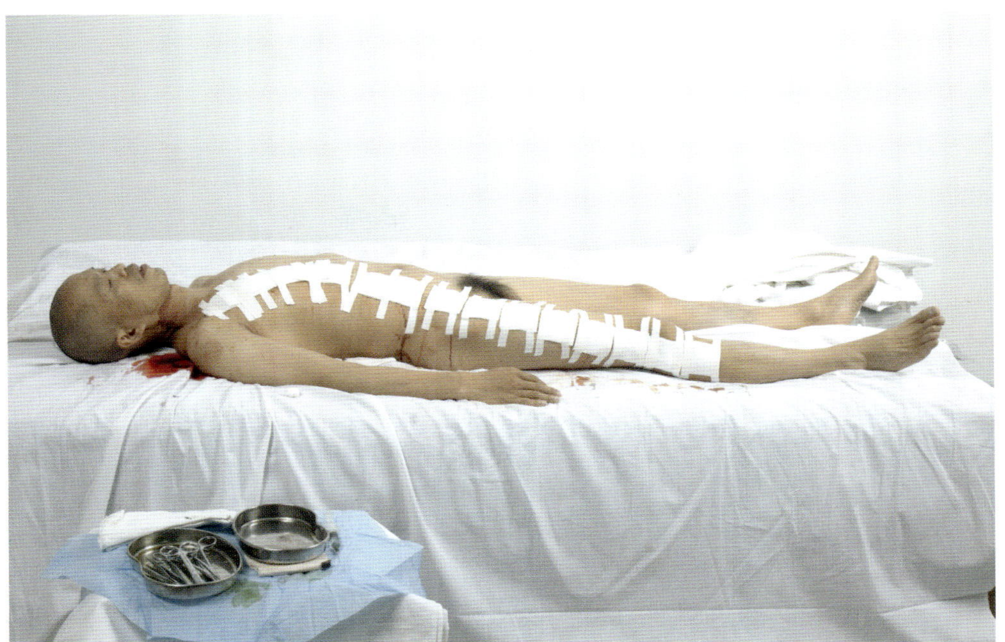

144 He Yunchang, *One Metre Democracy*, 2010 (photograph of performance)

real autonomy (on the part of the participants) that ordinary people experience in daily life. 'Where could we possibly find a metre of democracy? Not even a centimetre!'[42]

He Yunchang has never called his works 'performance art'. To some, they could be seen as 'incidents', in which he uses the body as a means to present his personal exploration of the human experience. As the artist has stated:

I repel the so-called performance. I use my body as an expressive medium and it must be differentiated from drama, film or music, without any rehearsals. There is no need for any additional performative element but the body can react naturally within the intensity that the artist sets for the piece. A replay could devalue or fail the work, or would become a 'performance'. [To me], every work can only be paid for [by my body] once.[43]

By pushing the limits of his body through self-harm, the artist effectively asserts his individual freedom and control, although there is a physical cost. In another work, *The Rock Tours Around Great Britain*, He Yunchang 'performed' in a Western democratic country as we understand it,[44] and spent

145

112 days, from 23 September 2006 to 14 January 2007, carrying out a circumambulation of Britain. Departing from the small town of Boulmer in Northumberland, He Yunchang picked up a rock and carried it while walking counter-clockwise along the perimeter of Great Britain, covering approximately 3,380 kilometres (2,100 miles). After more than sixteen weeks, he returned to the same spot and placed the rock at the very location from which it had been taken. We travel – from one place to another, from the local to the world and beyond, and from the familiar to the uncharted, and today we travel more than ever before, with various modes of transportation that make our globe smaller. To many, He Yunchang's long journey, with its innumerable trials and hardships, might seem to be a completely meaningless effort, and yet it is the very quality of that ineffectiveness which challenges mainstream perspectives of value, and which also, incidentally, attracts its own audience.

Solo journeys were also fundamental to the realization of Wang Sishun's work, *Truth*. From an accidental fire, the artist preserved a single flame, which he then kept as what he called the 'original blaze'. As he has commented:

145 He Yunchang, *The Rock Tours Around Great Britain*, 2006 (photograph of performance)

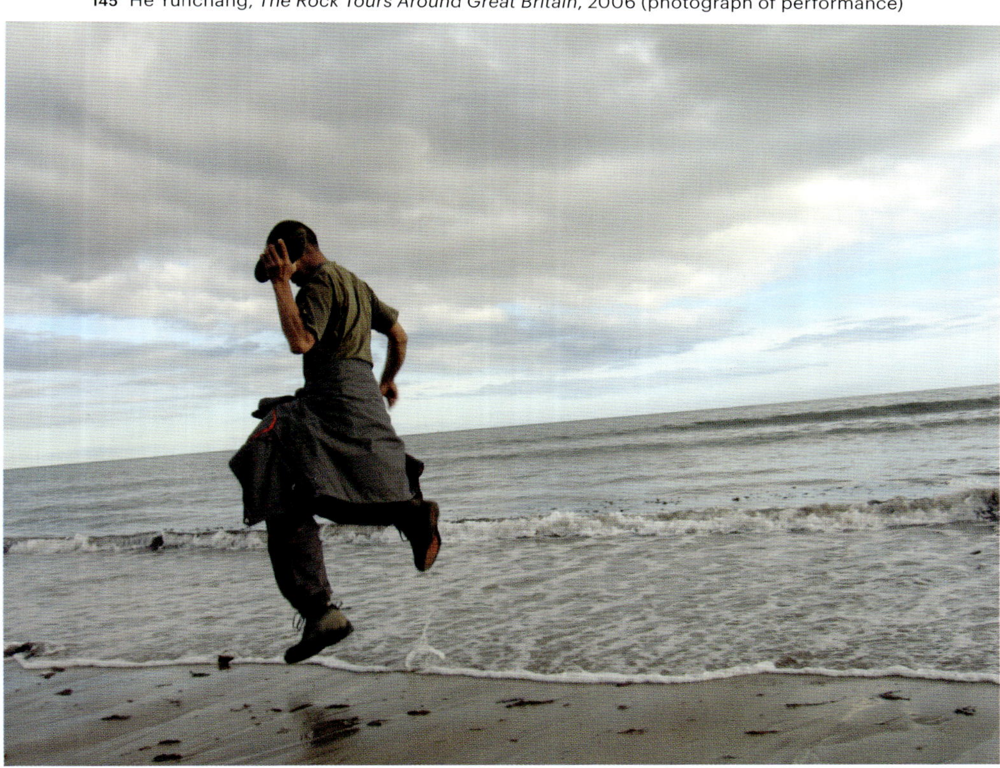

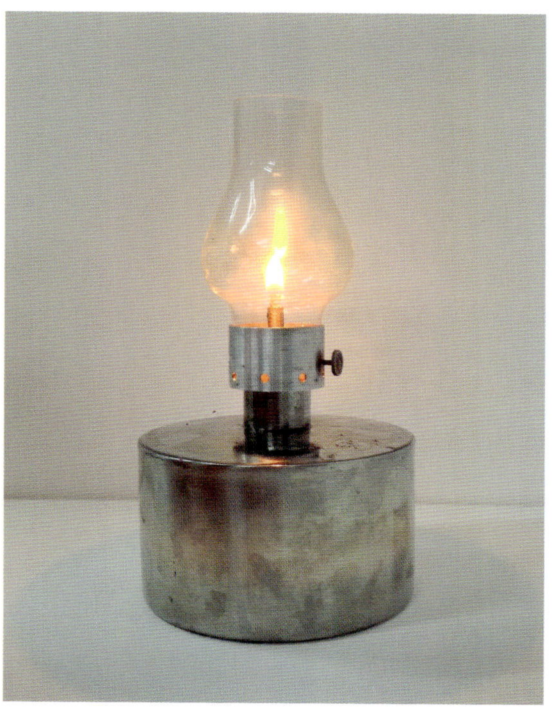

146 Wang Sishun, *Truth*, 2014

*The flame born from a disaster on the one hand can express
the status of being wild and evil, invasive and destructive;
on the other hand, it represents desire and vitality. It looks
weak – like a ghost raised with greed, but at any time, it could
grow expeditiously and spread widely beyond control, leading
to unforeseeable consequences.*[45]

The flame that emerged out of an accident was turned into
a piece of art through the efforts the artist made to transport
it to various venues. In 2014, Wang kept this flame in his
car and drove it all the way from his studio in Beijing to the
exhibition venue MadeIn Gallery in Shanghai. During the
exhibition period, the car was parked next to the entrance of
the gallery, housing the flame inside – ready to go to its next
destination. A year later, more ambitiously, the same flame was
carried by the artist, travelling alone in his car, for more than
16,000 kilometres (10,000 miles) from Beijing to Paris, across
the countries of Eurasia – Russia, Latvia, Lithuania, Poland,
Germany, the Netherlands, Luxembourg, and finally France.
The month-long journey began on 12 August 2015, and a series

of artworks was improvised during the trip, through the
artist's encounters with various weather and road conditions,
as well as different cultures. For example, he picked up
stones along the way, from the roadside, woods or grassland,
carved them into simple, small, symbolic objects, and then
threw them back. These were not to be exhibited in a gallery
space, but in the natural world. 'Many years later,' says
the artist, 'these stones might be discovered again. This
is how the present becomes a civilization for the future.'[46]
In another example, when a minor car accident left a mark
from a road barrier, he cut out the damaged part from the
body of the car as a piece of work that was made accidentally
during the drive. Apart from transporting the 'original blaze',
nothing was planned. The whole duration of the journey,
however, was faithfully documented by a driving recorder,
as a 180-hour-long documentary.

In the 2006 work *18 Days*, Xu Zhen drove to different sites
on China's state border, where he used a remote control to
'invade' neighbouring countries with toy military vehicles.
Although the act was seemingly meant to be provocative,
a sense of humour was divulged in the entire process of
the execution. In addition to the photographs and video
recordings of the events during the 18-day journey, the various
types of equipment used, including a range of toy tanks and
a Ford Escape vehicle, are all evidence of the implementation
of the 'incident'.

Although created in the softest and gentlest form, Yuan
Gong's ongoing series *Scented Air* can also be perceived

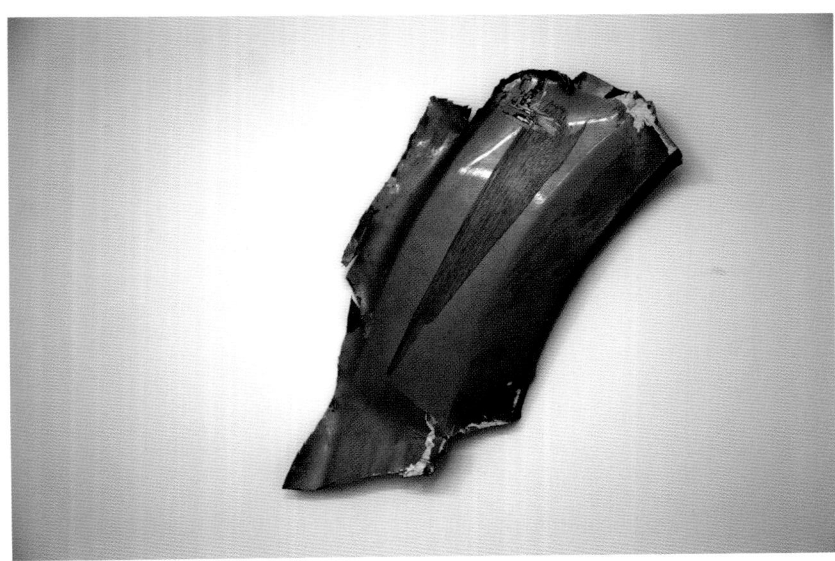

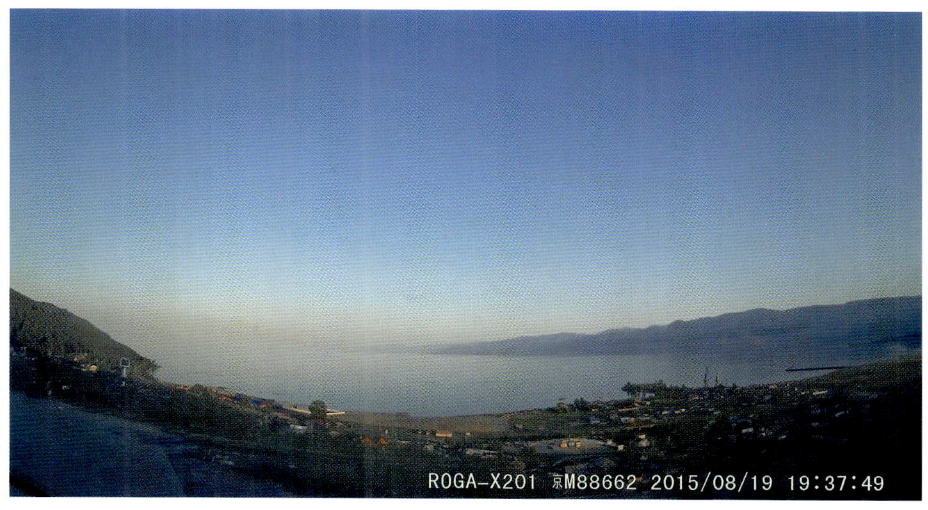

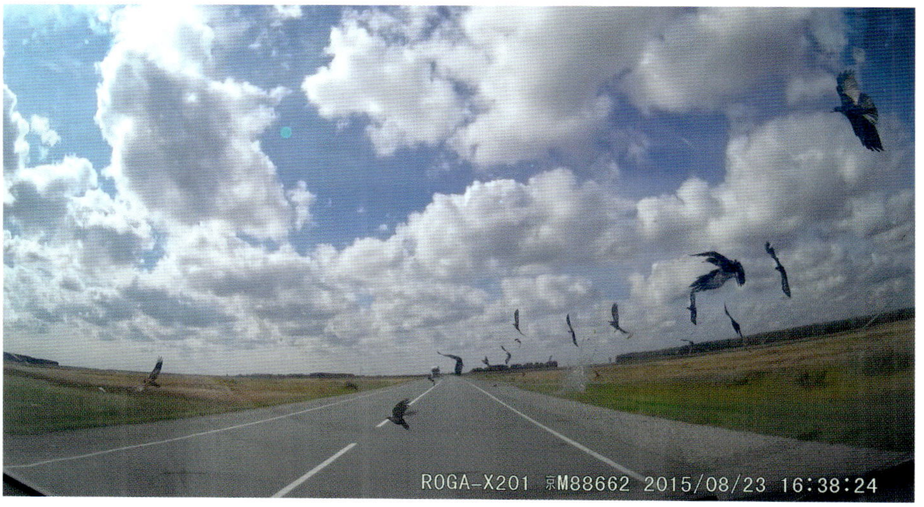

147 OPPOSITE Wang Sishun, *Truth 15.9.15*, 2015
148 ABOVE Wang Sishun, *Truth 15.8.13*, 2015 (video stills)

Art At Large

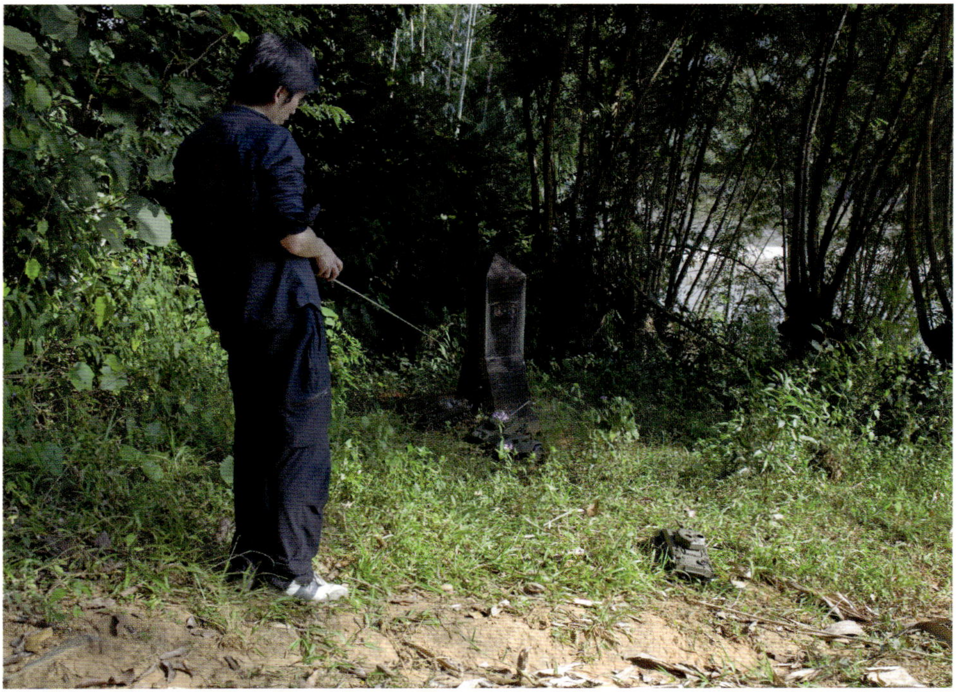

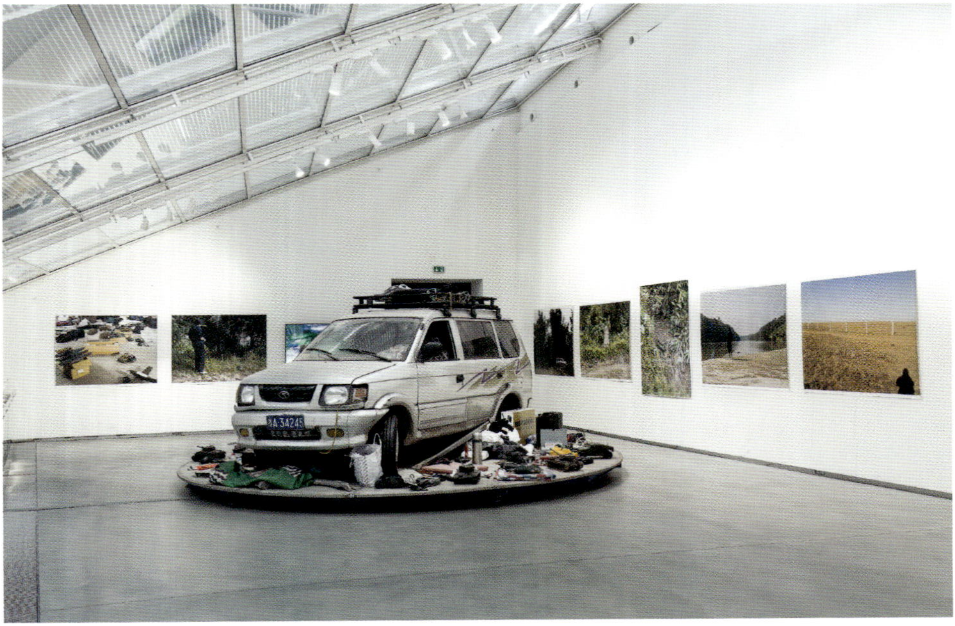

149 TOP Xu Zhen, *18 Days*, 2006 (detail of performance)
150 ABOVE Xu Zhen, *18 Days*, 2006 (installation view)

as invasive, interruptive and, sometimes, aggressive. The project was inspired by the artist's residency in Tibet in 2007. During his four-month stay on the plateau, the idea was forged by his personal bodily experiences – the lack of oxygen on the one hand, and, on the other, the endless smoke that proliferated with particular scents from the religious rituals taking place everywhere. Since then, *Scented Air* has travelled internationally, including to Berlin, Copenhagen, Hong Kong, Prague, Shanghai and Venice, in the form of *qi* (or *chi*), a curious substance. *Qi* is a complicated (and, indeed, somewhat nebulous) word in Chinese culture: it can be interpreted as 'breath', 'air', 'vapour', 'smoke' or 'energy' as life force. In Venice, the artist set the installation up to spray the specifically designed *qi* – sandalwood-scented air – to permeate the entire space of 6,000 cubic metres (over 210,000 cubic ft), thereby offering the audience an immersive experience. Rather than representing emptiness in a void, the artist instead fills the void – diffusing emptiness by occupying it. As Peng Feng, curator of the China Pavilion at the 2011 Venice Biennale, noted: 'It expands, pervades into time and space, physically and psychologically. It belittles boundaries, disrupts order, making order fall into chaos, the formless as form.'[47] The work has been extended to urban landmarks with different cultural contexts, such as the Oriental Pearl Tower in Shanghai and the Round Tower in Copenhagen. Using a portable *qi* producer, the artist has personally spread the scented air in the public spaces, for example, at the central railway station in Milan or in front of the Reichstag building in Berlin.

In Yuan Gong's work, *qi* seems to be a kind of expansive, substantial and visible happening; but at the same time, it is intangible, amorphous and, ultimately, invisible. Although in a sense it makes physically visible the ever-present currents of air around us, the work can be perceived in various other ways. On the one hand, in the post-9/11 era, it can be said to heighten vigilance, tension and fear. As the artist has noted: 'Around 2011 and 2012, people felt insecure when the world was haunted by terrorism – one day, one might suddenly lose his/her freedom, even life.'[48] On the other hand, paradoxically, its visual and olfactory form originally stemmed from the artist's Tibetan experience, and was inspired by the ritualistic prayers of believers, or the blessings from their gods, thereby symbolizing peace and good fortune. The 'incident' is constructed not by the artist, but by its audiences and participants, through their perception of *qi*, which thus always maintains its performative and provisional quality.

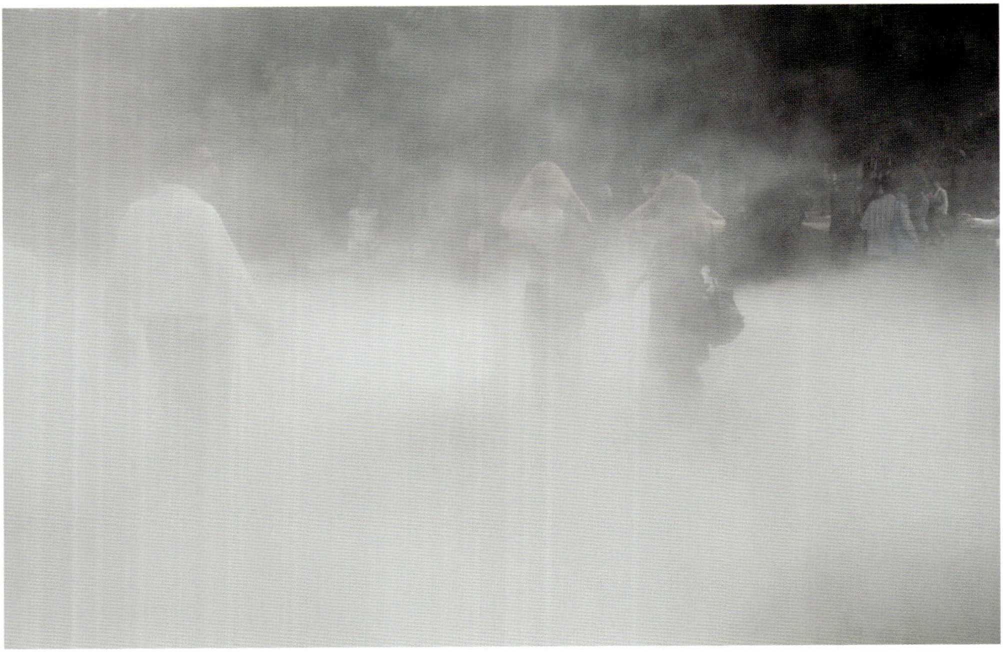

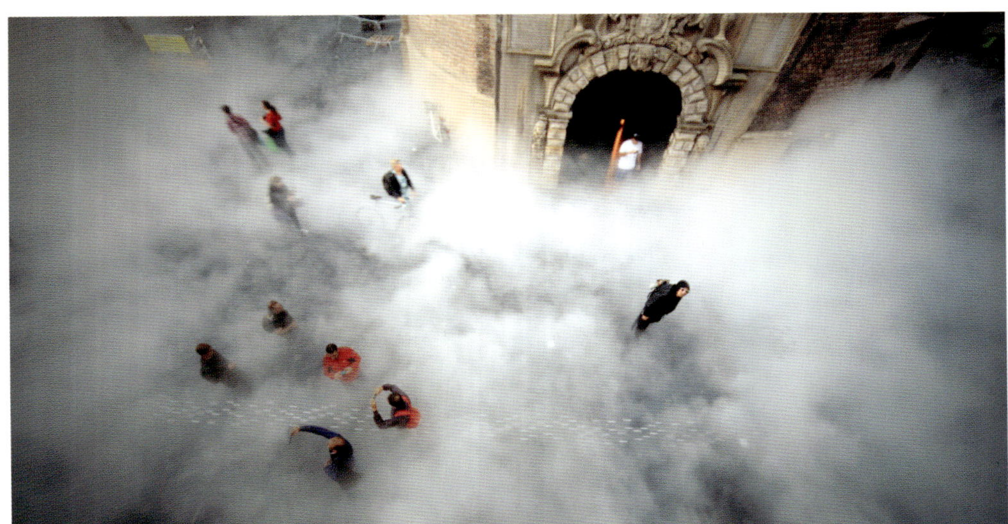

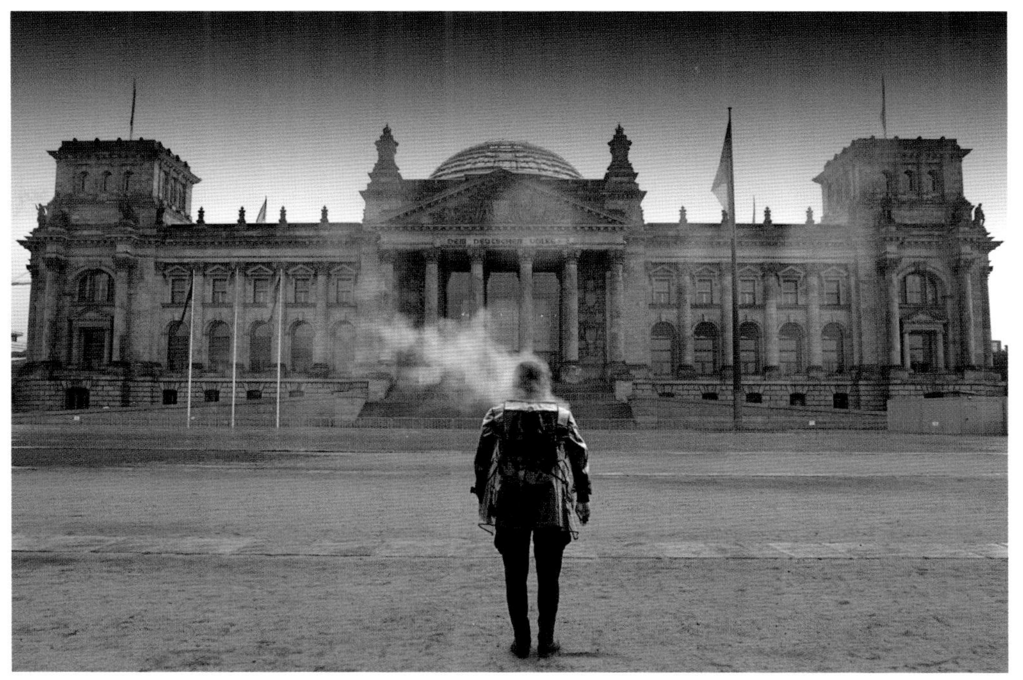

Coda

In the late 1980s, a group of avant-garde artists began to
live together as a community – later known as the 'artists'
village' – in the western suburbs of Beijing, near the ruins of
the former imperial park, Yuanmingyuan. During the following
decade, some of the Yuanmingyuan artists migrated to the
Songzhuang colony in Tongzhou District on the eastern outskirts
of the city, which has now become one of the largest artist
communities in Beijing. Since the start of the new millennium,
when the 798 Art Zone in Chaoyang District began to take
shape, artists have moved to various locations in that same
northeastern part of the city, to Feijiacun and Suojiacun, and
to Huantie and Heiqiao outside the fifth ring, and then further
on to Liqiaozhen in Shunyi, next to the Capital International
Airport. Studio moves are not always voluntary; on the contrary,
in some cases they are forced. Hundreds of artists have been
evicted by the authorities ahead of impending demolition,
making way for urban development, or allowing for the removal
of 'illegal constructions', or even, according to the authorities,
enabling the resolution of 'security problems' by breaking up
'unstable factors' and alleged crime rings. Similarly, in Shanghai,

artists have been moving their studios from Moganshan Art District to Taopu town, further out of the city, and more recently to the southwestern or northern edges of Shanghai, Songjiang and Baoshan. While relocating to such urban-rural fringes makes homes and large studios affordable due to low rents, these sites, far away from metropolitan centres, also seem to constitute a social and geographical statement of being 'at large'.

To visit one of these art communities – especially if one has to travel across Tiananmen Square, and thereby pass out of sight of the Chairman, whose gaze from the Tower is the same as the gaze that looked out from the top of every Chinese classroom blackboard in the 1970s – is to feel that one, too, is 'at large'. This is especially the case if an artist's studio is in an area without an official postal address. Even with the help of a smartphone, or an artist guiding the way at the end of the line, finding such studios can be a challenge.

This geographical and social distancing is mirrored in the fact that, from the beginnings of post-Mao China, a new artistic voice has been developed by those artist groups outside the mainstream, such as the April Photography Society, the No Name Painting Society and the Star movement. It has been quite a journey in the last forty years. In spite of the fact that in China artists can be expelled, studios can be moved, artworks can be censored and exhibitions can be cancelled, art continues to grow, and it grows tenaciously. Perhaps it suits a situation with a lack of stability, or a lack of art-market prosperity. Perhaps it is improved by being created beyond the comfort zone. Perhaps it is better 'at large'. When life is too smooth and steady, and ideas appear to be easy to execute and materialize, some artists fail to thrive. Without the need for alternative strategies, critical examinations and adventurous efforts in practice, for some, art is no longer art.

Alongside the increase of China's power in recent years, the rise of the so-called 'Global East' and the general pace of globalization, China's issues have also become the world's issues: climate change, the environment, urbanization, social conflict, and the problems of cultural legacy. This book has not sought to offer a comprehensive review of the forty-year development of Chinese art post-Mao simply to gather together what has happened in the past as a history; instead, through constructed perspectives, it has been designed to reflect on *why* these things have happened, and/or are still happening *now*, and so on towards the foreseeable future. Its aim has been not just to offer the latest fragment of a picture of Chinese contemporary art, like a jigsaw piece contributing to the world-atlas puzzle; this history is also a story, told so we can reimagine art and, together with the artists, reimagine China.

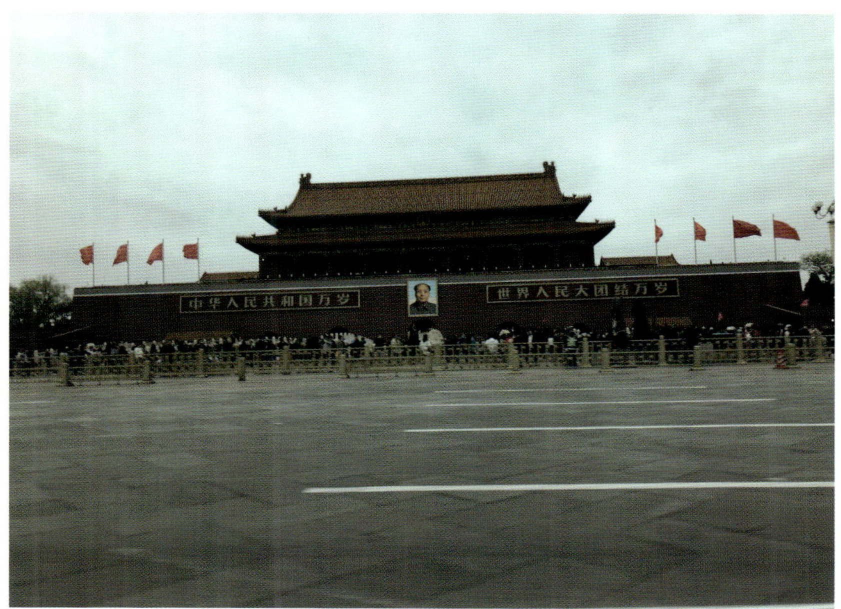

154 Tiananmen Square, photographed by the author from a moving taxi, 22 April 2018

Notes

Introduction

1 Hou Hanru, 'Towards an "Un-Unofficial Art": De-ideologicalisation of China's Contemporary Art in the 1990s', *Third Text*, 34, Spring 1996, p. 40.
2 Martina Köppel-Yang, *Semiotic Warfare: The Chinese Avant-Garde, 1979–1989. A Semiotic Analysis*, Hong Kong, 2003, p. 22.
3 For example, when the Institute of Contemporary Arts was established in 1947 in London, one of the co-founders, Herbert Read, recommended the use of 'contemporary' to mark a conceptual distance from the Museum of Modern Art in New York.
4 Terry Smith, *What Is Contemporary Art?*, London, 2009, pp. 6–8.
5 Wu Hung, *Contemporary Chinese Art: A History (1970s–2000s)*, London, 2014, pp. 126–8.
6 In 1942, around eighty people attended the forum organized by the Propaganda Department of the Central Government in Yangjia Ling, near the city of Yan'an, from 2 to 23 May, where Mao delivered two talks. The purpose of the forum was 'precisely to ensure that literature and art fit well into the whole revolutionary machine as a component part, that they operate as a weapon for uniting and educating the people, and for attacking and destroying the enemy, and that they help the people fight the enemy with one heart and one mind'. See Mao Zedong, *On Literature and Art*, Beijing, 1967, p. 2.
7 Wu Hung (ed.), *Contemporary Chinese Art: Primary Documents*, New York, 2010, p. 6.
8 Marc Augé, trans. Amy Jacobs, *An Anthropology for Contemporaneous Worlds*, Stanford, 1999, p. 89.
9 Hans Ulrich Obrist, *Ai Weiwei Speaks: With Hans Ulrich Obrist*, London, 2011, pp. 77–8.
10 Hans Belting, 'From World Art to Global Art: View on a New Panorama', in Hans Belting, Andrea Buddensieg and Peter Weibel (eds.), *The Global Contemporary and the Rise of New Art Worlds*, London, 2013, pp. 178–84.
11 Shu Qun, '*Wei beifang meishu qunti chanshi* (An Explanation of the Northern Art Group)', originally published in *Meishu sichao* (*The Trend of Art Thought*), no. 1, 1987, pp. 36–9, translated by Phillip Bloom, in Wu (ed.), 2010, op. cit., p. 79.
12 Köppel-Yang, 2003, op. cit., p. 152.
13 Gao Minglu, *Zhongguo qianwei yishu* (*Chinese Avant-Garde Art*), Nanjing, 1997, pp. 107–25.
14 Gao Minglu, *Total Modernity and the Avant-Garde in Twentieth-Century Chinese Art*, London, 2011, pp. 141–66.
15 The exhibition presented work by a number of young painters, including Fang Lijun, Liu Wei, Liu Xiaodong and Song Yonghong, and has been widely regarded as the beginning of the trend of new realistic painting.
16 Li Xianting, '*Hou 89 yishu zhong de wuliaogan he jiegou yishi: "wanshi xieshi zhuyi" yu "zhengzhi bopo" chaoliu xi* (Apathy and Deconstruction in Post-89 Art: Analyzing the Trends of "Cynical Realism" and "Political Pop")', originally published in *Yishu chaoilu* (*Art Trends*), no. 1, 1992, translated by Kela Shang, in Wu (ed.), 2010, op. cit., p. 159.
17 Wang Meiqin, *Urbanization and Contemporary Chinese Art*, London, 2015, p. 98.

Chapter 1
The Collective

1 David Bray, *Social Space and Governance in Urban China: The Danwei System from Origins to Reform*, Redwood City, CA, 2005, pp. 3–5.
2 Zhou Xueguang, 'Unorganized Interests and Collective Action in Communist China', *American Sociological Review*, vol. 58, no. 1, 1993, p. 55.
3 Li Xianting et al., 'Three Critical Perspectives on Wang Guangyi', in *Wang Guangyi*, Hong Kong, 2002, p. 38.
4 Lü Peng and Yi Dan, *Zhongguo xiandai yishu shi 1979–1989* (*A History of Contemporary Chinese Art 1979–1989*), Changsha, 1992, pp. 166–8.
5 Karen Smith, 'From Mao to Now: Wang Guangyi', in *Wang Guangyi*, 2002, op. cit., p. 10.
6 Interview with Yu Youhan, Shanghai, 9 October 2000. Unless otherwise stated, all interviews in this book were conducted by the author, and have been translated by the author.
7 Ibid.
8 Interview with Li Shan, Shanghai, 4 October 2000.

9   Francesca Dal Lago, 'Personal Mao: Reshaping an Icon in Contemporary Chinese Art', *Art Journal*, vol. 58, no. 2, Summer 1999, pp. 54–5.

10   Personal email correspondence with Sui Jianguo, 29 December 2016. Unless otherwise stated, all correspondence in this book has been translated by the author.

11   Interview with Sui Jianguo, online, 1 January 2017.

12   Wu Hung, *Remaking Beijing: Tiananmen Square and the Creation of a Political Space*, London, 2005, p. 130.

13   Michel Foucault, 'Two Lectures', in Michael Kelly (ed.), *Critique and Power: Recasting the Foucault/Habermas Debate*, Cambridge, MA, 1994, p. 34.

14   Bray, 2005, op. cit., p. 197.

15   Interview with Zhuang Hui, Beijing, 28 October 2003.

16   Karen Smith, *Representing the People*, Manchester, 1999, p. 140.

17   Mathieu Borysevicz, 'Zhuang Hui', in John Clark (ed.), *Chinese Art at the End of the Millennium*, Hong Kong, 2000, p. 252.

18   From 2013, the One-Child policy began to be phased out, until the Two-Child policy was introduced by the Chinese Communist Party in 2016 in order to relieve the foreseeable crisis of an ageing population.

19   Wang Jinsong, '*Biaozhun jiating* (Standard Family)', in Zeng Xiaojun and Ai Weiwei (eds.), *Huipishu* (*Grey Cover Book*), Beijing, 1997, p. 33, translated by Kristen Loring, in Wu (ed.), 2010, op. cit., p. 217.

20   Interview with Wang Jinsong, Beijing, 25 March 2006.

21   Interview with Zhang Xiaogang, Beijing, 30 October 2003.

22   Interview with Zhang Xiaogang, conducted by Huang Zhuan, 2 August 1996, Chengdu. Translated by Liu Yinjiu, in Wu (ed.), 2010, op. cit., p. 191.

23   For example, as discussed in Qin Hua, 'Rural-to-Urban Labor Migration, Household Livelihoods, and the Rural Environment in Chongqing Municipality, Southwest China', *Human Ecology*, 2010, available at https://www.ncbi.nlm.nih.gov/pmc/articles/PMC3241916/ [accessed 18 January 2019].

24   Jiang Jiehong, *An Era without Memories: Chinese Contemporary Photography on Urban Transformation*, London, 2015, pp. 108–15.

25   Zhang Dali, artist statement, 2003. Unless otherwise stated, all artist statements in this book were provided by the artist to the author, and are translated by the author.

26   Wu Hung, 'Instantaneous Copying and Monumentality: The Historic Logic of "Permanence and Impermanence"', in *Zhang Dali: Permanence and Impermanence*, Beijing, 2017, p. 37.

27   Chen Xiaoyun, artist statement, 2009.

28   Interview with Yue Minjun, 24 March 2006, Beijing.

29   Cited in Huang Zhuan, 'An Antithesis to the Conceptual: On Zhang Peili', in *Zhang Peili: Certain Pleasures*, Shanghai, 2011, pp. 23–4.

30   Katie Hill, 'Why the manic grin? Hysterical bodies: contemporary art as (male) trauma in post-Cultural Revolution China', in Jiang Jiehong (ed.), *Burden or Legacy: From the Chinese Cultural Revolution to Contemporary Art*, Hong Kong, 2007, pp. 76–9.

31   Yang Fudong, artist statement, 2001.

32   Interview with Yang Zhenzhong, online, 4 May 2019.

33   Interview with Zhou Xiaohu, online, 29 August 2019.

34   Claire Bishop, *Participation*, Cambridge, MA, 2006, p. 12.

35   *The Story of Spring* is a popular song, originally sung by the famous Chinese singer Dong Wenhua, in praise of the Chinese leader Deng Xiaoping, who is referred to as 'an old man' throughout the lyrics.

36   Cao Fei, artist statement, 2006, available at http://www.caofei.com/works.aspx?id=10&year=2006&wtid=3 [accessed 2 November 2019].

37   The performance was made at the two opening events of the 12th Shanghai Biennale, 'Pro-regress', at the Power Station of Art, Shanghai, November 2018. It was documented as a video piece, which was displayed on a small screen during the exhibition period, comprising the second phase of the work.

38   MadeIn Company, artist statement, 2011.

39   'China's Peaceful Development Road', *People's Daily*, 22 December 2005.

Chapter 2
Reinventing Tradition

1   Felice Beato (*c.* 1833–1907) was one of the first photographers to take pictures in East Asia. His photographs represent the first substantial oeuvre of what came to be called photojournalism.

2   Homi Bhabha, *The Location of Culture*, London, 1994, p. 3.

3   For further discussion, see Wu Hung, 'Negotiating with Tradition in Contemporary Chinese Art: Three Strategies', available at http://www.mplusmatters.hk/inkart/paper_topic10.php?l=en [accessed 11 August 2019].

4   Pi Li, 'Past as Future: The Discourse of *Chuantong* in Twentieth-century China', *Journal of Contemporary Chinese Art: Reinventing Tradition in Chinese Contemporary Art*, 6.2&3, pp. 181–2.

5   Interview with Yang Jiechang, conducted by Xin Wang, 3 May 2014, video available at https://www.metmuseum.org/metmedia/video/collections/asian/yang-jiechang-ink-art-2 [accessed 3 March 2019].

6   Hu Xiaoyuan, artist statement, 2010.

7   Nicolas Bourriaud, *States of Tension: Hu Xiaoyuan*, Milan, 2018, p. 10 [italics in original].

8   Liang Shaoji, artist statement, 1992.

9   Interview with Liu Jianhua, Shanghai, 19 July 2016. See details in *Journal of Contemporary Chinese Art: Reinventing Tradition in Chinese Contemporary Art*, 6.2&3, pp. 415–21.

10   Interview with Xiao Yu, Beijing, 18 August 2011.

11   Interview with Xiao Yu, online, 27 September 2019.

12   The work was presented at the Huangshan Symposium in 1988, but failed to arouse enough critical interest to be included in the seminal *China/Avant-Garde* exhibition in 1989.

13   Ai Weiwei, *Time and Place (Cishi cidi)*, Guilin, 2010, p. 119.

14   Interview with Yu Ji, Shanghai, 7 August 2015.

15   Interview with Hao Liang, Beijing, 6 August 2015.

16   Wu Chi-Tsung, artist statement, 2003.

17   Guo Xi and Guo Si, '*Linquan gaozhi*', reproduced in Xiong Zhiting et al. (eds.), *Songren hualun (Painting Theories by the Song Scholars)*, Changsha, 2000, p. 6.

18   See Chang Tsong-zung, 'Mesmerised by Power', in Jiang Jiehong (ed.), *Burden or Legacy: From the Chinese Cultural Revolution to Contemporary Art*, Hong Kong, 2007, p. 65.

19   Gu Wenda, artist statement, 2003.

20   Xu Bing, 'The Living Word', in Britta Erickson (ed.), *Words without Meaning, Meaning without Words: The Art of Xu Bing*, London, 2001, p. 16.

21   Alice Yang, *Why Asia? Contemporary Asian and Asian American Artists*, New York, 1998, pp. 24–9.

22   Norman Bryson, 'The Post-Ideological Avant-Garde', in Gao Minglu (ed.), *Inside Out: New Chinese Art*, London, 1998, p. 57.

23   Qiu Zhijie, artist statement, *A Personal Statement on Assignment No. 1 (zuoye yihao)*, 1994, text provided by the artist, English version translated by Kristen Loring, quoted from Wu (ed.), 2010, op. cit., p. 188.

24   Qiu Zhijie, artist statement, 2007.

25   Interview with Zheng Guogu, Yangjiang, 14 March 2018.

26   Ibid.

27   Lu Mingjun, '"Liao Garden" and Bodies of Energy: Everyday Madness and Temporal Magnetic Fields in the Work of Zheng Guogu', *Journal of Contemporary Chinese Art: Contemporary Chinese Artists in the Globalized Art World*, 5.1, p. 102.

28   Qiu Zhijie, 'Huang Yong Ping *sanlun* (On Huang Yong Ping)', available at https://xw.qq.com/cmsid/20160725017304O0 [accessed 8 May 2020].

29   Funded by the Leverhulme Trust, this research project was led by the Centre for Chinese Visual Arts at Birmingham City University, and included five international partnerships: the New Century Art Foundation and the Central Academy of Fine Arts in Beijing, Groningen University, Goldsmiths (London), and White Rabbit Foundation (Sydney).

30   Interview with Wen Tao, Pingyao, 30 May 2017.

31   Interview with Hui Dongcun, Dingxiang, 31 May 2017.

Chapter 3
The Art of Urbanization

1   For further discussions see, for example, John Friedmann, *China's Urban Transition*, Minneapolis, 2005; Wu Fulong, *China's Emerging Cities: The Making of New Urbanism*, New York, 2007; Hsing You-tien, *The Great Urban Transformation: Politics of Land and Property in China*, London, 2010.

2   See, for instance, Thomas J. Campanella, *The Concrete Dragon: China's Urban Revolution and What It Means for the World*, New York, 2008.

3   See Michael J. Meyer, *The Last Days of Old Beijing: Life in the Vanishing Backstreets of a City Transformed*, New York, 2008.

4   See Ian Johnson, 'China's Great Uprooting: Moving 250 Million into Cities', *New York Times*, 15 June 2013, available at http://www.nytimes.com/2013/06/16/world/asia/chinas-great-uprooting-moving-250-million-into-cities.html?pagewanted=all [accessed 18 January 2019].

5   See Bianca Bosker, *Original Copies: Architectural Mimicry in Contemporary China*, Honolulu, 2013, p. 119.

6   Built in 2001, Xintiandi is a leisure area of

reconstituted traditional *shikumen* houses that serve as shops, bookstores, cafés and restaurants.

7 Interview with Wang Gongxin, online, 2 November 2019.

8 Song Dong, artist statement, 2006.

9 Interview with Nabuqi, online, 30 October 2019.

10 Hu Weiyi, artist statement, 2019.

11 See www.chinadaily.com.cn/china/2014npc andcppcc/2014-03/05/content_17324203.htm [accessed 18 March 2019].

12 See Ingrid D'Hooge, *China's Public Diplomacy*, Leiden, 2014, p. 83.

13 Interview with Jiang Zhi, online, 26 October 2007.

14 Cao Fei, artist statement, 2007, see http://www.caofei.com/works.aspx?year=2007&wtid=3 [accessed 27 September 2019].

15 Chris Berry, 'Cao Fei's "Magical Metropolises"', in Wang Meiqin and Minna Valjakka (eds.), *Visual Arts, Representations and Interventions in Contemporary China: Urbanized Interfaces*, Amsterdam, 2018, pp. 213–21 [italics in original].

16 Interview with Zhao Zhao, online, 9 March 2019.

17 Zhang Ga, 'The Posthuman as a Condition of Art', in Zhang Ga (ed.), *Wang Yuyang: Tonight I Shall Meditate Upon That Which I Am*, Milan, 2015, p. 13.

18 Wen Bin and Weng Donghua, statement, 2019.

19 Mark Crinson, 'Urban Memory: An Introduction', in Mark Crinson (ed.), *Urban Memory: History and Amnesia in the Modern City*, London, 2005, p. xi.

Chapter 4
Art At Large

1 See Lucy Steeds, 'Contemporary Exhibitions: Art at Large in the World', in Lucy Steeds (ed.), *Exhibition (Documents of Contemporary Art)*, London, 2014, pp. 16–17.

2 See Roderick MacFarquhar and Michael Schoenhals, *Mao's Last Revolution*, London, 2006, p. 1.

3 See also Yan Jiaqi and Gao Gao (eds.), trans. D. W. Y. Kwok, *Turbulent Decade: A History of the Cultural Revolution*, Hawaii, 1996, p. 58. The Chinese term *zaofan* connotes turning all things upside down and has meanings ranging through the three English words 'revolution', 'revolt' and 'rebellion'.

4 Editorial, '*Women shi jiu shijie de pipanzhe* (We Are the Critics of the Old World)', *Renmin ribao*, 8 June 1966, p. 1.

5 Geremie R. Barmé, *Shades of Mao: The Posthumous Cult of the Great Leader*, Armonk, NY, 1996, p. 8.

6 Lu Na, *Mao Zedong xiangzhang shoucang yu jianshang* (*The Collection and Appreciation of Mao Zedong Badges*), Beijing, 1993, p. 14.

7 Jiang Jiehong, *Red: China's Cultural Revolution*, London, 2010, p. 60.

8 Cited in Li Xianting, '*Guanyu xingxing meizhan* (About the Star Art Exhibition)', *Meishu* (Fine Art), 1980, issue 3, pp. 8–9.

9 Jin Feng, artist statement, 2016.

10 Ai, 2010, op. cit., p. 124.

11 MacFarquhar and Schoenhals, 2006, op. cit., p. 118.

12 Birgit Hopfener, 'Tradition and Transmission: Shifting Epistemological and (Art-)historical Grounds of Contemporary Art's Relation to the Past', *Journal of Contemporary Chinese Art: Reinventing Tradition in Chinese Contemporary Art*, 6.2&3, p. 193.

13 Interview with Li Binyuan, online, 22 December 2019.

14 Josef Ng, 'Freedom', in *Sun Yuan & Peng Yu: Can't Have It All*, Beijing, 2009, p. 23.

15 Interview with Sun Yuan, conducted by Liang Shuhan, 15 March 2013, available at http://www.randian-online.com/np_feature/interview-with-sun-yuan/ [accessed 5 January 2020].

16 Ibid.

17 Bruce Altshuler, *Salon to Biennial: Exhibitions that Made Art History, Volume 1: 1863–1959*, London, 2008, pp. 12–13.

18 A number of international art events are today produced outside normal exhibition spaces. For example, since 2000, the Echigo-Tsumari Art Triennale has presented projects and initiatives developed in its outdoor Art Field. And in 2018, the Thailand Biennale staged its first edition in the tourist sites in Krabi, providing opportunities for artists to engage with local communities, culture and nature to develop site-specific and site-sustainable work.

19 Craig Clunas, *Chinese Painting and Its Audiences*, Princeton, 2017, p. 55.

20 With help from Liu Xun, an officer of the Beijing Art Association, the exhibition was eventually allowed to be shown from 23 November to 2 December 1979 in Beihai Park.

21 The Garage Show was organized by its artists at the underground garage of Shanghai Education Hall, 22–24 November 1991, presenting works by Geng Jianyi, Gong Jianqing, He Yang, Hu Jianping, Ni Haifeng, Song Haidong, Sun Liang and Zhang Peili.

22   Ai Weiwei and Feng Boyi, 'Preface to *Fuck Off* (*Buhezuo fangshi*)', China: privately published, 2000, p. 9, in Wu (ed.), 2010, op. cit., pp. 354–5.
23   Wu Hung, 'The 2000 Shanghai Biennale: The Making of a "Historical Event" in Contemporary Chinese Art', in *Making History: Wu Hung on Contemporary Art*, Hong Kong, 2008, p. 183.
24   Pauline J. Yao, 'Towards a Spatial History of Contemporary Art in China', *Journal of Contemporary Chinese Art: Chinese Art Outside the Art Space*, 5.2&3, pp. 119–20.
25   Ibid., p. 126.
26   Gao, 2011, op. cit., pp. 269–71.
27   Interview with Song Dong, conducted by Wu Hung, Beijing, February 2000; see Wu Hung, *Exhibiting Experimental Art in China*, Chicago, 2000, pp. 144–7.
28   Song Dong, Guo Shirui and Pang Lei (eds.), *Yesheng: 1997 nian Jingzhe shi* (*Wildlife: Starting from 1997 Jingzhe Day*), Beijing, 1998. English version quoted from Wu, 2000, op. cit., p. 143.
29   Ibid., p. 2.
30   http://www.arrowfactory.org.cn/?page=about [accessed 3 January 2020].
31   Arrow Factory closed permanently at the end of September 2019, due to reasons beyond its control.
32   Rania Ho, Wang Wei and Pauline J. Yao (eds.), *3 Years: Arrow Factory*, Beijing, 2011, pp. 44–7.
33   Rania Ho, Wang Wei and Pauline J. Yao (eds.), *Arrow Factory: The Next Four Years*, Beijing, 2015, pp. 116–21.
34   Wu, 2005, op. cit., pp. 227–33.
35   Interview with Huang Yong Ping, conducted by Jane DeBevoise, Museum of Modern Art, New York, 15 October 2010, available at http://www.aaa-a.org/programs/conversation-with-huang-yongping/ [accessed 31 December 2019].
36   Huang Yong Ping, text posted in the exhibition hall, translated by Wu Hung, in Wu (ed.), 2010, op. cit., p. 96.
37   Interview with Xiao Lu, conducted by Monica Merlin, Beijing, 12 November 2013, available at https://www.tate.org.uk/research/research-centres/tate-research-centre-asia/women-artists-contemporary-china/xiao-lu [accessed 31 January 2020].
38   Wu, 2014, op. cit., p. 87.
39   Wang Jin, artist statement, 1996, translated by Kristen Loring, in Wu (ed.), 2010, op. cit., p. 215.
40   Interview with He Yunchang, conducted by Jiang Ming, 8 April 2007, at the artist's studio in Caochangdi, Beijing, available at http://www.artda.cn/view.php?tid=305&cid=14/ [accessed 3 August 2019].
41   Artist's personal email communication with the author, 14 June 2019.
42   Interview with He Yunchang, online, 3 August 2019.
43   Interview with He Yunchang, conducted by Li Xuhui, 14 January 2011, available at http://www.artda.cn/view.php?tid=4817&cid=21 [accessed 8 May 2020].
44   According to Patrick Dunleavy, 'UK democracy has been in crisis ever since the Brexit referendum vote signalled a huge gap between elite, expert opinion and voters.' See P. Dunleavy et al., *The UK's Changing Democracy: The 2018 Democratic Audit*, London, 2018.
45   Wang Sishun, artist statement, 2014.
46   Interview with Wang Sishun, online, 1 February 2020.
47   Peng Feng, 'In-Between Existence', in *Programme* (Fang'an), Beijing, 2011, p. 392.
48   Interview with Yuan Gong, online, 6 January 2020.

Glossary

Chinese Names

Ai Weiwei (b. 1957) 艾未未
Cai Guo-Qiang (b. 1957) 蔡国强
Cao Fei (b. 1978) 曹斐
Chen Danqing (b. 1953) 陈丹青
Chen Shaoxiong (1962–2016) 陈劭雄
Chen Xiaoyun (b. 1971) 陈晓云
Chen Zaiyan (b. 1971) 陈在炎
Cheng Conglin (b. 1954) 程丛林
Deng Xiaoping (1904–1997) 邓小平
Dong Qichang (1555–1636) 董其昌
Emperor Taizong of Tang (598–649) 唐太宗
Fang Lijun (b. 1963) 方力钧
Feng Chengsu (617–672) 冯承素
Geng Jianyi (1962–2017) 耿建翌
Gu Wenda (b. 1955) 谷文达
Guo Shirui (b. 1952) 郭世锐
Hao Liang (b. 1983) 郝量
He An (b. 1970) 何岸
He Yunchang (b. 1967) 何云昌
Hu Jieming (b. 1957) 胡介鸣
Hu Jintao (b. 1942) 胡锦涛
Hu Weiyi (b. 1990) 胡为一
Hu Xiaoyuan (b. 1977) 胡晓媛
Huang Rui (b. 1952) 黄锐
Huang Yong Ping (1954–2019) 黄永砅
Jiang Zhi (b. 1971) 蒋志
Jin Feng (b. 1962) 金锋
Kan Xuan (b. 1972) 阚萱
Kangxi (r. 1661–1722) 康熙
Lam Tung Pang (b. 1978) 林东鹏
Li Bin (b. 1949) 李斌
Li Binyuan (b. 1985) 厉槟源
Li Shan (b. 1944) 李山
Li Xianting (b. 1949) 栗宪庭
Liang Shaoji (b. 1945) 梁绍基
Liang Sicheng (1901–1972) 梁思诚

Lin Yilin (b. 1964) 林一林
Liu Dahong (b. 1962) 刘大鸿
Liu Jianhua (b. 1962) 刘建华
Liu Wei (b. 1965) 刘炜
Liu Xiaodong (b. 1963) 刘小东
Luo Zhongli (b. 1948) 罗中立
Ma Desheng (b. 1952) 马德升
Mao Zedong (1893–1976) 毛泽东
Nabuqi (b. 1984) 娜布其
Peng Yu (b. 1974) 彭禹
Puyi (1906–1967) 溥仪
Qiu Anxiong (b. 1972) 邱黯雄
Qiu Zhijie (b. 1969) 邱志杰
Qu Leilei (b. 1951) 曲磊磊
Shao Yinong (b. 1961) 邵逸农
Shen Shaomin (b. 1956) 沈少民
Shu Qun (b. 1958) 舒群
Song Dong (b. 1966) 宋冬
Sui Jianguo (b. 1956) 隋建国
Sun Qinglin (b. 1974) 孙庆麟
Sun Yat-sen (1866–1925) 孙中山
Sun Yuan (b. 1972) 孙原
Tao Yuanming (365–427) 陶渊明
Wang Gongxin (b. 1960) 王功新
Wang Guangyi (b. 1957) 王广义
Wang Jin (b. 1962) 王晋
Wang Jinsong (b. 1963) 王劲松
Wang Keping (b. 1949) 王克平
Wang Sishun (b. 1979) 王思顺
Wang Wei (701–761) 王维
Wang Wei (b. 1972) 王卫
Wang Wenhai (b. 1951) 王文海
Wang Xizhi (303–361) 王羲之
Wang Yuyang (b. 1979) 王郁洋
Wen Bin (b. 1987) 文宾
Wen Tao (b. 1961) 温涛
Weng Donghua (b. 1989) 翁东华
Wu Chi-Tsung (b. 1981) 吴季聪
Xiao Lu (b. 1962) 肖鲁
Xiao Yu (b. 1965) 萧昱
Xing Zhibin (b. 1947) 邢质斌
Xu Bing (b. 1955) 徐冰
Xu Zhen (b. 1977) 徐震
Yang Fudong (b. 1971) 杨福东
Yang Jiechang (b. 1956) 杨诘苍
Yang Zhenzhong (b. 1968) 杨振中
Yu Ji (b. 1985) 于吉
Yu Youhan (b. 1943) 余友涵
Yuan Gong (b. 1961) 原弓
Yue Minjun (b. 1962) 岳敏君
Zhan Wang (b. 1962) 展望
Zhang Dali (b. 1963) 张大力
Zhang Huan (b. 1965) 张洹
Zhang Peili (b. 1957) 张培力
Zhang Xiaogang (b. 1958) 张晓刚

Zhao Zhao (b. 1982) 赵赵
Zheng Guogu (b. 1970) 郑国谷
Zhou Xiaohu (b. 1960) 周啸虎
Zhuang Hui (b. 1963) 庄辉

Chinese Terms

85 *Meishu xinchao* ('85 Art New Wave) 八五美术
新潮

85 *Meishu yudong* ('85 Art Movement) 八五美术运动

Beifang yishu qunti (Northern Art Group) 北方艺
术群体

Beijing zhi chun (Beijing Spring literary
organization) 北京之春

beiwo (literally, quilt nest) 被窝

biaozhun xiang (standard portraits) 标准像

Buhezuo fangshi (ways of non-cooperation) 不合
作方式

bupo buli (no construction without destruction)
不破不立

chaoshou yan (literally, hand-hold inkstone) 抄
手砚

chengxiang jiehebu (urban-rural fringe) 城乡结合部

Chi she (Pond Society) 池社

chuan qi (legend) 传奇

chuan tong (tradition) 传统

chuanghua (paper-cutting; literally, window
flowers) 窗花

dangdai yishu (contemporary art) 当代艺术

danwei (work unit) 单位

Dongting Chun (name of tea vendor in Changsha)
洞庭春

gaige kaifang (Reform and Opening policy) 改革
开放

gonggong hua (publicization) 公共化

gongyu yishu (Apartment Art) 公寓艺术

guangbo cao (broadcast calisthenics) 广播操

guangchang wu (square dancing) 广场舞

hanzi (Chinese character) 汉字

Hexie shehui (Harmonious Society) 和谐社会

Hong weibing (Red Guard) 红卫兵

Hong xiaobing (Little Red Guard) 红小兵

hutong (a type of narrow alley, commonly
associated with northern cities in China) 胡同

Jianchang (Arrow Factory; name of alley in
Beijing) 箭厂

jiashanshi (artificial rocks) 假山石

Jingzhe (one of the twenty-four divisions in
China's lunar calendar) 惊蛰

Jintian (Today literary organization) 今天

jiti (collective) 集体

kesi (a type of imperial tapestry with fine silks
and gold thread) 缂丝

Liao Yuan (Liao Garden) 了园

liaoyuan (to fulfil a destiny) 了缘

Ling zhan (*Zero Exhibition*) 零展

mingong (migrant worker, or peasant worker) 民工

neibu guanmo (showing internally) 内部观摩

qi (air, breath or energy) 气

qian kun chen fu (the ebb and flow of the universe)
乾坤沉浮

qianwei (avant-garde) 前卫

Sanji Zhai (name of bakery in Changsha) 三吉斋

Shanghen yishu (Scar Art) 伤痕艺术

shanshui (literally, mountains and waters; refers
to traditional landscape painting) 山水

shijian (event, or incident) 事件

shikumen (a traditional architectural style in
Shanghai since the 1860s) 石库门

shiwai taoyuan (a land of peach blossoms beyond
the world) 世外桃源

shiyan yishu (experimental art) 实验艺术

Shiyi yue huazhan (*November Painting Exhibition*)
十一月画展

shui (water) 水

shuimo (ink-wash) 水墨

sige weida (Four Greats) 四个伟大

siheyuan (a traditional style of residence in
Northern China) 四合院

sijiu (Four Olds) 四旧

simi hua (privatization) 私密化

wanghong (Internet-famous) 网红

Wanshi xianshi zhuyi (Cynical Realism) 玩世现实
主义

Wenheyou (name of restaurant in Changsha) 文
和友

wenren hua (literati painting) 文人画

Wuchan jieji wenhua da geming (Great Proletarian
Cultural Revolution) 无产阶级文化大革命

xiandai yishu (modern art) 现代

Xiangtu xieshi (Rustic Realism, or Native Soil Art)
乡土写实

xiao (raw silk) 绡

xiaoyao fawai (at large) 逍遥法外

Xin juxiang zhanlan (*New Figurative Exhibition*) 新
具象展览

Xinan yishu yanjiu qunti (Southwest Art Research
Group) 西南艺术研究群体

Xingxing meizhan (*Star Art Exhibitions*) 星星美展

Xinshengdai yishu zhan (*New Generation Art
Exhibition*) 新生代艺术展

yaji (elegant gathering) 雅集

yanzhi (rouge) 胭脂

zaofan (rebel) 造反

Zhengzhi bopu (Political Pop) 政治波普

Zhongguo (Middle Kingdom, or China) 中国

Zhongguo meng (China Dream) 中国梦

Zhongguo xiandai yishu zhan (*China/Avant-Garde*
exhibition) 中国现代艺术展

Select Bibliography

Ai Weiwei, *Time and Place* (*Cishi cidi*), Guilin, 2010

Altshuler, Bruce, *Salon to Biennial: Exhibitions that Made Art History, Volume 1: 1863–1959*, London, 2008

Augé, Marc, trans. Amy Jacobs, *An Anthropology for Contemporaneous Worlds*, Stanford, 1999

Barmé, Geremie R., *Shades of Mao: The Posthumous Cult of the Great Leader*, Armonk, NY, 1996

Belting, Hans, 'From World Art to Global Art: View on a New Panorama', in Hans Belting, Andrea Buddensieg and Peter Weibel (eds.), *The Global Contemporary and the Rise of New Art Worlds*, London, 2013

Berry, Chris, 'Cao Fei's "Magical Metropolises"', in Wang Meiqin and Minna Valjakka (eds.), *Visual Arts, Representations and Interventions in Contemporary China: Urbanized Interfaces*, Amsterdam, 2018

Bhabha, Homi, *The Location of Culture*, London, 1994

Bishop, Claire, *Participation*, Cambridge, MA, 2006

Borysevicz, Mathieu, 'Zhuang Hui', in John Clark (ed.), *Chinese Art at the End of the Millennium*, Hong Kong, 2000

Bosker, Bianca, *Original Copies: Architectural Mimicry in Contemporary China*, Honolulu, 2013

Bourriaud, Nicolas, *States of Tension: Hu Xiaoyuan*, Milan, 2018

Bray, David, *Social Space and Governance in Urban China: The Danwei System from Origins to Reform*, Redwood City, CA, 2005

Bryson, Norman, 'The Post-Ideological Avant-Garde', in Gao Minglu (ed.), *Inside Out: New Chinese Art*, London, 1998

Campanella, Thomas J., *The Concrete Dragon: China's Urban Revolution and What It Means for the World*, New York, 2008

Chang Tsong-zung, 'Mesmerised by Power', in Jiang Jiehong (ed.), *Burden or Legacy: From the Chinese Cultural Revolution to Contemporary Art*, Hong Kong, 2007

Clunas, Craig, *Chinese Painting and Its Audiences*, Princeton, 2017

Crinson, Mark, 'Urban Memory: An Introduction', in Mark Crinson (ed.), *Urban Memory: History and Amnesia in the Modern City*, London, 2005

Dal Lago, Francesca, 'Personal Mao: Reshaping an Icon in Contemporary Chinese Art', *Art Journal*, vol. 58, no. 2, Summer 1999

D'Hooge, Ingrid, *China's Public Diplomacy*, Leiden, 2014

Foucault, Michel, 'Two Lectures', in Michael Kelly (ed.), *Critique and Power: Recasting the Foucault/Habermas Debate*, Cambridge, MA, 1994

Friedmann, John, *China's Urban Transition*, Minneapolis, 2005

Gao Minglu, *Total Modernity and the Avant-Garde in Twentieth-Century Chinese Art*, London, 2011

— *Zhongguo qianwei yishu* (*Chinese Avant-Garde Art*), Nanjing, 1997

Guo Xi and Guo Si, '*Linquan gaozhi*', in Xiong Zhiting et al. (eds.), *Songren hualun* (*Painting Theories by the Song Scholars*), Changsha, 2000

Hill, Katie, 'Why the manic grin? Hysterical bodies: contemporary art as (male) trauma in post-Cultural Revolution China', in Jiang Jiehong (ed.), *Burden or Legacy: From the Chinese Cultural Revolution to Contemporary Art*, Hong Kong, 2007

Ho, Rania, Wang Wei and Pauline J. Yao (eds.), *3 Years: Arrow Factory*, Beijing, 2011

— (eds.), *Arrow Factory: The Next Four Years*, Beijing, 2015

Hopfener, Birgit, 'Tradition and Transmission: Shifting Epistemological and (Art-)historical Grounds of Contemporary Art's Relation to the Past', *Journal of Contemporary Chinese Art: Reinventing Tradition in Chinese Contemporary Art*, 6.2&3

Hou Hanru, 'Towards an "Un-Unofficial Art": De-ideologicalisation of China's Contemporary Art in the 1990s', *Third Text*, 34, Spring 1996

Hsing You-tien, *The Great Urban Transformation: Politics of Land and Property in China*, London, 2010

Huang Zhuan, 'An Antithesis to the Conceptual: On Zhang Peili', in *Zhang Peili: Certain Pleasures*, Shanghai, 2011

Jiang Jiehong, *An Era without Memories: Chinese Contemporary Photography on Urban Transformation*, London, 2015

— *Red: China's Cultural Revolution*, London, 2010

— (ed.), *Burden or Legacy: From the Chinese Cultural Revolution to Contemporary Art*, Hong Kong, 2007

Johnson, Ian, 'China's Great Uprooting: Moving 250 Million into Cities', *New York Times*, 15 June 2013: http://www.nytimes.com/2013/06/16/world/asia/chinas-great-uprooting-moving-250-million-into-cities.html?pagewanted=all

Journal of Contemporary Chinese Art: Reinventing Tradition in Chinese Contemporary Art, 6.2&3

Köppel-Yang, Martina, *Semiotic Warfare: The Chinese Avant-Garde, 1979–1989. A Semiotic Analysis*, Hong Kong, 2003

Li Xianting, 'Guanyu xingxing meizhan (About the Star Art Exhibition)', *Meishu* (Fine Art), 1980, issue 3

— et al., 'Three Critical Perspectives on Wang Guangyi', in *Wang Guangyi*, Hong Kong, 2002

Lu Mingjun, '"Liao Garden" and Bodies of Energy: Everyday Madness and Temporal Magnetic Fields in the Work of Zheng Guogu', *Journal of Contemporary Chinese Art: Contemporary Chinese Artists in the Globalized Art World*, 5.1

Lu Na, *Mao Zedong xiangzhang shoucang yu jianshang* (The Collection and Appreciation of Mao Zedong Badges), Beijing, 1993

Lü Peng and Yi Dan, *Zhongguo xiandai yishu shi 1979–1989* (A History of Contemporary Chinese Art 1979–1989), Changsha, 1992

MacFarquhar, Roderick, and Michael Schoenhals, *Mao's Last Revolution*, London, 2006

Mao Zedong, *On Literature and Art*, Beijing, 1967

Meyer, Michael J., *The Last Days of Old Beijing: Life in the Vanishing Backstreets of a City Transformed*, New York, 2008

Ng, Josef, 'Freedom', in *Sun Yuan & Peng Yu: Can't Have It All*, Beijing, 2009

Obrist, Hans Ulrich, *Ai Weiwei Speaks: With Hans Ulrich Obrist*, London, 2011

Peng Feng, 'In-Between Existence', in *Programme* (Fang'an), Beijing, 2011

Pi Li, 'Past as Future: The Discourse of *Chuantong* in Twentieth-century China', *Journal of Contemporary Chinese Art: Reinventing Tradition in Chinese Contemporary Art*, 6.2&3

Qin Hua, 'Rural-to-Urban Labor Migration, Household Livelihoods, and the Rural Environment in Chongqing Municipality, Southwest China', *Human Ecology*, 2010: https://www.ncbi.nlm.nih.gov/pmc/articles/PMC3241916/

Qiu Zhijie, 'Huang Yongping *sanlun* (On Huang Yongping)': http://review.artintern.net/html.php?id=66864

Smith, Karen, 'From Mao to Now: Wang Guangyi', in *Wang Guangyi*, Hong Kong, 2002

— *Representing the People*, Manchester, 1999

Smith, Terry, *What Is Contemporary Art?* London, 2009

Steeds, Lucy, 'Contemporary Exhibitions: Art at Large in the World', in Lucy Steeds (ed.), *Exhibition (Documents of Contemporary Art)*, London, 2014

Wang Meiqin, *Urbanization and Contemporary Chinese Art*, London, 2015

'Women shi jiu shijie de pipanzhe (We Are the Critics of the Old World)', *Renmin ribao*, 8 June 1966

Wu Fulong, *China's Emerging Cities: The Making of New Urbanism*, New York, 2007

Wu Hung, *Contemporary Chinese Art: A History (1970s–2000s)*, London, 2014

— *Exhibiting Experimental Art in China*, Chicago, 2000

— 'Instantaneous Copying and Monumentality: The Historic Logic of "Permanence and Impermanence"', in *Zhang Dali: Permanence and Impermanence*, Beijing, 2017

— 'Negotiating with Tradition in Contemporary Chinese Art: Three Strategies': http://www.mplusmatters.hk/inkart/paper_topic10.php?l=en

— *Remaking Beijing: Tiananmen Square and the Creation of a Political Space*, London, 2005

— 'The 2000 Shanghai Biennale: the Making of a "Historical Event" in Contemporary Chinese Art', in *Making History: Wu Hung on Contemporary Art*, Hong Kong, 2008

— (ed.), *Contemporary Chinese Art: Primary Documents*, New York, 2010

Xu Bing, 'The Living Word', in Britta Erickson (ed.), *Words without Meaning, Meaning without Words: The Art of Xu Bing*, London, 2001

Yan Jiaqi and Gao Gao (eds.), trans. D. W. Y. Kwok, *Turbulent Decade: A History of the Cultural Revolution*, Hawaii, 1996

Yang, Alice, *Why Asia? Contemporary Asian and Asian American Artists*, New York, 1998

Yao, Pauline J., 'Towards a Spatial History of Contemporary Art in China', *Journal of Contemporary Chinese Art: Chinese Art Outside the Art Space*, 5.2&3

Zhang Ga, 'The Posthuman as a Condition of Art', in Zhang Ga (ed.), *Wang Yuyang: Tonight I Shall Meditate Upon That Which I Am*, Milan, 2015

Zhou Xueguang, 'Unorganized Interests and Collective Action in Communist China', *American Sociological Review*, vol. 58, no. 1, 1993

List of Illustrations

Dimensions are in centimetres, followed by inches, height before width before depth (where applicable)

1   Zhao Zhao, *Project Taklamakan*, 2016. Performance. Taklamakan Desert, Xinjiang, 2016. Courtesy of the artist
2   Wang Guangyi, *Great Criticism: Coca-Cola*, 1993. Oil on canvas, 200 × 200 (78¾ × 78¾). © Wang Guangyi Studio
3   Yu Youhan, *On the Tiananmen Tower*, 1990. Acrylic on canvas, 131 × 160 (51½ × 63). Courtesy of the artist and ShanghART Gallery
4   Liu Dahong, *A Tale of Two Cities*, 1999. Oil on canvas, 240 × 200 (94½ × 78¾). Courtesy of the artist
5   Zhang Peili, *1989 Standard Pronunciation*, 1991. Single-channel video, 10 minutes. Courtesy of the artist
6   Wang Jinsong, *Taking a Picture in Front of Tiananmen*, 1992. Acrylic on canvas, 128 × 185 (50⅜ × 72⅞). Courtesy of the artist
7   Wang Guangyi, *Mao Zedong: Red Grid No. 1*, 1988. Oil on canvas, 150 × 130 (59 × 51⅛). © Wang Guangyi Studio
8   Yu Youhan, *Mao and His People*, 1995. Oil on canvas, 2 pieces, 182 × 127 each (71⅝ × 50). Courtesy of the artist and ShanghART Gallery
9   Yu Youhan, *Talking with Hunan Peasants*, 1991. Oil on canvas, 167 × 118 (65¾ × 46⅜). Courtesy of the artist and ShanghART Gallery
10   Li Shan, *Rouge No. 22*, 1992. Acrylic on canvas, 140 × 258 (55⅛ × 101½). Courtesy of the artist and ShanghART Gallery
11   Sui Jianguo, *Sleeping Chairman Mao*, 2003. Painted fibreglass, 120 × 240 × 40 (47¼ × 94½ × 15¾). Courtesy of the artist
12   Zhuang Hui, *Mao*, 2007. Wax and plexiglass, 160 × 320 × 110 (63 × 126 × 43⅜). Courtesy of the artist
13   Geng Jianyi, *People Do Exist*, 1994. Certificates, handwriting on paper, 18 pieces, dimensions variable. Courtesy of ShanghART Gallery
14   Geng Jianyi, *Definitely Her*, 1998. Certificates, colour chromogenic prints, 10 pieces, 50 × 30 each (19⅝ × 11⅞). Courtesy of ShanghART Gallery
15   Geng Jianyi, *The Second Series of Eight Steps*, 1991. Collage on wood, 122 × 158 (48 × 62⅛). Courtesy of ShanghART Gallery
16   Geng Jianyi, *Two Series of Five Steps of Wearing Clothes*, 1991. Collage on wood, 122 × 147 (48 × 57⅞). Courtesy of ShanghART Gallery
17   Geng Jianyi, *To Be Your Correct Self*, 2005. 20-channel video installation, 4 minutes 57 seconds. Courtesy of ShanghART Gallery
18   Zhuang Hui, *The One and Thirty*, 1995–96. Photograph, 30 pieces, 60 × 50 each (23⅝ × 19⅝). Courtesy of the artist
19   Zhuang Hui, *Group Portraits: Luoyang Cadre Police Academy Students and Staff, Henan Province, May 13, 1997*, 1997. Photograph, 19 × 133 (7½ × 52⅜). Courtesy of the artist
20   Wang Jinsong, *Standard Family*, 1996. Photograph, dimensions variable. Courtesy of the artist
21   Zhang Xiaogang, *Big Family No. 1*, 1996. Oil on canvas, 180 × 230 (70⅞ × 90½). Courtesy of the artist
22   Zhang Xiaogang, *Big Family: Red Scarf*, 1998. Oil on canvas, 150 × 150 cm. Courtesy of the artist
23   Wang Jin, *100%*, 1999. Photograph, 109 × 127 (42⅞ × 50). Courtesy of the artist
24   Zhang Dali, *Migrant Workers*, 2000. Meat jelly and mixed media, dimensions variable. Courtesy of the artist
25   Zhang Dali, *One Hundred Chinese No. 56*, 2001. Resin, life-size. Courtesy of the artist
26   Zhang Dali, *Chinese Offspring*, 2003–5. 15 life-size cast figures, mixed media, average height 170 each (66⅞). Installation view at the Saatchi Gallery, London, 2008. Courtesy of the artist
27   Zhang Dali, *Monuments*, white marble, 147 × 43 × 62 (57⅞ × 16⅞ × 24⅜), 2016 (left); 169 × 52 × 38 (66½ × 20½ × 15), 2015 (right). Courtesy of the artist
28   Chen Xiaoyun, *Night/2.4KM*, 2009. Single-channel video, 9 minutes 30 seconds. Image courtesy of the artist
29   Chen Xiaoyun, *Fire/3000KG*, 2009. Single-channel video, 9 minutes 50 seconds. Image courtesy of the artist
30   Yue Minjun, *Great Joy*, 1992. Oil on canvas, 185 × 250 (72⅞ × 98⅜). Courtesy of the artist
31   Yue Minjun, *Romanticism and Realism Study No. 6*, 2003. Acrylic on fibreglass-reinforced plastics, 88 × 163 × 90 (34⅝ × 64⅛ × 35⅜). Courtesy of the artist

32 Zhang Peili, *Happiness*, 2006. 2-channel video, 6 minutes 39 seconds. Courtesy of the artist
33 Yang Fudong, *Backyard – Hey, Sun is Rising!*, 2001. 35 mm black-and-white film, 13 minutes. Courtesy of the artist and ShanghART Gallery
34 Yang Zhenzhong, *Disinfect*, 2015. 6-channel video, 15 minutes. Courtesy of the artist
35 Zhou Xiaohu, *Concentration Training Camp*, 2007–8. 8-channel video, installation view, 2008. Courtesy of the artist
36 Zhou Xiaohu, *Concentration Training Camp*, 2007–8. 8-channel video. Courtesy of the artist
37 Yang Zhenzhong, *Spring Story*, 2003. Single-channel video, 12 minutes. Courtesy of the artist
38 Cao Fei, *Whose Utopia*, 2006. Video, 20 minutes. Courtesy of Cao Fei and Vitamin Creative Space and Sprüth Magers
39 Yang Fudong, *Indeed, the Only Way*, 2018. Performance. Installation view at the Power Station of Art, Shanghai, 2018. Courtesy of the artist and ShanghART Gallery
40 Xu Zhen, *Physique of Consciousness*, 2013. Single-channel video, 52 minutes 3 seconds. Courtesy of the artist and MadeIn Company
41 Xu Zhen, *Physique of Consciousness*, 2016. Performance, dimensions variable. Installation view at Somerset House, London, 2016. Courtesy Art Night London and XU ZHEN®, photographed by Hugo Glendinning
42 Square dancing in Xuanwuhu Park, Nanjing, photographed by Chen Qiwei, 20 January 2020. Courtesy of Chen Qiwei
43 Yang Jiechang, *100 Layers of Ink, No. 1*, 1990. Ink on rice paper and gauze, mounted on canvas, 320 × 218 (126 × 85⅞). Courtesy of the artist
44 Hu Xiaoyuan, *Wood*, 2009–10. 31 pieces, size variable, wood, ink, silk and white paint. Courtesy of the artist
45 Liang Shaoji, *Snow Cover Series: Snow in the Woods*, 2016 (details). Willow branches, silk, porcelain, cocoons, burned keyboard, wooden board, 3 pieces, 35 × 122 × 244 each (13¾ × 48 × 96). Photos by Lin Bingliang
46 Liang Shaoji, *Chains: The Unbearable Lightness of Being / Nature Series No. 79*, 2003–16. Polyurethane colophony, iron powder, silk and cocoons, iron and silk, dimensions variable. Installation view at ShanghART Gallery, 2007. Photo by ShanghART Gallery
47 Liu Jianhua, *Blank Paper*, 2012. Porcelain, 120 × 90 × 0.5 each (47¼ × 35⅜ × ⅛). Courtesy of the artist
48 Liu Jianhua, *Filled*, 2016. Porcelain, 3 × 68 diameter (1⅛ × 26¾). Courtesy of the artist
49 Xiao Yu, *Translocation, No. 17*, 2017. Bamboo, 240 × 993 × 73 (94½ × 390⅞ × 28¾). Courtesy of the artist
50 Xiao Yu, *Infinitive, No. 1*, 2018. Cast copper with chemical stain, 170 × 250 × 166 (66⅞ × 98⅜ × 65⅜). Courtesy of the artist
51 Xiao Yu, *Thinking Too Much That... No. 5*, 2015. Single-channel video, 6 minutes 29 seconds. Courtesy of the artist
52 Zhao Zhao, *Lighter*, 2016. Jade, 8 × 2 × 0.8 (3⅛ × ¾ × ⅜). Courtesy of the artist
53 Zhao Zhao, *Again*, 2014. Damaged Buddhist statues from various dynasties, limestone and white marble, 150 × 150 × 150 (59 × 59 × 59). Courtesy of the artist
54 Zhao Zhao, *Countless*, 2014. Damaged Buddhist statues from various dynasties, limestone and white marble cubes, 1 × 1 × 1 each (⅜ × ⅜ × ⅜), total dimensions variable. Installation view at Shanghai Minsheng Art Museum, 2016. Courtesy of the artist
55 Hu Xiaoyuan, *Useless*, 2008 (detail). Rice paper, scotch tape and sound recording, 664 × 66 (261⅜ × 26). Courtesy of the artist
56 Zhang Peili, *30 × 30*, 1988. Single-channel video, 180 minutes. Courtesy of the artist
57 Zhan Wang, *Artificial Rocks, No. 164*, 2013. Stainless steel, 66 × 45 × 32 (26 × 17⅝ × 12½). Courtesy of the artist
58 Zhan Wang, *Artificial Rocks, No. 175*, 2013. Stainless steel, 252 × 160 × 97 (99⅛ × 63 × 38⅛). Installation view at Arthur M. Sackler Museum of Art and Archaeology, Peking University, Beijing, 2013. Courtesy of the artist
59 Shao Yinong, *The Nine Twigs*, 2011. Stainless steel and tourmaline, dimensions variable. Installation view at Shanghai Minsheng Art Museum, 2016. Courtesy of the artist
60 Yu Ji, *Flesh in Stone, No. 6*, 2016. Cement and iron, 75 × 43 × 39 (29½ × 16⅞ × 15⅜). Courtesy of the artist
61 Yu Ji, *Flesh in Stone, Component 1*, 2015. Cement and iron, 100 × 40 × 30 (39⅜ × 15¾ × 11⅞). Courtesy of the artist
62 Hao Liang, *The Tale of Clouds*, 2013 (detail). Ink and colour on silk, 42 × 1,000 (16½ × 393⅝). Courtesy of the artist
63 Wu Chi-Tsung, *Wire I*, 2003. Metal, glass, acrylic, dimensions variable. Courtesy Wu Chi-Tsung Studio
64 Wu Chi-Tsung, *Wire II*, 2003. Metal, glass, acrylic, dimensions variable. Courtesy Wu Chi-Tsung Studio

97 Wang Wei, *Hypocritical Room*, 2002.
Installation and performance at the exhibition
Fan Mingzhen & Fan Mingzhu, Shanghai,
23–24 November 2002. Courtesy of the artist
98 Nabuqi, *A View Beyond Space No. 13*, 2016.
Concrete, acrylic, 24 × 24 × 7 (9⅜ × 9⅜ × 2¾).
Courtesy of the artist
99 Nabuqi, *A View Beyond Space No. 16*, 2017.
Bronze, 800 × 210 × 45 (315 × 82⅝ × 17¾). Courtesy
of the artist
100 Nabuqi, *A View Beyond Space No. 4*,
2015. Stainless steel, varnish, 400 × 80 × 10
(157½ × 31½ × 3⅞). Courtesy of the artist
101 Yang Zhenzhong, *Light as Fuck*, 2002.
Photograph (and video, 1 minute). Courtesy of
the artist
102 Yang Zhenzhong, *Let's Puff*, 2002. 2-channel
video installation, 15 minutes. Courtesy of the
artist
103 Hu Weiyi, *The Window Blind*, 2019. Video
installation, 3 pieces, 175 × 115 × 25 each
(68⅞ × 45¼ × 9⅞). Courtesy of the artist
104 Hu Weiyi, *The Window Blind, No. 1* (detail).
Courtesy of the artist
105 Hu Weiyi, *The Rule of the Wind*, 2019, video
installation, 7 minutes 10 seconds, and *The Rule
of the Water*, 2019, video installation, 6 minutes
1 second. Courtesy of the artist
106 Jiang Zhi, *Rainbow, No. 3*, 2005. Photograph.
Courtesy of the artist
107 Jiang Zhi, *Rainbow*, 2007. Video installation,
dimensions variable. Courtesy of the artist
108 Hu Jieming, *Somewhere: Square*, 2004.
Photograph. Courtesy of the artist
109 Hu Jieming, *Where Is My Home*, 2011.
Photograph. Courtesy of the artist
110 Wang Wei, *What You See Is Not What You See*,
2017. Mosaic wall, 1,650 × 330 (649⅝ × 129⅞). Site-
specific installation at Edouard Malingue
Gallery, Shanghai, 2017. Courtesy of the artist
and Edouard Malingue Gallery, Hong Kong and
Shanghai
111 Wang Wei, *Shadow*, 2017. Mosaic tiles,
1,350 × 1,020 (531½ × 401½). Site-specific
installation at the West Bund Art Centre,
Shanghai, 2017. Courtesy of the artist and
Edouard Malingue Gallery, Hong Kong and
Shanghai
112 Cao Fei (SL avatar: China Tracy), *RMB City:
A Second Life City Planning*, 2007. Video, 5 minutes
57 seconds. Courtesy of Cao Fei and Vitamin
Creative Space and Sprüth Magers
113 Zhao Zhao, *Project Taklamakan*, 2016.
Performance. Taklamakan Desert, Xinjiang,
2016. Courtesy of the artist

114 Zhao Zhao, *Project Taklamakan*, 2016.
Courtesy of the artist
115 Zhao Zhao, *Project Taklamakan*, 2016.
Courtesy of the artist
116 Wang Yuyang, *Artificial Moon*, 2007. Energy-
saving lights, metal, 400 diameter (157½).
Courtesy of the artist
117 Wang Yuyang, *Singularity*, 2015. LED lights,
metal, motor and computer, 400 diameter (157½).
Courtesy of the artist
118 Wenheyou Old Changsha Restaurant, 2019.
Courtesy Weng Donghua
119 'Teacher Zhou' room, Wenheyou Old
Changsha Restaurant, photographed by the
author, 16 October 2019
120 Li Bin, *Revolution Is No Crime, Rebellion
Is Justified*, 1966. Woodcut print, 100 × 78
(39⅜ × 30⅝). Courtesy of the artist
121 Wang Keping, *Idol*, 1978. Birch, 57 × 29 × 15
(22⅜ × 11⅜ × 5⅞). Courtesy of the artist
122 Jin Feng, *Chinese Plates*, 2014 (detail). Wood
panels, dimensions variable. Courtesy of the
artist
123 Jin Feng, *Aesthetics of Violence No. 1*, 2016
(detail). Steel bar, dimensions variable. Courtesy
of the artist
124 Jin Feng, *Aesthetics of Violence No. 1*, 2016
(detail). Rubber, dimensions variable. Courtesy
of the artist
125 Ai Weiwei, *Study of Perspective: The White
House*, 1995. Photograph. Courtesy of Ai Weiwei
Studio
126 Ai Weiwei, *Dropping a Han Dynasty Urn*,
1995. Photograph of performance. Courtesy of Ai
Weiwei Studio
127 Ai Weiwei, *Dust to Dust*, 2008. 30 glass jars
with powder from ground Neolithic pottery on
wood shelves, 200 × 240 × 36 (78¾ × 94½ × 14⅛).
Courtesy of Ai Weiwei Studio
128 Li Binyuan, *Board 100×40*, 2017. Single-
channel video of performance, 8 minutes
56 seconds. Courtesy of the artist
129 Li Binyuan, *Gravity*, 2013. Single-channel
video of performance, 7 minutes 54 seconds.
Courtesy of the artist
130 Sun Yuan and Peng Yu, *Freedom*, 2009.
Metal plate, high-pressure hydraulic pump,
fire hose, hydrant, and electronic control
system. Courtesy of Tang Contemporary Art
and the artists
131 *Star Art Exhibition*, Beijing, China, 1979.
Courtesy Huang Rui
132 Wang Gongxin, *It's Not about the
Neighbourhood*, 2009. Site-specific installation.
Courtesy Arrow Factory and the artist

Index

References in italics indicate
illustration figure numbers

A

Ai Weiwei 8, 83, 162–4, 170, 177;
125, 126, 127
animation 94, 116; *83, 84*
Apartment Art 171–2
April Photography Society 8,
196
Arrow Factory (Beijing) 171,
173–4
*Art Chinois 1990: Chine Demain
pour Hier* exhibition 15
Augé, Marc 9
avant-garde art 7, 9–12, 169,
172, 184, 195

B

Badaling (Beijing) 177
Beato, Felice 67
Beijing 10, 20, 21, 45, 65, 94,
115, 116–17, 119, 127, 130,
144, 145, 156, 160, 162, 166,
169, 171, 172, 173, 174, 177,
178, 182, 183, 189, 195; *131,
143*
Beijing Opera 24, 117
Beijing Spring 178
Belting, Hans 9
Berry, Chris 144
Bhabha, Homi 68
Bishop, Claire 57
Borysevicz, Mathieu 40
Bosker, Bianca 115
Bourriaud, Nicolas 72
Bray, David 19, 34
Bryson, Norman 102
Buddhism 29, 71, 80, 87, 108,
158, 162

C

Cai Guo-Qiang 69, 177; *136*
calligraphy 69, 87, 96–105, 107,
108, 169; *74, 75, 76, 77*
Cao Fei 58, 143; *38, 112*
carving 67, 79, 95, 99, 110
Chairman Mao Memorial Hall
(Beijing) 29, 138
Chang Tsong-zung 97
Changsha (Hunan Province)
151–2; *118, 119*
Chen Danqing 8
Chen Shaoxiong 126, 173;
95
Chen Xiaoyun 51, 58; *28, 29*
Chen Zaiyan 105
Cheng Conglin 8
Chengdu (Sichuan Province)
172
China Art Museum Beijing 182
China/Avant-Garde exhibition
11, 15, 20, 182
'China Dream' 136–7
communism 7, 17, 19, 24, 25,
29, 64, 116, 155, 158
Crinson, Mark 153
Cultural Revolution 6–8, 11, 18,
21, 24, 37, 51, 53–4, 67, 80,
100, 115, 155–6, 158–9, 162
Cynical Realism 11–13

D

Dal Lago, Francesca 24
danwei (work unit) 17, 19–20,
31, 34, 37, 64
Deng Xiaoping 58
Dingxiang (Shanxi Province)
111, 113
Documenta 6
Dong Qichang 88
drawing 111, 169
dynastic China 69, 80, 94, 96,
115, 151

E

Eastern Jin dynasty 89
'85 Art New Wave/Movement
10, 11, 178, 182
Emperor Puyi 116
Emperor Taizong of Tang 101

F

Fang Lijun 13
Feng Boyi 170
Feng Chengsu 101

film 34, 51, 53, 54, 57, 58, 60,
174, 184, 187; *33; see also*
video
Foshan (Guangdong Province)
58
'Four Greats' 158
'Four Olds' 51, 156
Fuck Off exhibition 170–71
Fujian Provincial Art Museum
179; *140*

G

Gao Minglu 10, 171–2, 182
Garage Show (exhibition)
170
Geng Jianyi 30, 34; *13, 14, 15,
16, 17*
Gobi Desert 177
Great Hall of the People
(Beijing) 20, 116
Great Leap Forward campaign
116
Great Wall of China 116, 177;
135
Gu Wenda 96–7; *69, 70*
Guangzhou (Guangdong
Province) 126, 141, 172
Guo Shirui 172
Guo Xi 92

H

Haikou (Hainan Province) 172
Han dynasty 162; *126*
Hangzhou (Zhejiang Province)
66
Hao Liang 89–90; *62*
'Harmonious Society' 66, 136
He An 120, 174; *87, 88, 133*
He Yunchang 184, 186–8; *143,
144, 145*
Henan Province 37, 173; *19*
Hill, Katie 53
Ho, Rania 173
Hong Kong 93, 193
Hopfener, Birgit 164
Hu Jieming 138–41; *108, 109*
Hu Jintao 136
Hu Weiyi 133–6; *103, 104, 105*
Hu Xiaoyuan 71, 82–3; *44, 55*
Huang Rui 8, 178
Huang Yong Ping 108, 178–9;
80, 139
Huangshan Symposium 11
Hui Dongcun 111, 113
Hunan Province 22, 151, 165; *9*

'The single most influential series of art books ever published' *Apollo*

'Outstanding ... exceptionally authoritative and well-illustrated' *Sunday Times*

Comprehensive in coverage and accessible to all, the World of Art series explores both the newest and the perennial in all the arts, covering themes, artists and movements that straddle the centuries and the gamut of visual culture around the globe.

You may also like:

Central and Eastern European Art Since 1950
Maja and Reuben Fowkes

Contemporary African Art
Sidney Littlefield Kasfir

Movements in Art Since 1945
Edward Lucie-Smith

World of Art